AF262997

MEMOIR
OF A
COLLECTION

Steven Kasher

MEMOIR

OF A

COLLECTION

FINDING

MEANING THROUGH

ART

ABBEVILLE PRESS
New York London

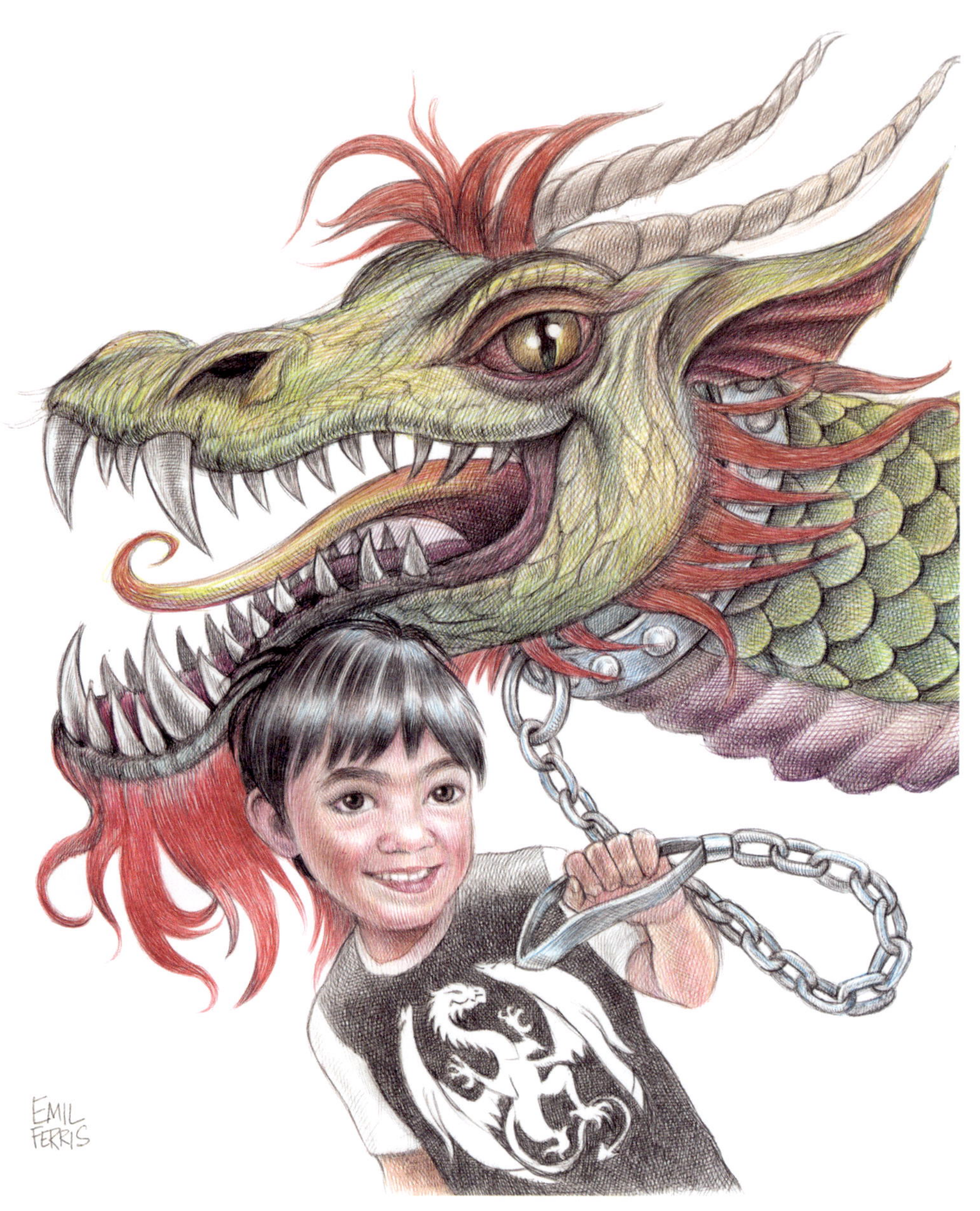

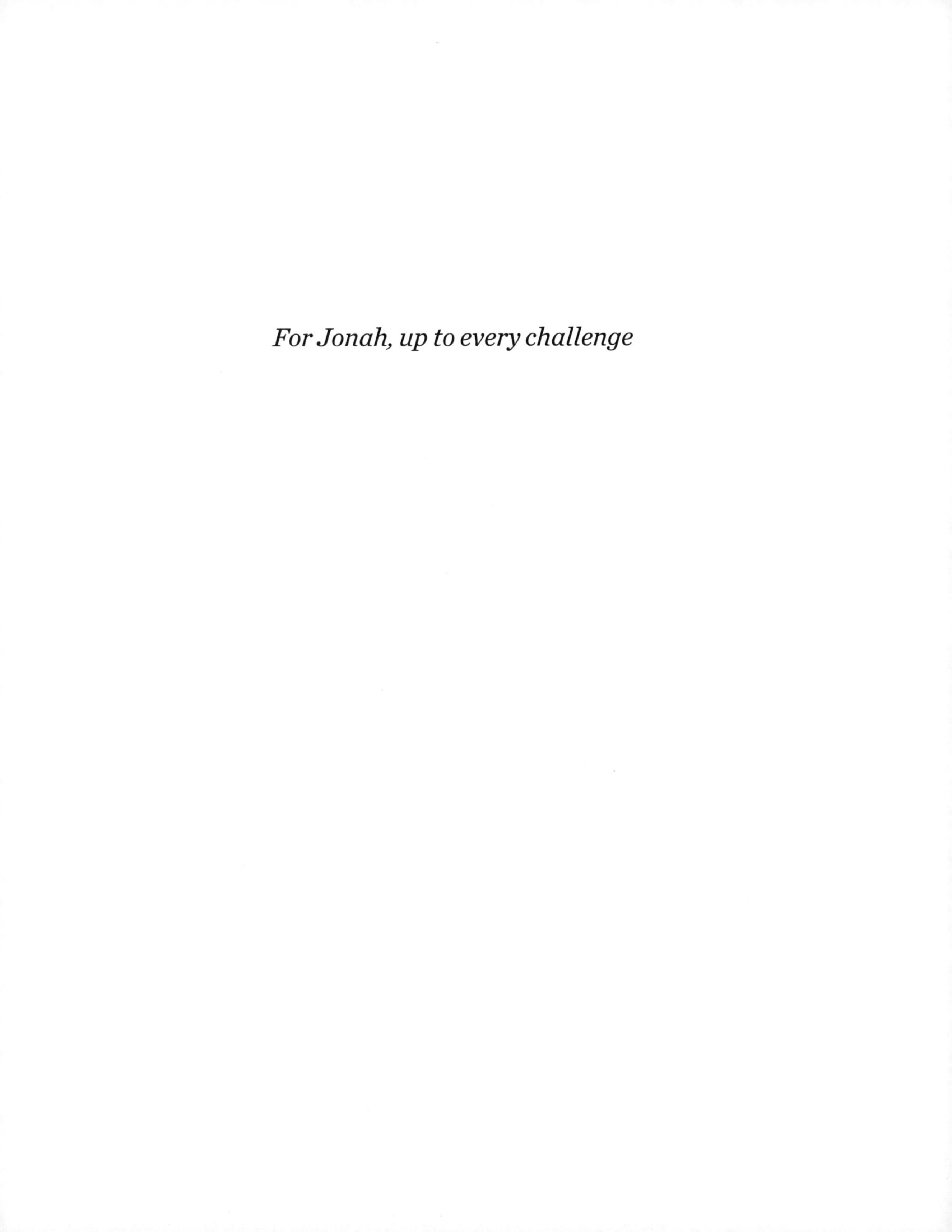

For Jonah, up to every challenge

Nighttime falls and the water
*   is flooded with moonlight.*
Here in the Dragon's jaws:
Many exquisite jewels.

—Setcho Juken (980–1052)

Contents

Introduction

I'm writing this introduction in a shaky place. It's December 2024. One president is packing up, another is taking over. I am in temporary housing after our home caught fire.

As I watched the flames surge, I imagined it all burning down, I thought nothing would remain but ashes. But I remained calm: the fire started just four hours after my return from a forty-two-day retreat spent meditating on impermanence, unreliability, and non-self.

Soon the volunteers of five local firehouses arrived. They were so fast, skillful, and gentle. No one was hurt. None of our belongings were harmed by fire, smoke, or water. The artworks illustrated in this book would have been destroyed. We were spared. We felt blessed.

I began these writings in the summer of 2020, the summer of COVID. I had been musing about this project for a decade; now I had the time and quiet to attempt it. The idea was to write a book made of a chain of images that changed my life. It would start with a TV cartoon, Bugs Bunny confronting the shadow-faced Martian (*The Hasty Hare*, 1952), and travel through my years as an art student, an artist, an art dealer.

As I wrote, the project evolved into what you hold here: a book about artworks that hang on my walls, about images that live large in my mind, about the meanings I find in them.

The title *Memoir of a Collection* points in a couple of directions. It points to how we can use art around us to remember, to recollect essential things. It proposes that a collection can be thought of as a living thing that collects and recollects meanings. I see my collection as a magnet for meanings. The magnetic field is wide, encompassing personal history, art history, and history at large.

The twenty-five pieces in this book are not quite essays, memoirs, or stories. They are hybrids—or fables, because of their moral flavor. They are written from the perspective of the dharma path. I took a couple of steps on that path in my teens, but began walking it in earnest only a dozen or so years ago. You'll find in these writings many echoes of what the Buddha said about the path that leads us on a journey to a freedom we can find.

Some years ago it struck me that each artwork I have—what has grabbed me, what I cherish—tells a singular story. Each picture portrays human struggle coupled with its overcoming. In every face and every body in these pictures I see both suffering and succor. These images may have been made with other intentions, but I attune to their message of pain and healing, their message of struggle transcended—through courage, through solidarity, through wisdom, through joy.

I seek out this two-sided message over and over. I gather this couplet to hang on my walls, to have around me as I go through my day. As an artist, a gallerist, a publisher, a writer, I set out to share these images and their messages.

Something else is now clear to me: the theme of compassion. Various tastes of compassion can be found throughout these writings. This theme came into focus after that long meditation retreat. The melody of that retreat was compassion as the opening of the heart to one's own suffering and to the suffering of others. The dharma teaches compassion and wisdom. Wise compassion and compassionate wisdom. They are like two wings; without both, we can't fly.

You'll find here fables about artists Philip Guston, John Chamberlain, June Leaf, Andy Warhol; about graphic artists Basil Wolverton, Gabrielle Bell, Leela Corman, Lauren Weinstein. There are writings that focus on photographs by Ernest Withers, Weegee, Mike Disfarmer, Robert Frank, Charles Moore, Edward Curtis. There are writings about vernacular photographs—people's pictures—and writings about Insider (Outsider) artists. I write about Lou Reed and Laurie Anderson and about Janis Joplin and Leonard Cohen. I write about my mother and father—Ursula and Charlie—about my Uncle Del and Aunt Ada, about my grandparents Rose and Justin. You will find in these pages men acting badly, but they are not condemned.

Each of these pieces can be read on its own. If you read them in the order presented you will join me on a journey from youth to age, from dumb wonder to dumbfounded wonderment. We'll walk through the valley of the shadow of death reaching for the red star sky. We'll arrive at a different place.

Big Cats, Under-Cats

When I was a kid, this painting hung prominently in the living room of my father's Greenwich Village home. It was my favorite thing of all his possessions. When he died, I claimed it. It hangs in my home, still in its original Mexican carved-wood frame. And it pulses like a backbeat always in some corner of my mind.

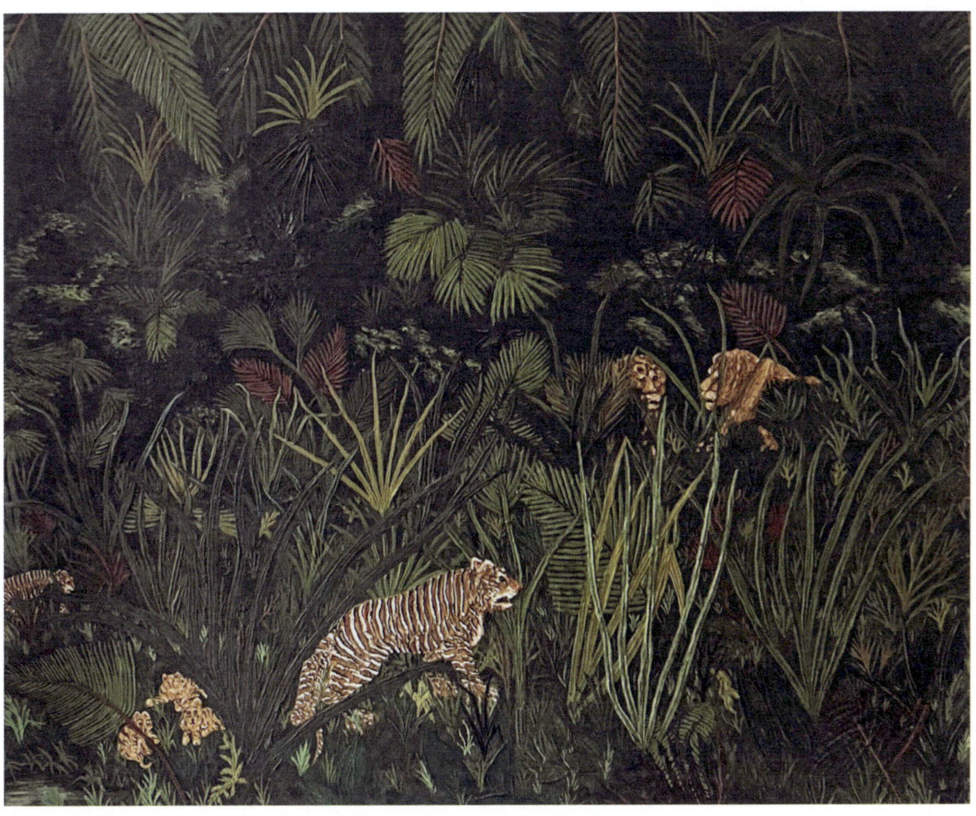

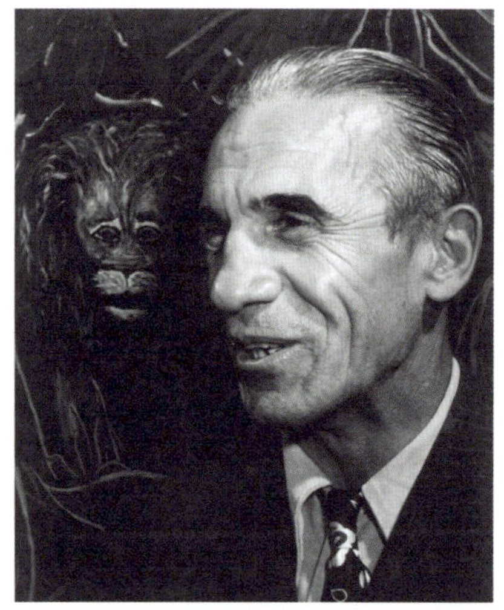

Dad told me the painting was by a Greenwich Village artist named Joe Gatto. Dad knew Gatto from the neighborhood. He told me Gatto was a follower of the famous French painter Henri Rousseau, that Gatto and Rousseau were "primitives" (self-taught artists). Dad liked paintings of recognizable things, paintings like this. He thought abstracts were snow jobs, even Picassos. Though Dad admired Picasso's success and his virility.

Victor Joseph Gatto was born in 1893 in Greenwich Village. In his early twenties he was a professional prizefighter. He was connected to the Mob and served time in Dannemora prison. When he got out, he noticed that Village street artists could make a living without getting their noses broken. He took up painting and was successful, graduating from street fairs to art galleries. His big break came in 1948, when he was profiled by *Life* magazine, photographed by their star photographer W. Eugene Smith. Gatto's work was collected by bigwigs such as the Bloomingdales, the Hearsts, the Warburgs, the Rockefellers, John Steinbeck. Muse-

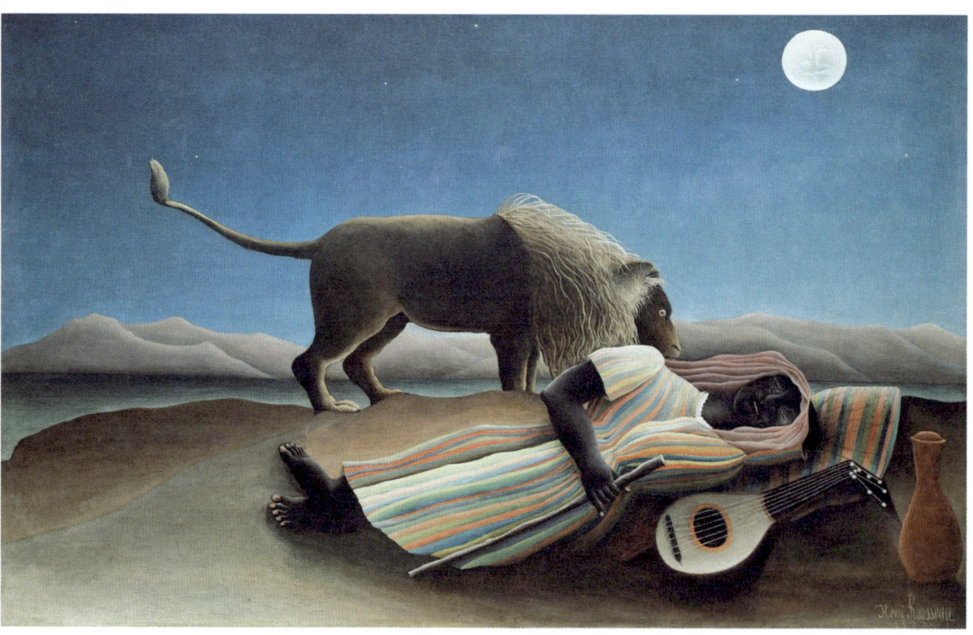

ums holding his paintings include the Whitney, the Smithsonian Museum of American Art, MoMA.

Gatto died in poverty in Miami in 1965. He is now forgotten. Rousseau is a tough act to follow. Rousseau's brushwork and colors are exciting and precise, Gatto's are more murky and managed. When told his paintings resembled Rousseau's, Gatto shot back: "The guy's been stealing my stuff for years."

The Museum of Modern Art houses two masterpieces by Henri Rousseau, *The Sleeping Gypsy,* 1897, and *The Dream,* 1910. On a fourth-grade field trip to MoMA I selected *The Sleeping Gypsy* as my favorite painting, and wrote a report. I wrote about wild beasts and scary dreams.

The Sleeping Gypsy should be called *The Sleeping Egyptian* because to Rousseau "Gypsy" meant Egyptian. Rousseau called her "a wandering Negress." She sleeps stiffly in a coat of many colors in a moonlit night. A wide-eyed lion sniffs at her pink veil, his rapt stillness echoed by the stiff tendrils of his mane. Across the chill and starry void the full-faced moon and the lion's erect tail stare each other down. Foregrounded are a lute, a vase, and a staff—each a potentiality from which good or evil may issue, as is dreaming sleep.

In *The Dream* we are again in Africa and under the same full moon. Here it lights a jungle luxuriant with bananas, oranges, and purple lotus. We see

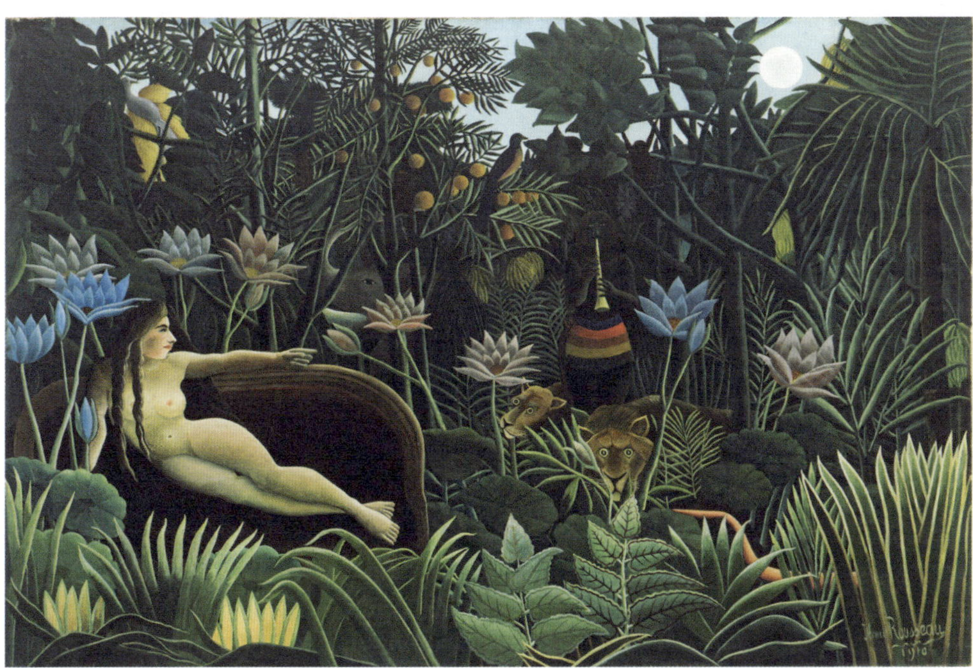

another reclining woman, this one awake, a fulsome odalisque undulating on an incongruous couch. Here the music flows, piped by an African flautist in a rainbow skirt. In the resplendent foliage an elephant trumpets and a lion observes the rhythmic curves of the nude. A second lion stares out at us, the intruders.

A pair of contrasting fantasies: cold and hot, sleeping and awakened, tense and refulgent, hushed and musical. We wonder at these visions so unlikely yet somehow so familiar. Rousseau's dreams become our dreams.

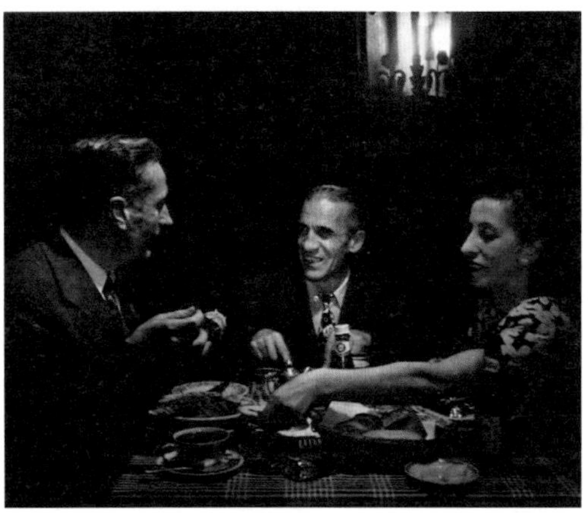

Rousseau knew he was a great painter. His main rival, in his own mind, was Picasso. Picasso admired Rousseau. In 1908, Picasso, already king of the Parisian avant-garde, threw a gala banquet for the much older painter. Rousseau told Picasso, "You and I are the two most important artists of the age—you in the Egyptian style, and I in the modern one." Rousseau was telling Picasso: your work is great in an austere, formalized, hieratic mode, while mine drips with the juices of today. Picasso and his guests laughed at Rousseau's bold presumption.

But humility is not useful when you are cultivating a new style, raising it up in the tangled jungle of modernity. Rousseau is still considered the king of the Outsider Artists. These artists from the margins speak to us today. They are more of our moment than Picasso, who can feel of the past. The Black Outsider Artists I love—Thornton Dial, Bill Traylor, William Hawkins, William Coleman, the Gee's Bend quilters—thrill us with their unexpected turns of line and color, their flute work and lute work, their fierce emotions rendered carefully. They have achieved their wisdom by shaking off the callousness of the masters. They have the energy of underdogs overcoming. I call them Insider Artists. They speak from the heartwood of human experience.

In 1965, eleven years old, I was fifth wheel at a double date with my father, Charlie, and his friend Al and two young ladies. We dined at a round table at an elegant restaurant in London, where Dad was living then. Charlie sat next to

Al. I sat next to my father's date. She was pretty and funny and closer to me in age than to Dad by two decades. Only many years later did I figure out what she was. Charlie picked up the dinner tab, and certainly the tab for the two escorts too: London was his turf, and Al was his special guest in the jungle that night. Anyway, Dad always picked up the tab. He always played the central character around which the supporting cast revolved: he played the godfather.

My father's friend Al, born Alfredo Lettieri, became well-known as Al Lettieri, known for his role in *The Godfather*. He played Virgil "The Turk" Sol-

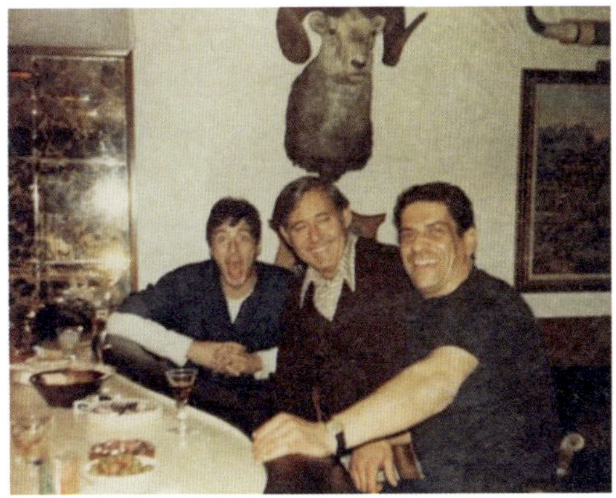

lozzo, the drug-dealing mobster who gets whacked at dinner in a Bronx restaurant by Al Pacino's Michael Corleone in his crucial coming-of-age scene. This snapshot shows the two Als flanking "Patsy Ryan" Eboli, a real-life mobster related to Lettieri by marriage. Patsy's brother, "Tommy Ryan" Eboli, was acting boss of the Genovese crime family. In July of 1972, four months after the premiere of *The Godfather*, Tommy Ryan was gunned down, some say because of his indiscreet clowning around with movie stars.

For Dad, life was a jungle. The daily hunt for a mate was inexorable. He stalked a consistent prey. In every decade of his life, from his teens until his eighties, he seduced, fucked, lived with, and married women who were twenty-five years old when he met them. He organized his work, his homes, his haberdashery, his hours, his charming speech, his friendships, his nights on the town to flush out and tumble these women. One day, in a taxi, he offered me a valuable lesson. He taught me his endgame. When he tired of a girlfriend or wife, he would convince her she was to blame for the breakup. This succeeded, he told me, to keep the women on friendly terms and to ease his remorse.

To me, when I was young, my father was the tiger-king, commanding the jungle, ruler without peer. I was the under-tiger, trailing behind King Tiger's tread. I was moon to his sun, reflecting his radiance, but dimly. Quoting TV's Charlie Chan, he called me "Number-One Son." I was prince to his king. I was the godfather in line.

In Joe Gatto's *Jungle Scene*, plant forms spring up and droop in undulant rhythms. A tiger prowls, bright-lit, the protagonist. In a corner three tiger cubs rest, looking more like puppy dogs. An adolescent tiger slinks in from the left, mimicking his father. Two intimidated lions hide in the foliage. This painting is not just a Rousseau wannabe. It feels sincere, feels like something real, like something Gatto felt.

This scene is familiar to me. The stalking tiger is my father. The three cubs are my younger siblings. The intermediate tiger imitating his sire is me. The unthreatening lions are Dad's women: off to the side, not part of the main action.

For many years I lived in that jungle, in that mob-land, hunting prey. Lonely years, repetitive, horizonless, claustrophobic. Eventually, I would find my way out. Like Rousseau's Negress, I would learn to dream in many colors. Like Rousseau's desert lion, I would learn to salute the moon. I would learn how to cut through the overgrowth, learn how to clear open space in my heart—cool, tranquil space for intimacy.

Genius

I n high school an idea of Genius was planted in my brain; it took root and grew. So much else was squeezed out. To be a Genius became my life's goal. All problems would be solved. I would get all the attention and affection I so deserved. Nothing else much mattered—not decency, not kindness. My circle of bookish high-school friends studied Dostoevsky's Raskolnikov, who justified his axe-murders by Genius. We talked about whether Genius excused all, trumped all.

This was at Horace Mann School for Boys, considered one of New York's best prep schools. The most highly regarded English teacher was Robert Berman. He taught *Hamlet*, *Moby Dick*, Milton, and Russian literature to juniors and seniors. His students were expected to write down every word he said, on pain of banishment. Each year he gathered a fresh cult following. The most dedicated Bermanites mimicked his uniform of tight wool suit, white shirt, thin black tie. A few even copied his shaven head—in an era when only Yul Brynner and *Goldfinger's* Oddjob shaved their heads—though nobody dared imitate his dark glasses, worn ostensibly for medical reasons, never removed. Though I was a long-haired hippie type, I was on the fringe of the Berman cult. I enthusiastically signed up for all of his courses.

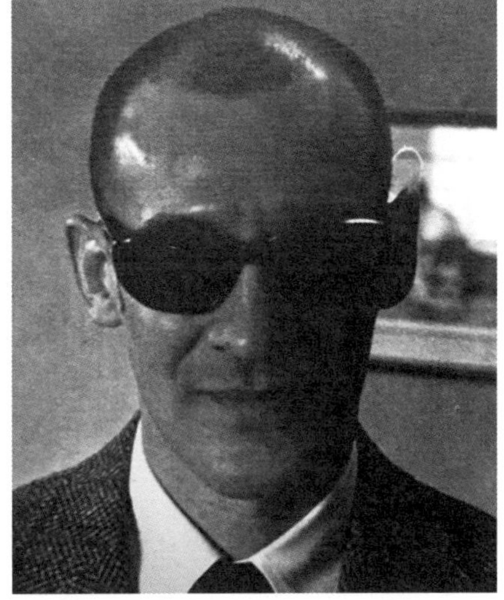

Berman was a coolly fanatic proponent of the doctrine of the exceptional Genius. Every year he published a new edition of his list of *The One Thousand Greatest People Who Ever Live*d. He sold mimeographed copies to his students. The chapters were "The First One Hundred," "The Second One Hundred."... Blazoned on a special introductory page were the words: "Leonardo da Vinci: Off the Human Scale."

Berman believed himself a Genius. His confidence was impenetrable. He impressed upon his followers that if they sufficiently embraced his Genius, they might become Genius too. He encouraged certain students to meet him after school in his classroom decorated with reproductions of Renaissance paintings. Or to meet with him at his apartment.

The most dedicated Bermanite of all, Robert Simon, who was two grades above me, used family money to buy a house for Berman and his cult. They still live there today. Simon became a dealer in Renaissance art. He was instrumental in discovering and promoting the (disputed) Leonardo da Vinci painting *Salvador Mundi*, which is currently the most expensive painting ever sold. Almost off the monetary scale. Sold first to a lackey of Vladimir Putin, and then to Saudi Crown Prince Mohammed bin Salman (MBS).

Berman forced himself sexually on the most vulnerable of his followers. One of them was my best friend, molested in Berman's hotel room while on a class trip to Washington to visit the Renaissance paintings in the National Gallery of Art. I was on that trip too. After the assault by his hero, my friend clammed up; I learned of it only decades later. I learned that with his mother, who was a high official in the New York City government, my friend went to the headmaster to report Berman's abuse. Nothing was done. Berman boasted to my friend that he would be his thirteenth victim, thirteenth to commit suicide. In fact, there were many suicides of Horace Mann students in the days of Berman. Despite his later exposure, which included a feature story about

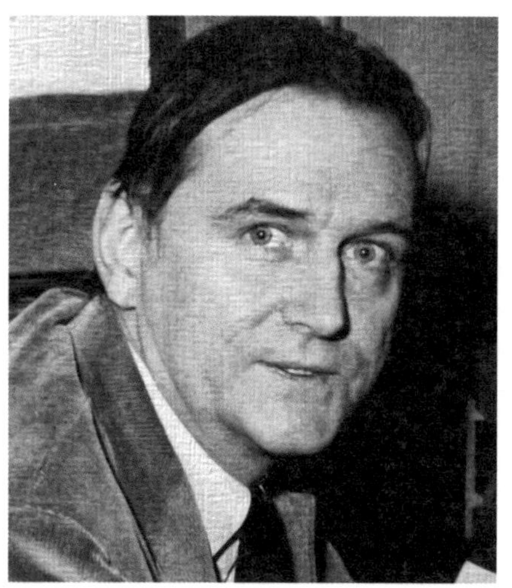

him in the *New Yorker*, Berman has not been brought to justice. Statutes of limitation.

Another adored Horace Mann English teacher was Robert Cullen. It was Cullen who taught me to love Shakespeare, Keats, Yeats, Blake. Cullen was Berman's close friend and knew about his doings. Cullen too was a seducer of boys, though, as far as I know, he stopped at platonic affairs, and was not sadistic like Berman. Cullen encouraged his favorites to meet him after class, to discuss our problems, air out our secrets. To be granted one of these meetings was considered a rare privilege. I applied for that privilege as often as I could because I adored Cullen, valued his attention and advice. One day I got up the nerve to ask him—who else could I ask?—if it was normal that my girlfriend got strangely rigid as we finished sex. He said it was probably her way of orgasm. I was reassured.

My meetings with Cullen were loaded with long, breathless silences. Melancholic Irish Cullen would gaze out the casement windows of his classroom onto the central campus field. One snowy afternoon, he turned back from the window and said: "I have a poem for you."

> Far off Broadway, in matinee snow,
> Children sledding stage a hit show.
> Gnomic dancers, lying low,
> They throw away lines,
> Fortissimo.

It's a lovely and loving poem. I've recited it to myself many times. It's a gift I have cherished. Even if it came from a problematic writer.

It has taken me decades to exorcise the doctrine of the Genius, the Genius entitled to break the bonds of human solidarity, entitled to use people. That doctrine laid waste to friendships and love affairs in my life.

By dint of my gallery—and it was not just a perk, but one of its reasons for being—I have been friends with a number of geniuses. By friends I mean being invited to their homes, eating together, exchanging personal histories, meeting one another's families. By geniuses I mean lions in their fields, creators of things unforeseeable that have had worldwide influence: documentarian Eugene Richards, writer Gunter Grass, filmmaker Albert Maysles, sculptor John Chamberlain, musician Lou Reed, performance artist Laurie Anderson, graphic novelist Emile Ferris, painter June Leaf, photographer Robert Frank.

I first met the couple Robert Frank and June Leaf in December of 2011. After an exhibition opening at my gallery, I was hosting a dinner at a big round table in a Chinese restaurant. At another round table a different dozen folk were celebrating a June Leaf opening. I was excited to see Robert Frank there, one of my heroes. Sitting next to him was a recent acquaintance of mine, Ayumi Furuta, a photographer and Frank's assistant. I had hung out with Ayumi that summer at the Steidl publishing house in Germany. I sidled over and crouched down between Ayumi and Frank; Ayumi introduced us. I told them that we were about to open a Weegee show. I told Frank that in my press release I had written that Weegee's great first book, *Naked City*, had influenced him. I asked him if he agreed. He paused. In his chewy Germanic accent he said "no" in a way that I knew meant "yes." I invited him to come preview the show.

A day or two later Frank showed up with a strange entourage: Ayumi and June, but also the photographers François-Marie Banier and Martin d'Orgéval. Banier was then famously on trial for seducing and cadging from Liliane Bettencourt, the heiress of the notoriously anti-Semitic company L'Oreal. (Four years later, Banier was convicted, sentenced to three years in prison and restitution payments of over $173 million.) I knew all these folk were in the Steidl inner circle, but that a melancholy Jewish genius like Frank should be hanging out with a poseur like Banier struck me as odd. Banier sprawled across my viewing room table like a wizened odalisque, snapping pictures and making his presence never unfelt. Robert sat quietly, admiring the Weegee prints I brought out for him. He too had a small camera in hand, occasionally lifting it to discreetly snap pictures.

Despite Banier's shenanigans, or because they broke the ice, the visit was good. As he was leaving, Robert came close to me and said, "If there is anything I can do for you, let me know." It was as if I had never heard those words before. When Robert said them to me, they opened two doors. They opened a door to many visits I had with Robert and June at their Bleecker Street and Nova Scotia homes. And they opened the door to a room in my heart from which I speak those words often, an offer of openness, of solidarity, of generosity.

Robert had a reputation for testiness, but I saw him lose his temper only once. It was in a hospital. June had banged her head and was having an amnesiac incident. I happened to visit just minutes after the event. I realized June needed attention, so I took her and Robert to a clinic, and then the hospital. Robert was calm throughout, shuffling along patiently. Until he suddenly decided June wasn't being attended well. He let the nurses know, loudly, angrily.

Visiting Robert at Bleecker Street meant sitting with him at his favorite perch, a second-story window overlooking the street. I would bring apple cake or apple pie, his favorites. He would offer me a chair. We would look at each other, exchange a few words, look out the window. We would sit in silence. At

first, the silences made me nervous. Shouldn't we be talking? But I came to
cherish the silences. What needed to be said? Spending time together was the
point. I came to think of Robert as some sort of sage.

Robert was a Swiss Jew who relocated to New York after World War II. He
made photographs for magazines and for himself, and made friends among the
Beats, Allen Ginsberg and Jack Kerouac for instance. In 1955 he was awarded a
Guggenheim grant to travel across the United States taking pictures. His book
of those pictures, *The Americans,* is the most influential photography book of
the late twentieth century. It is a compassionate look at people in power and
out, monied and poor, their commonalities, their sufferings, their joys.

Robert made this picture in Hollywood in 1956. It shows fans yearning for
the stars on a bleacher set up for a movie premiere. It is Robert Frank's genius
in this picture that he holds the energy of every one of these individuals of his
adopted America, holds each singular human, each uncommon beauty, holds
them up for us. Each one seen as seeing, as taking in the world, as sensitive, as
engaged. None of them off the human scale, none of them second-listers.

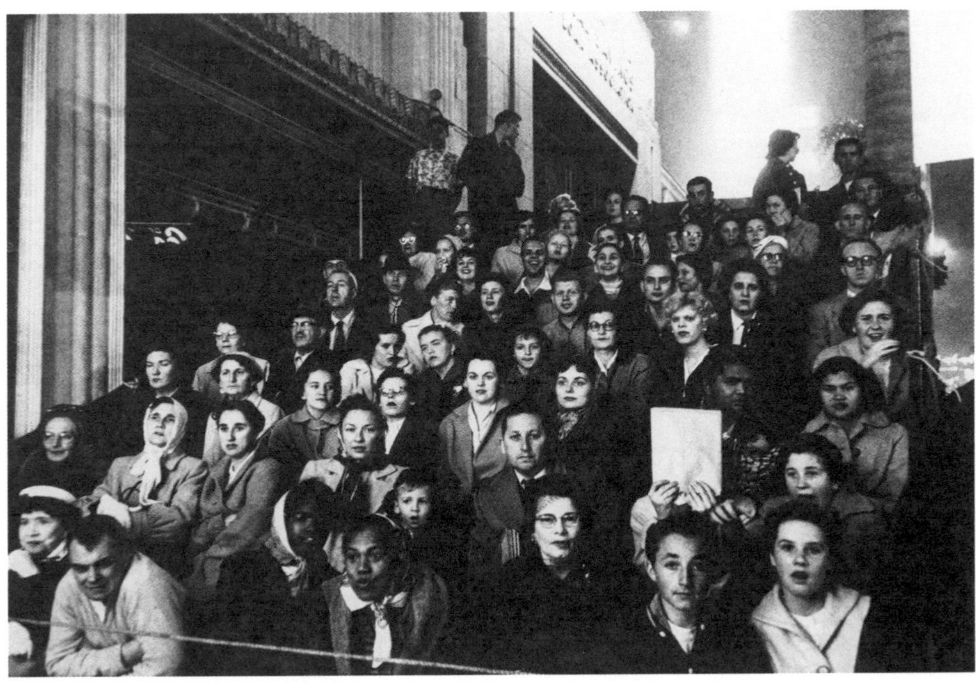

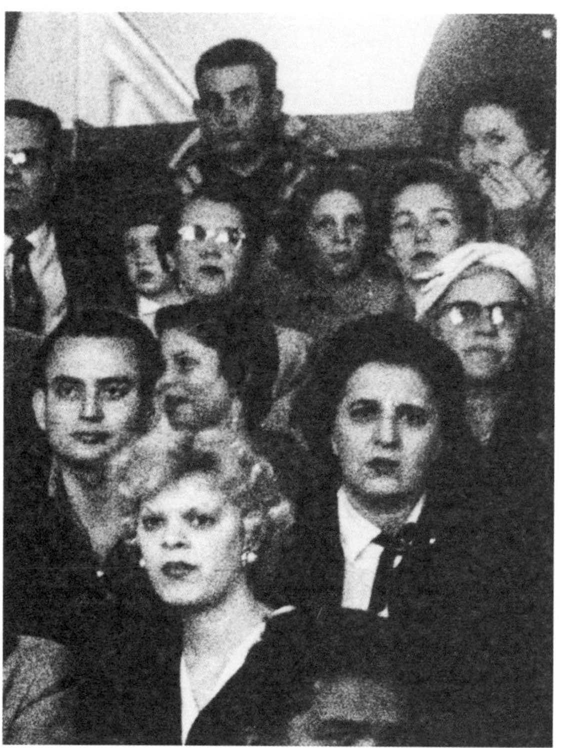 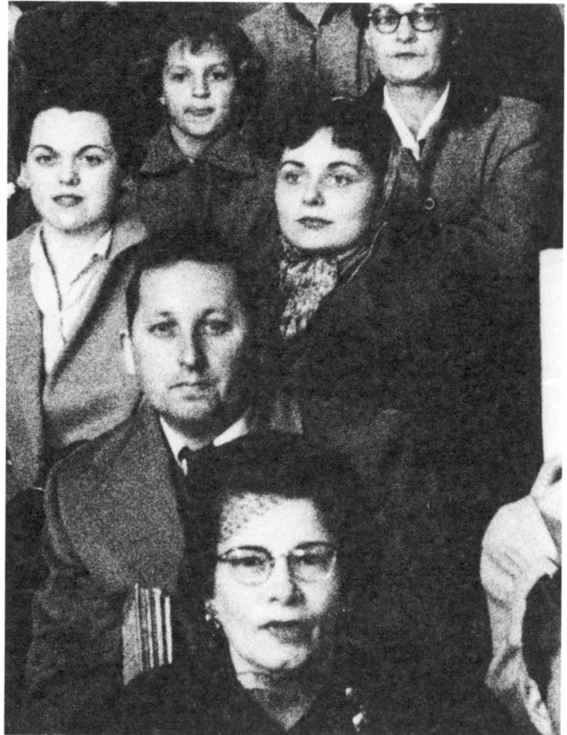

Have a good look at each of those faces, at each of those beings as they sit awaiting the show. Not one is uninteresting. Each has his or her own special light. Even the hidden one, the shy one, the one with secrets. Take your time. They are held up for us to love.

June was always talkative, full of stories. I learned about her childhood in Chicago, about her grandmother introducing her to art-making, about her difficult life caring for Robert. In her studios she showed me works old and new—which were often the same ones, because the works took years to complete. She would hold up a small steel sculpture, bending it with unsteady fingers, reshaping it, still making it. She was marvelously rich with questions about me, my gallery, my family, my past. Her mindful listening was such a gift to me,

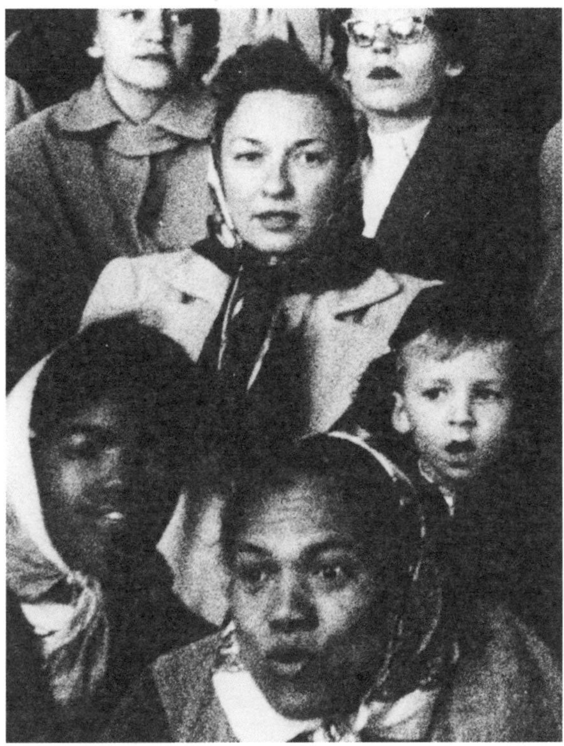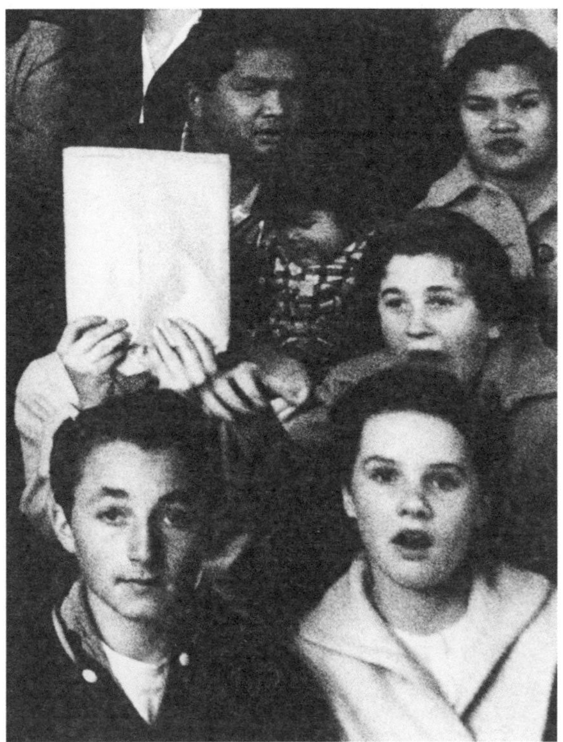

such a solace for one who has not felt heard enough. June was born one week to the day before my mother.

Thinking of the genius artists I have known, I don't think of their sense of privilege, their acts of callousness. I think of their fragility, their struggles with shyness. I think of their secrets held and revealed. I see them putting their best selves into their work. I see their ascensions above known ground. I see their maverick leaps into the air.

Look at the small figure in this June Leaf painting that hangs in my living room. He is grounded, he rests embedded. He is also groundless, floating free. A word is painted above him, faintly, almost erased: "fly." Look at his right arm and hand: they are doubled, one curling in, one reaching out. Reaching out to that ambiguous reaching hand above, that big white vulnerable yearning hand. That godlike hand. The hand of God, the hand of June, the hand of

Robert? Big hand and small hand, both hands reaching out for contact, for comfort.

This painting is genius. Walking the tightrope. Maybe falling off. Falling into the unknown. To say something in a new way. Something that we all know. Saying that we are all suffering. That we need each other. That we need to see, to feel, to hear, to say our suffering. Together. And our relief. Yearning is met with responsiveness, with communion, with love.

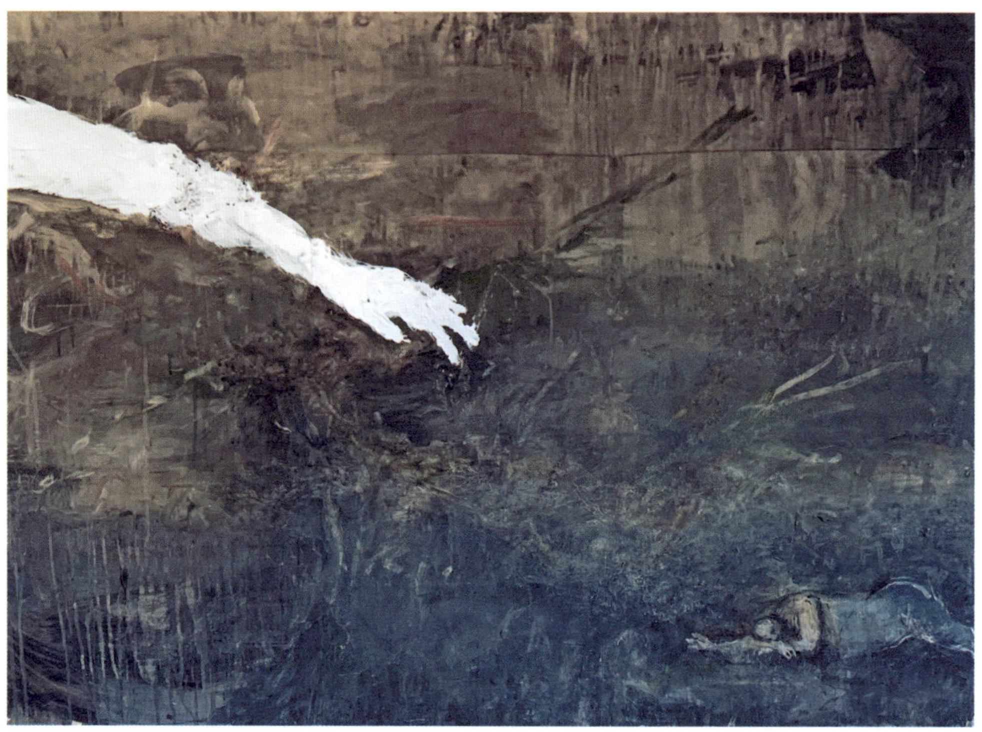

The Artist, Then and Now

In 1970, the summer after my junior year of high school, I strapped on a backpack to hitchhike and hop trains around Europe. Flown from Amerika, rid of parents and teachers, I made pilgrimage to the museums and churches of London, Paris, Madrid, Rome, Florence, Venice. I couldn't get my fill of classical European painting. I also visited hashish cafés in Amsterdam, and international-hippie nude beaches on Ibiza. I was haunted by the teenage riddles: Who am I? Who can I be?

I looked for answers in the paintings I saw, Renaissance altarpieces and frescoes telling melodramatic Christian tales. They were like the comic books that had so engrossed me a few years earlier, likewise full of heroes and villains, good and evil, apocalypse and redemption. These stories were even more compelling. With Adam and Eve, I shed tears as we were driven from Paradise. With St. Francis, I tendered my only garment to a leper and preached Gospel to my brothers and sisters the birds. I shuddered with guilt and fear at the Last Judgment. Most devastating was Grünewald's Isenheim Altarpiece, his skin-

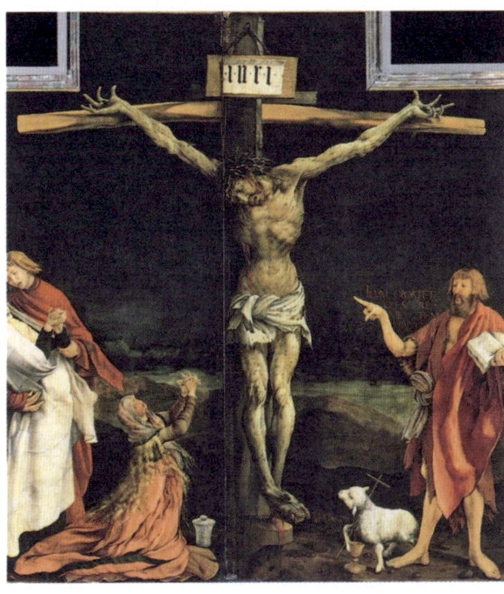
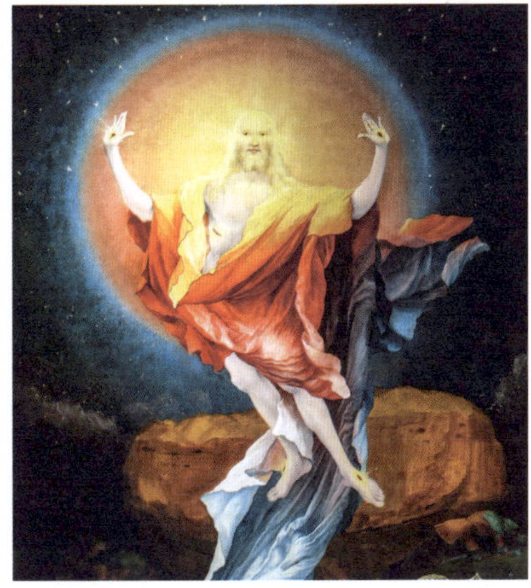

ripped Jesus, his irradiated Christ. I saw Jesus as a superhero bringing an end to war and evil. His superpowers were suffering and detachment.

I summoned Jesus to lead me out of the maze and mishegas of my family. I memorized these lines from Blake:

> Thou, mother of my mortal part,
> With cruelty didst mold my heart,
> And with false self-deceiving tears
> Didst bind my nostrils, eyes, and ears.
> . . . .
> The death of Jesus set me free:
> Then what have I to do with thee?"

Even more real to me than Jesus and his saints were the painters and sculptors who told their stories. I dreamed of adding my voice to their choir. I imagined painting my way to redemption and glory. I felt like the 1971 Bob Dylan song set in Rome—a song in which he sings, "I've got me a date with Botticelli's niece."—"Someday everything is gonna be smooth like a rhapsody / When I paint my masterpiece."

Five decades later, I am amazed to find a drawing that sums up my adolescent yearning for a sanctified art world: Lauren Weinstein's 2017 cartoon *The Artist, Then and Now.*

Then: An aged Renaissance artist alone with his devotions, drawing saints and angels. With delicate pen Weinstein gathers the fifteenth-century iconography of sainthood—the beard, the cave, the crucifix, the skull, the receding Tuscan landscape. She melds that with the cross-legged Eastern sage of many a *New Yorker* cartoon. This beatified artist is drawing a tender Madonna and Child. His drawing is inspired by holy texts; it is a study for a work to be displayed in a holy temple.

Now: The artist of today, a young woman, like Weinstein herself, attached by both hands to electronic devices, drawing mechanically. She's been sipping soda and eating crap. She's haunted by a Hieronymus Bosch cacophony of kids' characters, her inescapable crappy imaginary. She draws a demented smiley face, a cliché to be piped into the marketplace.

Lauren told me about her discomfort making comics for the internet, about the pressure to capture big online audiences. She told me about the "tyranny

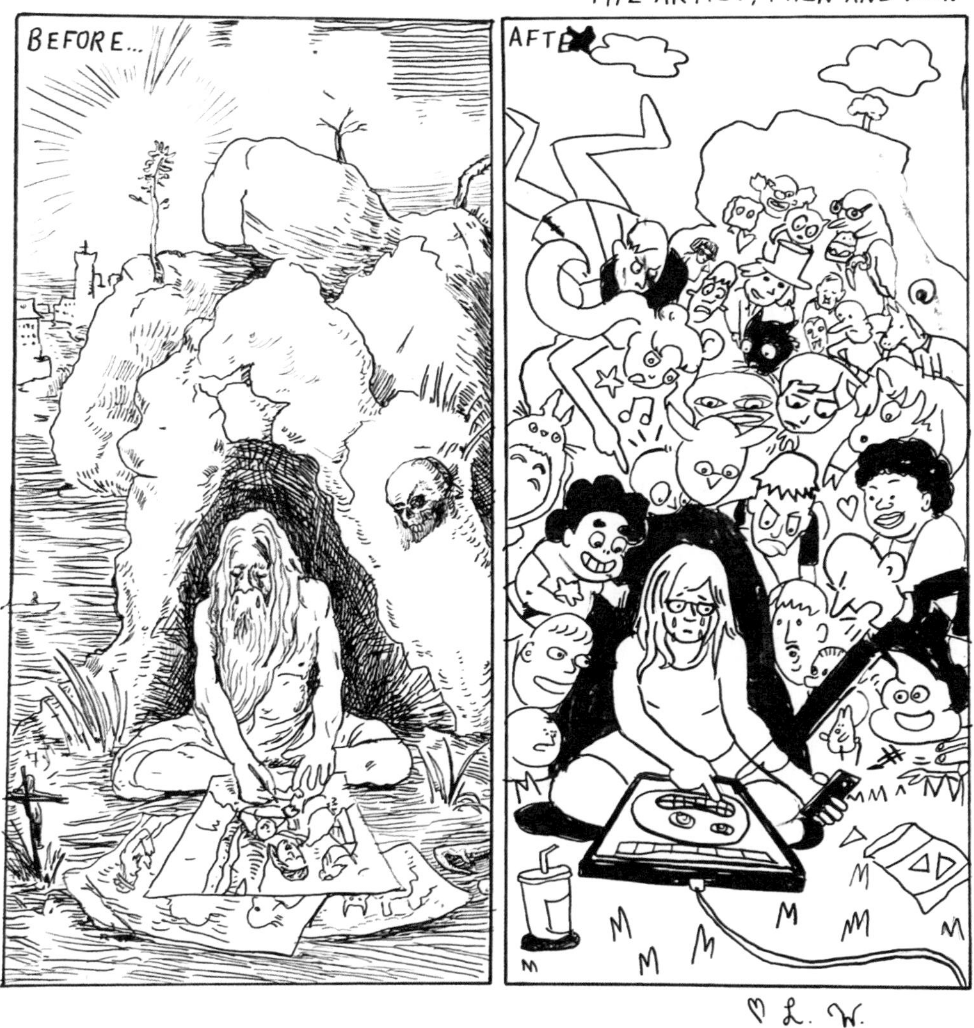

of cute," how female comics artists are pressured to candy-coat experience. She talked about feeling smothered by the neediness of the Internet audience, about making a comic for AOL called *Am I Fat?* and receiving hundreds of photographs from girls asking her if they were fat. She talked about longing to make work from a quiet, offline place.

The dichotomy of *The Artist, Then and Now* is gendered. The woman is buried in an avalanche of ideograms, is beleaguered by a maelstrom of kitsch. She is beset by the ever-lurking online critic (the angry man pointing, just above the grinning turd). The female artist cries tears of frustration, of feeling overwhelmed. While Weinstein's artist of yore, male, sits alone at the mouth of his sanctuary, all the time in the world, shedding slow tears of holy compassion. That is his privilege.

In Weinstein's cartoon *Preferences*, she again addresses privilege, the Internet, tyranny. Topical when it was drawn in the 2017 lead-up to the election of President Trump, it was just as apt when I discovered it in 2020.

I couldn't help laughing at how precisely it predicted/portrayed my wife's 2020 Summer of Fear obsessions—and not just her's. The first five panels were the memes that mattered most in our pandemic brain fog: cats to love, Trump to hate, cute kids to love, systemic racism to hate, infatuating foods to love. Weinstein sums us up in that last panel: an apocalypse of the addicted and the oblivious, a hell of relentless aversions and needs.

Weinstein's dystopia is the flip side of her imagination of a better world. Where Black lives matter. Where Trump is just a cartoon. Where cats are forever kittens. Where babies play in ever-loving menageries. Where every bowl of soup is sustenance to the core. She imagines a world where love and hate are not assigned with the flick of an electrified finger, where attraction and aversion are not programmed reactions. She imagines a world where the genders, all of them, create characters born in the holy caves of the heart. She imagines an earthly paradise, a social nirvana.

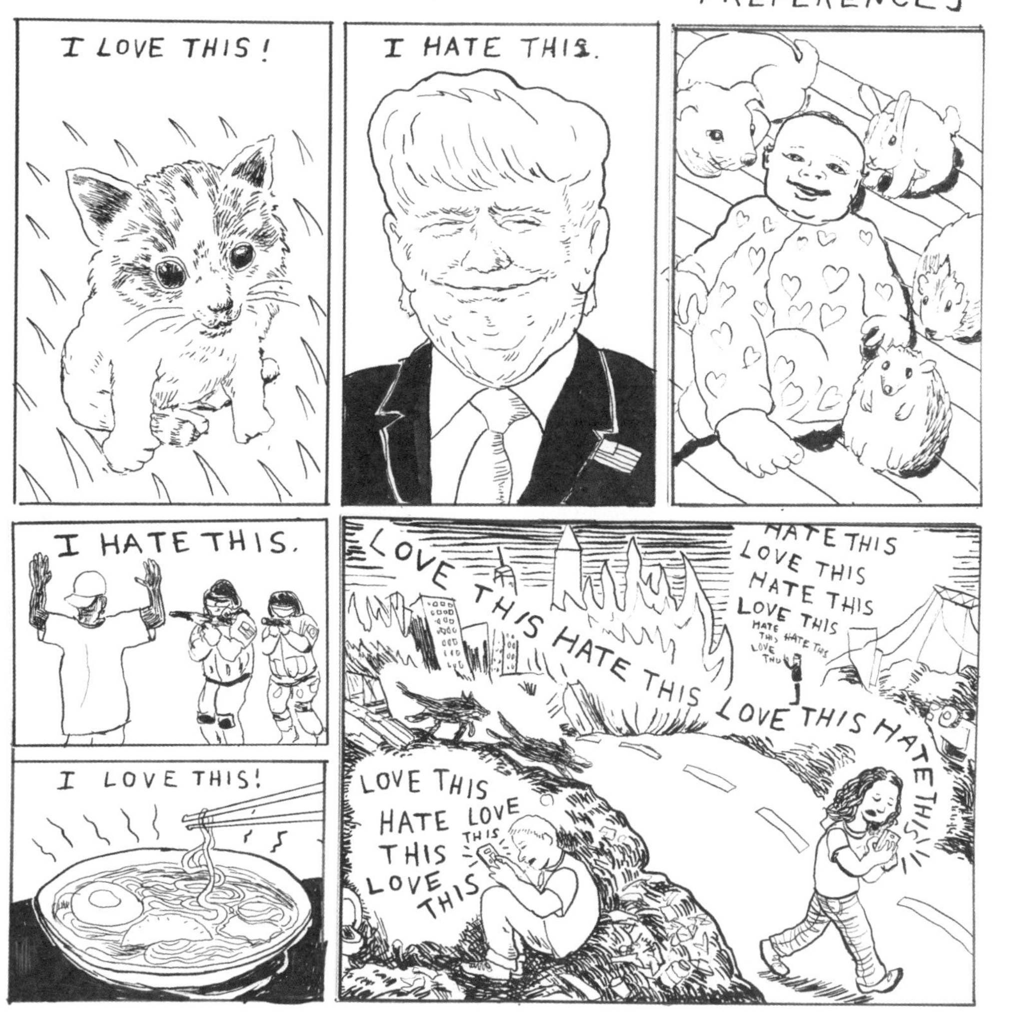
I LOVE THIS!
I HATE THIS.
I HATE THIS.
I LOVE THIS!
LOVE THIS HATE THIS HATE THIS LOVE THIS HATE THIS
HATE THIS
LOVE THIS
HATE THIS
LOVE THIS
HATE THIS HATE THIS LOVE THIS
LOVE THIS HATE LOVE THIS
THIS
LOVE THIS
BY   LAUREN R. WEINSTEIN

Lady Day

Graduating high school, I flew to Florence and enrolled in the Accademia di Belle Arti, the art-school branch of the Università di Firenze. It was free for foreign students. I rented the second floor of a hillside stuccoed farmhouse with a fellow art student named Alan. It was ten minutes from city center via Vespa. I would park out front, walk past chickens scratching in the dusty courtyard, mount concrete steps. We had no running water or electricity; we drew water from a well and lit kerosene lamps. I built a fireplace out of firebricks to heat my bedroom. Our rooms were above an old wooden olive press. We stashed empty Chianti bottles for the days the elderly proprietor forgot to lock the oil storage. We would sneak in, plunge the bottles in the huge ceramic vat: virgin oil for months, for our friends too! The whole setup was ridiculously bohemian, *The Whole Earth Catalog* goes to Tuscany.

One summer evening I walked the hill above the farmhouse and sat beneath an olive tree. I watched blood-red poppies in the breeze folding and unfolding their wrinkled petals. I felt a sadness that I had no one to share this vision with. Beauty wants to be shared, sadness too.

Billie Holiday was my dear companion there on that hill in my first home away from home. I had come to Billie through my father. Looking to expand my musical horizons, I asked him who was his favorite singer. Billie Holiday, Lady Day. He had listened to her in the 52nd Street clubs. He had met her, Dizzy Gillespie too. He had tried to option her biography for a movie. From the moment I heard her, Billie was for me too the greatest singer of all. In the Florence farmhouse I had a small mono record player, turntable and speaker in one box, battery operated. An Italian best-of-Billie album helped me through a cold, lonely winter of wondering who I was. I warmed to the heat of Billie's desire. I was consoled by hearing her pain tempered by her lilt.

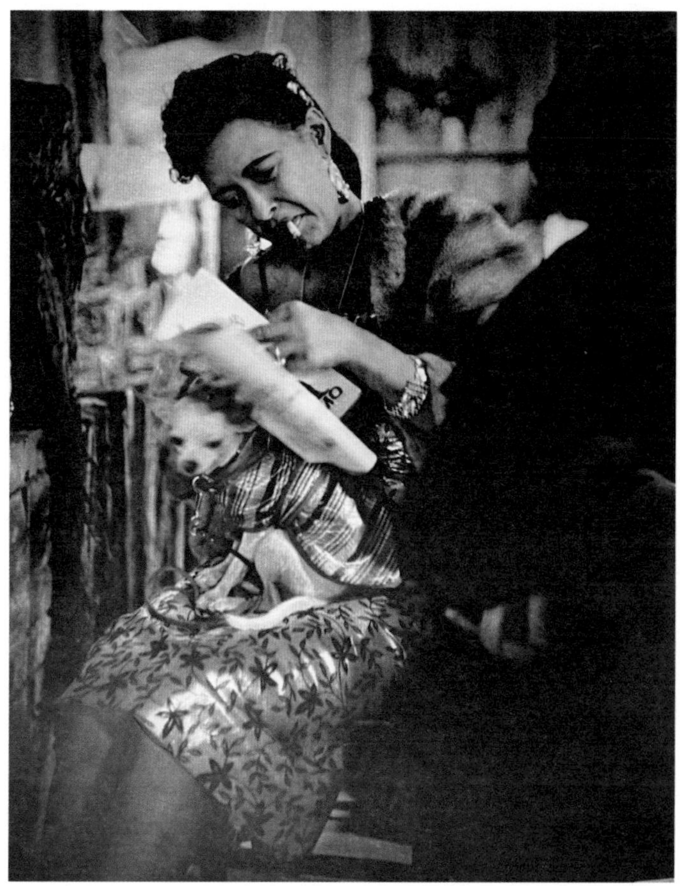

Oh, my man, I love him so
He'll never know
All my life is just despair
But I don't care

When I was eight, nine, ten, my dad was married to a young white jazz singer named Lodi Carr. Lodi had recorded an album titled *Ladybird* in tribute to Lady Day. Dad and Lodi were friends with Nat Hentoff, the *Village Voice* writer. Nat's columns were about jazz and the First Amendment: free expression, the pressing issue of the era. I remember Hentoff mostly for his full beard—beards were not for cowards then—and for his daughter Joie, pronounced not "Joey" like the gangster Joey Gallo, who was in their social set, but *joie*, French for "joy." Hentoff wrote of Holiday: "Lady's sound—a texture simultaneously steel-edged and yet soft inside; a voice that was almost unbearably wise in disillusion and yet still childlike, again at the center." He is describing Billie's Buddha-nature, her enlightenment gained through her suffering.

Hanging on my walls are two Billie Holiday photographs by Jerry Stoll. I first encountered Jerry on a trip to San Francisco in 2000. At the Hotel Bohème in North Beach, I noticed the enlarged black-and-white photographs decorating the hallways. They were pictures of the neighborhood in the sixties, Beat-infused scenes of cats and chicks cuddling in smoky clubs, a painter singing aloud as he strokes his canvas, a café chess game played beneath a poster for "6 Poets at the Six, 3119 Fillmore, Sat. 8:30."

These were scenes I recognized from hanging out as a kid at the off–Central Park West apartment of my beloved Uncle Del and Aunt Ada. Dear Aunt Ada with her stiletto ebony and silver cigarette holder, her black Edith Piaf hair and black capris, and her X-ray vision that saw my forlornness and comforted it like no other. Del, born Joseph Del Negro, was a painter in the style of Rauschenberg. Del's masterpiece was a salvaged crate painted janitor green and collaged with a blood-red bullfight poster, pink theater stubs, a yellowing wine cork, all shellacked to a high sheen. At front and center Del screwed on a worn nickel bath faucet from which he hung a lacquered half salami.

I asked the desk clerk, "Who took the pictures?" "Jerry Stoll." I got his phone number, rang him, was invited to visit. I found Jerry living in a sprawling former factory in Oakland. A long hose ran from an oxygen tank to his nose. Jerry was not well, but he was game to show me his prints. In addition to the North Beach Beat pictures, he had a cache of wonderful jazz prints. As official photographer for the Monterey Jazz Festival from 1958 through 1965 (in later years side by side with his mentee Jim Marshall), Stoll took photographs onstage and backstage. He lined some up for me: Ella, Pops, Dizzy, Trane, Mingus, Monk, Miles and Lady Day, a Parthenon frieze of musical titans. He wanted to share his pictures with the world. He felt I was excited about them. I left Oakland with a box of prints for my gallery.

Stoll's 1955 portrait of Billie was printed from a copy negative for extra grain, extra pop. This is Lady Day like a sibyl from the Sistine Chapel. Her head strains away searchingly. Her hair is a smoldering nimbus in a neon halo. Her eyes burn through the air, her nostrils flare, her parted lips are saying something we cannot hear. Her earrings spin like galaxies. She plummets into view like a black comet, her eroded beauty and her sadness shining in the cold white space of the negation of Black lives in America.

The photograph of Holiday at the beginning of this chapter was taken by Stoll three years later. Billie is hunched in a cluttered space, a makeshift dressing room. On her lap she cradles her beloved Pepi, outfitted lavishly in a striped wrap. Pepi looks out soulfully. He supports on his back the magazine that Billie is reading. She is elegant in an embroidered dress and mink stole. Her right eye is wide open in concentration; her left is squinting from her cigarette smoke. There is tragedy on her face. There are bruises on her legs. She would be dead a year later.

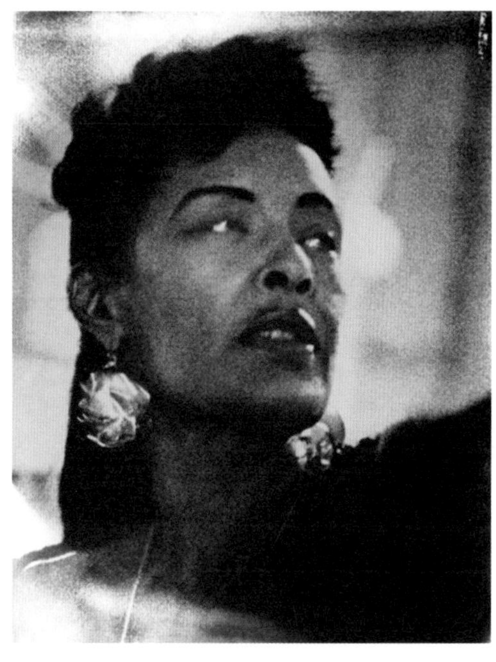

At the age of twenty-three, in 1939, Holiday first sang "Strange Fruit." It is a song about lynching, about the torture and murder of Black bodies. The song was written in 1937 by Abel Meeropol, a New York Jewish Communist who would later adopt the two orphaned boys of Ethel and Julius Rosenberg after they were executed as Communist spies. It is well documented that Billie Holiday died of "Strange Fruit." For decades she was hounded by Harry Anslinger, the first commissioner of the Federal Bureau of Narcotics, a rabid racist. Anslinger promoted the first national campaign against marijuana, saying, "Reefer makes darkies think they're as good as white men." Anslinger had particular hate for jazz musicians. He pursued Holiday relentlessly because she would not obey his command to stop singing "Strange Fruit." Anslinger arrested Holiday repeatedly. In 1958 he chained her to a hospital bed, where she died.

For twenty years Holiday ended her nightclub sets with "Strange Fruit." The waiters stopped serving. The audience went still. The lights were cut. A spotlight snapped on, encircling Billie's face. She sang—softly, slowly. "Black bodies swinging in the Southern breeze / Strange fruit hanging from the poplar trees…" The light was killed. A black stage. No encore.

Guston Unobstructed

The New York Studio School of Drawing, Painting, and Sculpture was the place for me. There were no credits or degrees, we each got our own studio space, we made art all day long. It occupied a rundown building that had been the original Whitney Museum. It was across the street from the Eighth Street Bookshop, a haunt of the Beats. Entering up a curvaceous marble staircase, you met a reek of turpentine and oil paint wafting off a gunky washout sink. The sink was the hub of a warren of studios linked by various contradictory staircases. I was always getting lost.

The Studio School had an Abstract Expressionist pedigree. It was descended directly from the Hans Hoffman School of Fine Art. Mercedes Matter, the founding director, had been friends with Jackson Pollock. Morton Feldman, the composer who along with John Cage brought indeterminacy into music, had been dean. Philip Guston was our most eminent teacher.

Guston's annual visit was the big event. Mercedes would pick her favorite students; they would each bring a painting into a big studio. Guston would look them over and speak his mind. The whole school crowded in to listen. Guston, in professorial woolens, perched on a stool, crossed his legs languidly, chain-smoked. He held forth in passionate sentences. He could also be generous, could rave about a blue table or emphatic thigh in a student's painting. He could be impatient, domineering, not to be contradicted. He would put the finishing touch on an argument by summoning up Piero della Francesca.

I was just back from being an art student in Florence. I had been twice to Arezzo to visit Piero's celebrated frescoes. Piero was my favorite too! A great living painter loved what I loved! And Guston was in the mold of my father: tall, handsome, loquacious, charming. He was born Philip Goldstein in Montreal in 1913 to Jewish Ukrainian immigrants escaping pogroms; my dad was born Charles Kashevitz in Chicago in 1912 to Jewish Ukrainian and Belarusian immigrants escaping pogroms. I adopted Guston as my mentor.

Around 1950 Guston met John Cage and Morton Feldman; the three became

close friends. They attended
D. T. Suzuki's lectures on Zen
at Columbia University. Suzuki
was the great introducer of Zen
to America. Affected by Suzuki's
Zen teachings and by the "indeterminacy" of his friends Cage
and Feldman, Guston made his
first abstract paintings. Paintings like the one shown here,
White Painting I, 1951. Cage
wrote, "The doctrine which he
[Suzuki] was expressing was that
every thing and every body, that
is to say every nonsentient being
and every sentient being, is the
Buddha. These Buddhas are all,

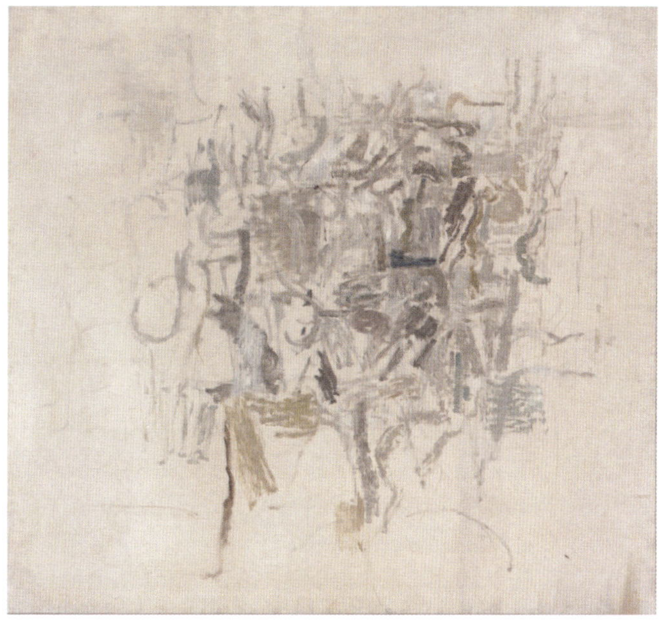

every single one of them, at the center of the Universe. And they are in inter-
penetration, and they are not obstructing one another." Cage's most famous
lecture dated from this time: "Lecture on Nothing."

Already under the spell of Zen, at the Studio School I gravitated to the Zen
in Guston's paintings. With pictures like White Painting I in mind, I impro-
vised emotive painterly shapes feathered out into indefinite infinite space.
I painted my way to that certain indeterminate Zen groove. When I slotted in, I
felt all my cares slough off. I was light, balanced, unobstructed. For a moment,
a resonant moment.

But by then, Guston was onto something quite different. 1968 had inter-
vened. On April 4, 1968, Martin Luther King Jr. was assassinated. On June 3,
Andy Warhol was shot in the gut and barely survived. On June 5, Robert Kennedy was shot dead. In August, Chicago police rioted against anti–Vietnam
War protestors as the whole world watched. In November, Richard Nixon was
elected President.

In 1968, Philip Guston waged war against himself. He fought to escape from
abstraction. He said, "I'm sick of all that Purity! I want to tell Stories." He said,
"The war, what was happening to America, the brutality of the world. What
kind of man am I, sitting at home, reading magazines, going into frustrated

fury about everything—and then going into my studio to adjust a red to a blue?" He added: "I knew ahead of me a road was laying. . . . I wanted to be complete again, as I was when I was a kid. . . . Wanted to be whole between what I thought and what I felt."

Guston returned from Florida and an affair, returned to his wife, his dear Musa, his muse. He began to paint simple objects known and strange. A fat cigar, a lightbulb, a book, a nail, a hooded Klansman. He infused comics he admired—Mutt and Jeff, Krazy Kat—with Piero della Francesca's monumentality and de Chirico's urban foreboding. He used thick pinks, scummy greens, and leaden blacks brushed with a touch both completely self-assured and utterly erasable. He birthed an unforeseen figurative art. Guston was, in his friend Philip Roth's words, "painting a new American landscape of terror."

Many in the art world took Guston's turn to figuration as a betrayal. Cage and Feldman cut him off. In 1968 Guston left New York City, retreating upstate to Woodstock, a place artists went to homestead away from intrusions, to escape the prodding, the demanding, the seducing of the world. A place to lick one's wounds. Guston built himself a studio there, on Maverick Road.

Guston's best friend in Woodstock was not Zen Cage but Jewish Roth. Roth was in Woodstock escaping, as he put it, "my new reputation as a crazed penis." Roth admired Guston's everyday-wasteland imagery, comparing it to the work of two of his heroes, Kafka and Beckett. Roth said that he used Guston, twenty years his senior, as a model for E. I. Lonoff, the Berkshires recluse genius, the magnetic father figure of his celebrated novel The Ghost Writer. Guston was bowled over by Roth's 1971 satiric novel Our Gang, the story of Trick E. Dixon. It inspired Guston to devote six months to making two hundred cartoonish pen-and-ink drawings of President "Tricky Dick" Nixon and his seedy cronies. Nixon is portrayed as a walking, talking penis, scrotum-jowled. Guston shared his drawings with Roth, who loved them, but otherwise kept them to himself.

Bob Dylan was in Woodstock then too, in a three-year recovery from a motorcycle crash, bringing up a son, secretly recording songs with the Band at Big Pink. Guston, Roth, Dylan: the Three Jews of Woodstock, three Jews who stayed fresh into old age, who did not burn out. They were blessed and cursed with unrelenting restlessness and with enormous confidence. Roth said, "He who is loved by his parents is a conquistador." Conquistadors kill. Dylan killed folk music with prophetic lyrics transcribed from some dire muse. Roth killed Jewish decorum with Portnoy's flagrant ejaculations. Guston killed pure modernist painting with his ultraserious comics. The world greeted all three murders with bewilderment and anger (before sanctifying them). They were murders committed not to destroy. They were committed for freedom.

While I was a student at the Studio School, a show of these new Guston paintings was mounted at Boston University. I traveled up to see it. Thirty-odd canvases hung in two awkwardly repurposed rooms. No one else was there. Just me and some casual Klansmen performing a vaudeville show of evil, me and some cigarette-smoking mummies dreaming of Holocaust hobnail boots, me and the tired lonely racist bones of the world. I felt what I had felt once or twice before—in front of Piero's Arezzo frescoes, in front of Grünewald's Isenheim Altarpiece. I was in a world illuminated differently, a world darker and brighter.

One picture stood out: *Painting, Smoking, Eating.* In the background, soles of boots piled high, paint cans stuck with brushes—a nightmare land-scape bracketed by a bloated lightbulb (seeing) and a window-blind cord (the unseen). In the foreground, the Self, rigid, noseless, smoking in bed between

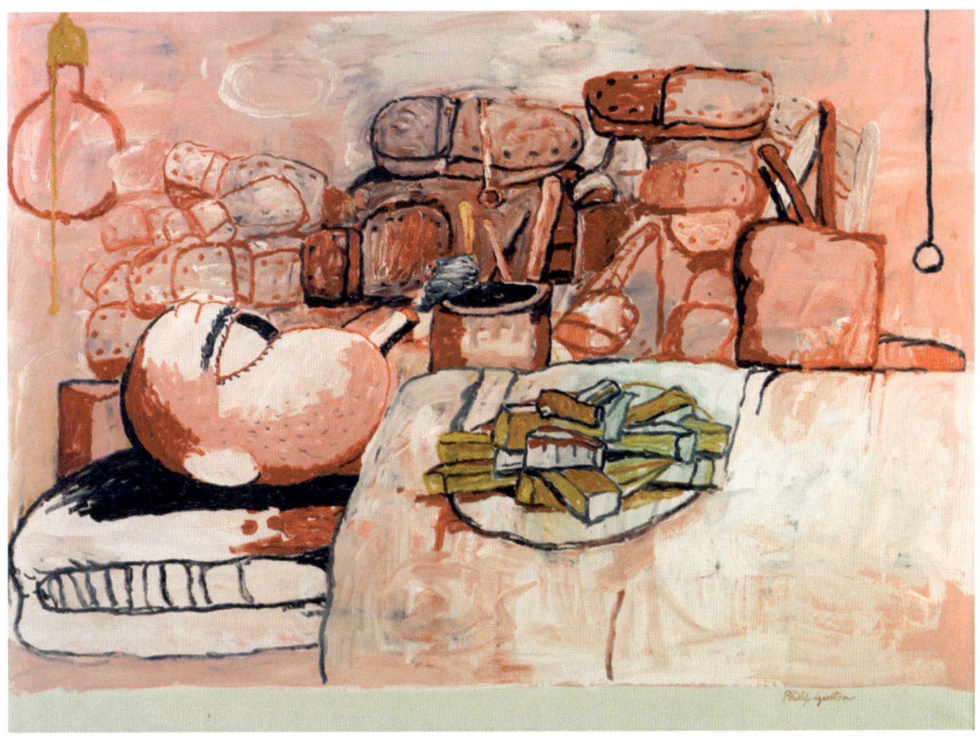

a hard mattress and an overbearing blanket. On his chest a monumental stack of french fries like the ruins of some acropolis. Swaddled in his sarcophagus, the Self can't reach them. If he breathes, they'll slide right off. Not eating, not painting. He's trapped. His staring cyclops eye sees the dream and sees the reality. Somehow we know what all this means.

I bought this signed poster when David McKee Gallery mounted an offshoot of the Boston show. It's a version of *Painting, Smoking, Eating* that is less claustrophobic but still tragic. The one-eyed smoking painter. A bare canvas nailed to a wall. A quartet of smoke puffs like the clouds in Guston's favorite Piero painting, The Flagellation of Christ, a copy of which hung prominently in his Woodstock kitchen. Clouds that are casual, unattached, transcending the cruelty below.

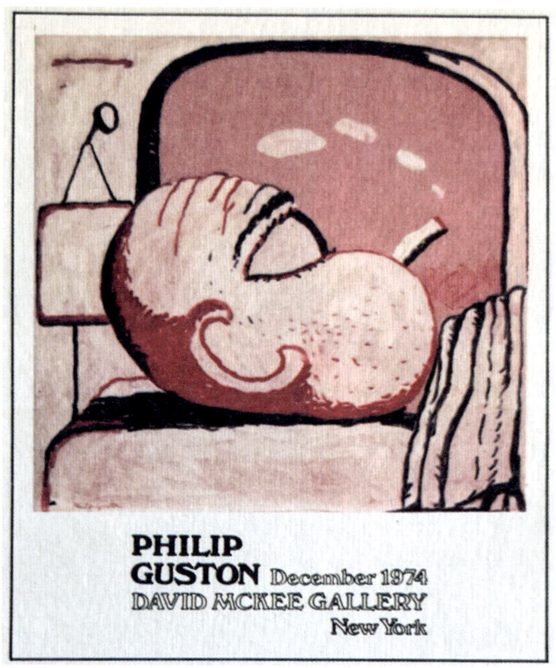

In the 1980s Guston's vivified mummies, his tormented boots, his immobilizing fries taught me ways to make art after the Holocaust and after AIDS. I shaped white plaster, red wax on wood, ceramic glazes like melting skins, formed them into statues like banshees, like mushroom clouds. Like Guston, I was shaping forms suspended between falling into ruin and rising above it.

In his last years, bereft by his wife's mental impairment, weakened by his own heart disease and depression, Guston produced furiously. He painted mostly at night, making works keyed to melancholy. He painted his insomniac nightscapes and his daily woe. He rehearsed a litany of motifs that compose a map of samsara, of the inescapable. The unclosing Cyclops eye. The smoking head. The amputated limb. The empty book. The demanding fat canvas. The doomsday clock. The sunset over the black sea. The forehead of his dying wife. The hand of God scribing an indelible line. The brick wall.

In 1978, two years before he died, Guston painted more than sixty large canvases, none of them trivial. After one particularly rewarding studio bout, he wrote an excited letter to his friend, the writer Ross Feld. He wrote about a set of three paintings he had made in a single week, a set he considered a major breakthrough. He wrote the letter in short thought-strokes both self-assured and marveling. He starts: "Now the contest is between knowing and not knowing." Of Mid-Day, the first painting in the set: "It is a painting of crumbling—of dissolution. As I look at it now—today—I was heading for another state of feeling not known to me." Of the second painting, Conversation, he says, "No—all there finally is left is just the moment—the second— of life's gesture—fixed forever—in an image—there—to be seen." He points to the stunning revelation of the final painting, Pink Sea, a negative revelation of a place both in and beyond Art: "Ah, so that's what 'art' is—lets you stop—isolate it—lets us 'see' it—but here in this new picture there is 'nothing' to see."

Feld quotes this letter at the very beginning of his book on Guston. Next he relates Guston's primal formative encounter, faced at ten years of age, a frightful tale of knowing and not knowing, of seeing, and of nothing. "[Guston's father] hawked junk and scrap metal but did not do well, and in a few years' time he killed himself by hanging, with young Philip discovering the body. The trauma of losing a parent to suicide (to say nothing of witnessing the horror face to face) is something that could easily close up a child's desire for seeing the unexpected ever after. In Guston it seemed to work in reverse, like an immunization: his hunger to see what he wasn't expecting only increased."

After a near-fatal heart attack, as he lay wide-eyed in his hospital bed, Guston stated his last wishes. He asked that Kaddish, the traditional Jewish prayer for the dead, be said for him: "May there be abundant peace from heaven, and satisfaction, help, comfort, refuge, healing, redemption, forgiveness, atonement, relief, and salvation." He asked that it be recited by three men: Ross Feld, Philip

Roth, and Morton Feldman. Guston and Feldman had not spoken in decades. Feldman showed up, but he still could not forgive Guston his betrayal of purity. When Feld saw that even at the funeral Feldman remained blind to Guston's achievement, he felt pierced by an "existential splinter." Feldman could not see that Guston had found a new way to paint himself to "nothing."

In his last months, too sick to work on large canvases, Guston made small acrylic paintings on paper. One of these last paintings is of a mound of cherries. Each cherry is its own particular red, each has its own antic stem; they balance in an impossible pyramid. Another painting is of a sandwich. The sandwich is very specific: salami and cheese on seeded rye, no mustard. It's so animated you can hear it talk Yiddish. These are pictures of small but real consolations.

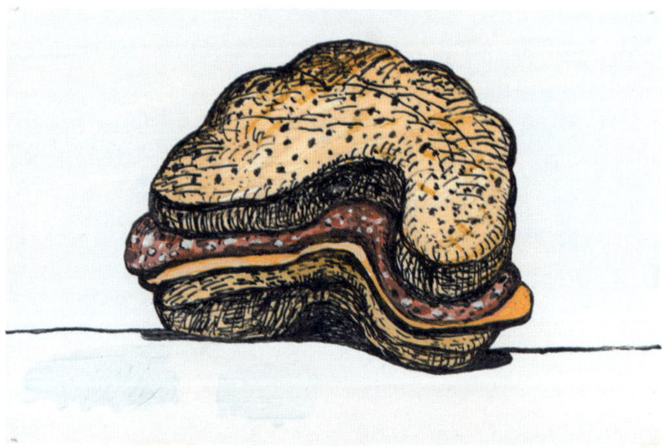

Guston had not forgotten Zen. His last paintings summon up Sengai, the Zen abbot whose drawings Cage had shown to Guston in the fifties. Sengai retreated in his final days to an abode called Empty White House. There he inked drawings of good-humored saints, of fishes, of eggplants, of tigers. Suzuki's commentary on this painting: "Here the mighty tiger is meekly beating a retreat as he is being charged by a fiercely insistent cat. Observe the tiger's troubled expression." A drawing about surprise. A drawing about fear. A drawing about the brawny overawed by the brave. Sengai gifted such drawings to his parishioners to give them relief, to give them courage, to give them enlightenment.

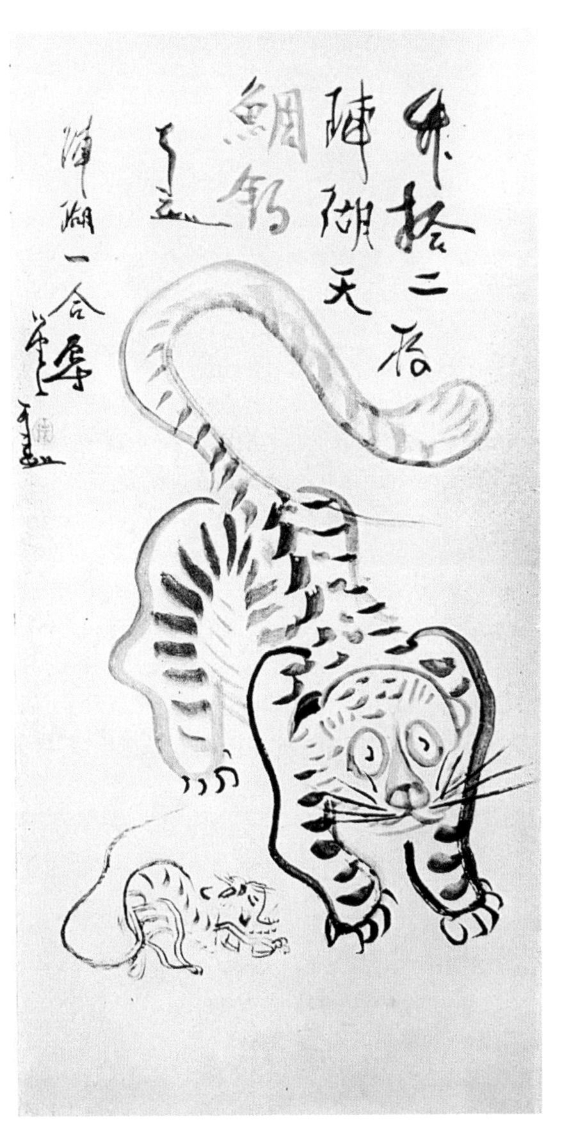

John Chamberlain and Max's

John Chamberlain built sculptures from mangled carcasses of automobiles. He crushed steel and twisted it into muscular arabesques. He splayed metal through space the way a painter, de Kooning for instance, might splash a loaded brush across a canvas. He worked calmly on his sculptures to achieve a deranged yet lyrical balance. He was looking for how an addled man can balance himself. John struggled with how to be a man in America.

I knew of Chamberlain from my earliest days. My beloved Uncle Del the artist was friends with him, worked on a film with him. As a teenager I heard about him from a girlfriend who frequented a bar where Chamberlain hung out, Max's Kansas City. One day in 1985, soon after I moved into a loft on the Hudson River, my ceiling seemed to explode so brutally loud was a hydraulic press crushing car parts on the floor above me, the floor of Chamberlain's studio. In the years when I was a sculptor, Chamberlain's work was a touchstone for how to mount material in space so it would feel both ominous and effervescent. Towards the end of John's life we became friends.

I own two vintage photographs portraying John. They show him in the thick of New York nightlife, drunk or stoned. In this unsavory 1971 print by Anton Perich, the light tones are blown out, and the black negative spaces creep around like hungry reptiles. Chamberlain sports dirty shirt cuffs, chin stubble, a single wayward tooth, half-seeing slit-eyes. He places a finger-pistol deliberately dead center on his drinking partner's brow—the universal symbol for "You're dead!" I find this ugly picture beautiful. It captures John's macho energy, his drive to destroy in order to create.

This picture was taken in the bar/restaurant Max's Kansas City, perhaps the single coolest hangout in the world in the 1960s. It was so cool that Patti Smith and Robert Mapplethorpe couldn't get in until, on one of their many attempts, Danny Fields, a major scenester and a friend of the owner, took pity and ushered them past the velvet rope. Lou Reed was a regular. From its opening night and for many years, John Chamberlain was the ringmaster and capo

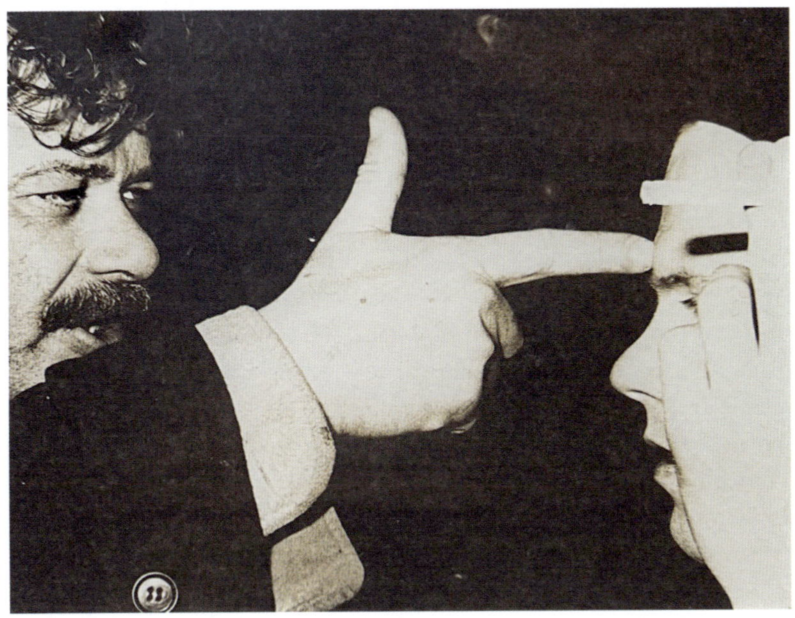

of the main room, the front barroom where the sculptors and painters drank each night.

Anton Perich was an innovative photographer, videographer, painter, magazine publisher—and a busboy at Max's Kansas City. Almost all the photographs and video taken at Max's (the bar/restaurant, not the later music venue) are by Anton, because Mickey Ruskin, the legendary owner/manager of Max's, wouldn't permit photographers to importune his guests, except Anton, whom he trusted as a respectful and artistic insider, an integral part of the scene that Ruskin orchestrated there each night. The flavor of Ruskin's relationship to Anton is captured on an audiotape recorded at Max's late one night in 1974, a conversation between Ruskin and Danny Fields (who was then manager of the Ramones):

> DF: Oh, did you see the videotape we made with Anton?
> MR: Is there another one on tonight?
> DF: Yeah.
> MR: Is it anything good?
> DF: I didn't see it, I don't know, I guess it is good, with Taylor [Mead] and Susan [Blond]. Anton is great, he has a lot of energy.

MR: Yeah, he really seems to move. I still keep waiting for one of my
   ex-employees to make it big.
DF: Did he work for you?
MR: Sure, he was a busboy for a long time. One of the worst. God, all my
   managers used to beg me to fire him and I carried him and carried
   him. . . .
DF: Oh, his photographs of Max's would be a great book.

In 2010 I put together a book and exhibition about Max's, full of Perich pictures. I first heard about Max's when I was fifteen, from Ivy Strick, who had been there. I fell for Ivy—beautiful Ivy, clad always in faded blue jeans and faded blue work-shirt—as we marched in DC in November of 1969 for the Moratorium to End the War in Vietnam. Ivy was a couple of years older than me. She told me about her visits to the sanctum sanctorum of cool, Max's. Her stories fascinated, frightened, and challenged me. Was I man enough for Max's, for Ivy? Cool enough? Decades later, I tried to get into Max's by organizing the posthumous retrospectives.

Mickey Ruskin opened Max's in December of 1965. It was on Park Avenue at 17th Street, deadsville. It was an immediate success because clients, hard-drinking artists from his former bar, the Ninth Circle, followed him there. Joined by some artists who had lofts nearby, they established themselves at the front bar. First among equals was John Chamberlain.

A Chamberlain sculpture of crushed galvanized steel, 60 × 60 × 60 inches, an ironic monument, stood at the entrance near the jukebox. Past the bar was a middle room of booths doled out by Ruskin to the famous and the beautiful. Frosty Myers, the sculptor who designed Max's, installed a futuristic laser sculpture. From his studio across the street, Frosty projected a red laser beam onto a small jiggling mirror mounted on the jukebox. The red ray hovered across the smoky barroom, the booth room, and the back room. It landed on the farthest back room wall, whirling like a red-fezzed dervish to whatever beats were being played on the jukebox up front.

The backroom was lit by a red-fluorescent-light sculpture—Dan Flavin's 1966 *monument 4 those who have been killed in ambush (to P.K. who reminded me about death)*—a pioneering Minimalist sculpture protesting the Vietnam

War. Originally an overflow room, the back room became the clubhouse of Andy Warhol and his Factory. They had dibs every night on the large central table.

Across its barroom, booth room and back room, Max's became the site of a unique cross-pollinating traffic as the macho artists, the Beautiful People, and the multifarious queens intermingled. In a picture shot in the back room of Max's by Elliott Landy on the March 1968 night that the Fillmore East first opened, the headline artist, Janis Joplin, stares past Warhol as she nurses a pack of Marlboros. The opening act, Tim Buckley, cradles a coffee and laughs. Warhol's consigliere Paul Morrissey scowls at the camera.

Three months later and five blocks south, Valerie Solanas, the author of *The S.C.U.M Manifesto* (S.C.U.M.: Society for Cutting Up Men) walked into Warhol's studio, the Factory, and shot him in the stomach. The night of the shooting, as Andy struggled to survive in the hospital, his friends posted a note on The Factory's front door: "If you are looking for us you'll find us at Max's."

In an Anton Perich photograph taken at Max's, the pale figure holding a louche cigarette, its shadow like a censor bar on his skull, the guy John is blowing away, that guy is the young Andrew Wylie. Wylie had just moved to New York from Harvard to nurture literary ambitions and hang out with the Warhol crowd. Shortly after this photograph was made, a book of Wylie's poetry came out, *Yellow Flowers*, which contains poems such as this:

> THIGHS
>> thighs
>>
>> on my neck
>>
>> I suck
>> the clit

Wylie went on to become the world's top literary agent, his achievements in that realm unequaled. He is literature's most feared operator, known as the Jackal for his poaching of authors and for his aggressiveness with publishers. I once encountered Andrew in full feral force. We were guests at an event; Andrew drew me aside. "You work with Gerhard Steidl, right? I represent the Warhol Foundation. Steidl's been stalling on a book for the foundation. You tell Gerhard if he fucks with me, I'll make him eat his balls." His apoplectic face had me believing his male animus entirely.

My other John Chamberalin picture was made by Takayuki Ogawa in the summer of 1967—the Summer of Love. John and his girlfriend Ultra Violet are dolled up for an event in the Sculpture Garden of the Museum of Modern Art. Both John and Ultra have noticed the camera and smile. John's smile is smirking; he seems drunk or stoned. Ogawa catches the couple against the musicality of the tiled wall. A sign reading Metropolitain hovers above them like an Art Nouveau blimp advertising their urbanity.

Takayuki Ogawa (1936–2008) was a Japanese photographer known for the pictures he made in New York during a one-year visit from April 1967 to March 1968. Robert Frank was Ogawa's mentor in New York; Frank gave Ogawa's photographs one of his highest compliments: he dubbed them sad. For me they are inquisitive, amused, celebratory—Ogawa's youthful take on a cosmopolis he could visit but not inhabit.

Chamberlain and Ultra Violet had been introduced by Andy Warhol, most likely at Max's. Ultra Violet, born Isabelle Collin Dufresne, was a Warhol Superstar. She was an actress, artist, and writer. She was a muse to Salvador Dalí, John Graham, Warhol, and Chamberlain. Chamberlain made her the star of his 1967 experimental film *The Secret Life of Hernando Cortez*. James Rosenquist recalls them visiting his Hamptons' studio while they were working on the film:

Not all my visitors were as provocative as John and Ultra. On Easter Sunday John arrived and immediately began to unroll a big length of tar paper across my lawn. Ultra took her top off and began crawling on her hands and knees across the tar paper, then climbing up in a tree like an animal—all of which John was recording on film. This was all going on just as church was getting out, and my neighbors and postman stood there watching it with their mouths open. "It's an artwork," I said.

Working on my Max's project was a way for me to meet John Chamberlain. I asked a mutual friend, eminent Condé Nast photographer Jonathan Becker, to introduce us. Jonathan brought me to Chamberlain's Shelter Island home/ studio. I wanted to borrow one of his sculptures from the heyday of Max's,

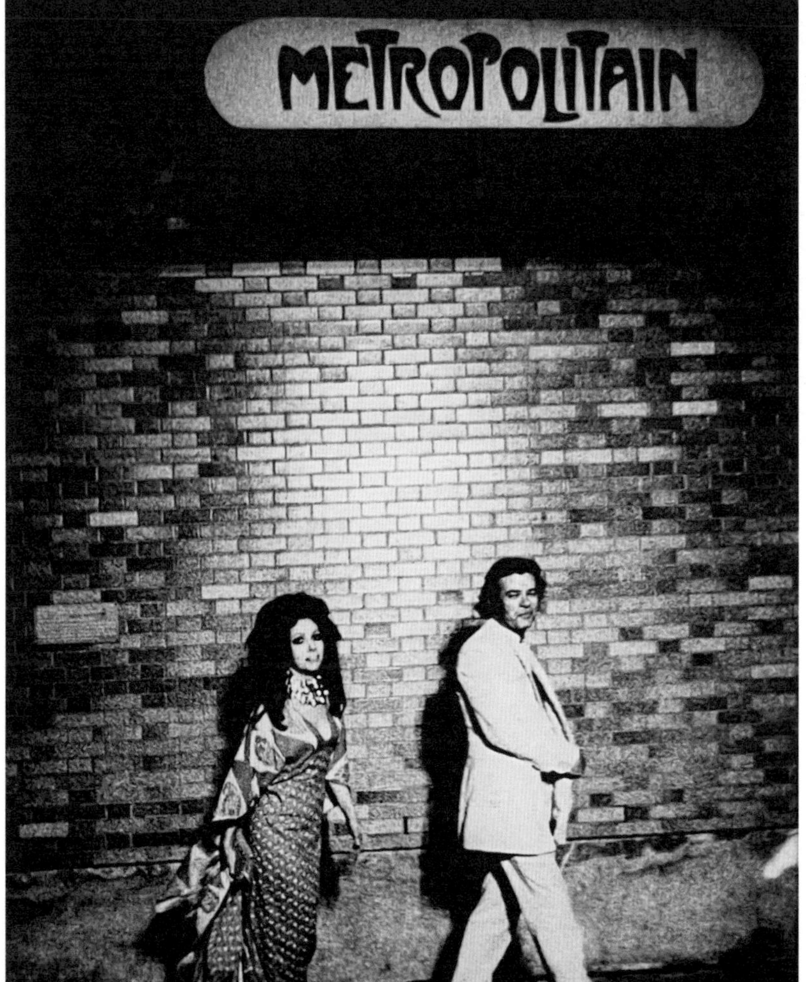

METROPOLITAIN

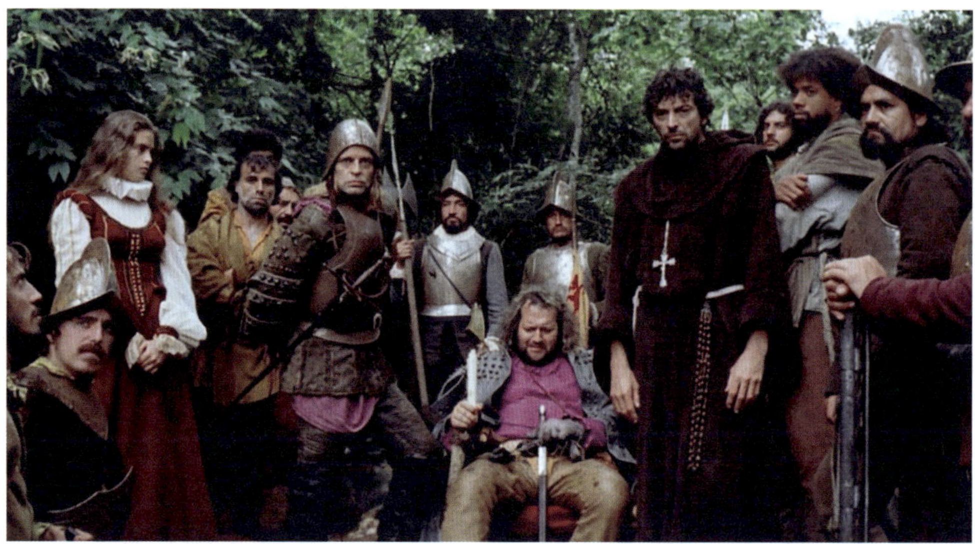

preferably a crushed metal box like the one that had stood by the front entrance. I wanted to hear his Max's stories.

I was especially curious to hear what Chamberlain would have to say about my beloved Uncle Del. Del had worked on experimental films with Chamberlain. Del, short for Joseph Nicolas Antonio Del Negro, was a jack of all trades: painter, actor, con artist, seducer of women. He was a tall, handsome, witty, outrageous Punch of a man, a bit unpredictable, a bit dangerous. He's best known for playing the priest in Werner Herzog's mad 1972 film *Aguirre, the Wrath of God*. When I met Chamberlain, I told him I was Del's nephew. John lit up with a nostalgic glow. He told me how Del was one of the few guys that could keep up. Those memories of Del, still alive in John, watered our budding friendship.

Chamberlain's film *The Secret Life of Hernando Cortez* plays on a continuous loop in Marfa, Texas, in a building dedicated to a permanent Chamberlain exhibition installed by Chamberlain and his friend Donald Judd. The anteroom features one of Chamberlain's sprawling foam and silk sculptural couches; visitors can loll in this irreverent den to watch the film, to watch the sexual and psychedelic shenanigans of Ultra Violet and of Taylor Mead, the fey stalwart of many Warhol films. Most of the film is double-exposed and has an incomprehensible soundtrack. The film and the couch are meant to be orgiastic. The wall label next to this installation quotes Chamberlain:

I deal with new material as I see fit in terms of my decision making, which has to do primarily with sexual and intuitive thinking. I am told, to a lesser degree, what to do by the material itself.

Sexuality is the childlikeness in me and the articulation comes through my intuition. My sense of nature is my ability to make decisions based on the sexual and intuitive aspects of my psyche. The intellectual and emotional aspects have little role in my work.

Even for the 1960s, John's sexual notions were old-school. His favorite story about Max's was about his pickup technique. "It was easy. I just hung around till closing time. There'd always be some chick left who hadn't found anyone else. I'd take her home." John told me this story more than once. He wasn't bragging or apologizing, just reminiscing. As in, "I took a lot of drugs then." Except they weren't drugs; they were women.

I mounted in my gallery John's last exhibition before he died. We selected from his studio nine of his immense canvas photocollages. John came to the gallery to oversee their installation. Though dealer-collector Heiner Friedrich put the whole show on hold, I sold none of those works. Those fiery, funny, weird two-dimensional late Chamberlains still await their moment.

In the years I was friends with John, he was making monumental sculptures with urgency, and he had cancer. He had moved his bed into his studio. His wheelchair circuit was from his bed to the enormous kitchen counter where he twisted aluminum foil into maquettes, to his photographic studio down the hall, to the vast welding studio. The welding studio was an elephants' graveyard of car parts sorted by color—big chrome, black, white piles, smaller red, blue, green, yellow piles. Toward the back there was a clearing where John directed his assistants. From his wheelchair he pointed out the part he wanted, pointed to where it should go, had an assistant fidget with it until it clicked into place and was spot-welded there. John said that when the fit was right, he could hear it. I watched John work like this on his final masterpieces, the late great mountains of metal that dominated his final sculpture show at Gagosian. He worked with concentration and clarity. He made some of his greatest works then at the end.

To experience the full power and beauty of the High Renaissance, one should travel to Michelangelo's Cappella Sistina in Rome. To fully experience postwar American sculpture, one should travel to Chamberlain's Wool and

Mohair Building in Marfa. If you walk past the foam couch and absurd movie, you will find a spread of twenty steel Chamberlain sculptures from the 1970s. The sculptures are massive, orotund. They take time to circumnavigate. They will make you feel small. They have hidden interiorities you will struggle to glimpse through the surface ruptures. The colors are not Pop or Minimal, not natural or industrial or metropolitan. Maybe alien. The place looks like a UFO crash site. The sculptures feel like nuclear fission about to explode. They feel like precisely the right response—smashed to ground yet poised on tiptoes—to the crumble of war and peace, of murder and loving-kindness, of machismo and embrace, of stoned-drunk-crazy-glee-without-a-pilot at the center of America in the middle of the twentieth century, where John was.

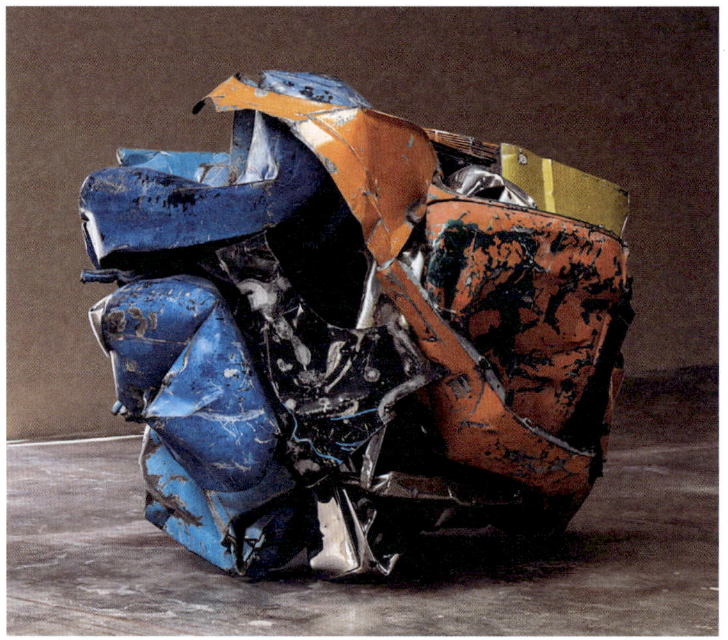

Lou's The Past

From 2005 to 2013 I represented Lou Reed as an art photographer. We mounted shows in New York and in Milan, Rome, Amsterdam, Palma de Mallorca, and Pittsburgh.

I enjoyed travelling with Lou, but there were challenges. It once fell to me on a holiday weekend in Rome, all stores closed, to find Lou a Tai Chi sword. There was an ill-planned book signing In an Amsterdam gallery where I had to puff myself up into some likeness of a bouncer to fight off a scrum of scary fans. In Milan, when Lou was scheduled to take questions from forty Italian journalists at the Palazzo Marino, the city hall, I had to finagle some words to explain their ninety-minute wait. When Lou finally showed up, he charmed them with contemptuous answers—some just a grunt, some with the stiletto wit that will keep Lou's songs alive forever. The next day Lou was on the front pages of forty Italian newspapers, quoted with affection.

Lou made it a priority to be late. He shouldn't wait for anyone; everyone should wait for him. One time we were flagrantly late for a flight out of JFK. The cabin doors were already shut. They opened the sealed doors for Lou (and me in tow).

Some people enjoyed letting Lou have the upper hand, enjoyed being masochists to his sadist. In his sadism I saw the eruption of the short, kinky-haired, Long Island Jewish kid electroshocked by his parents who didn't want him to be gay. Lou's celebrity gave him compensatory power.

Lou's pulling rank made me uncomfortable. But I got used to it. When I was in Lou's orbit, some of his celebrity, his power, attached to me. I reveled in that.

With Lou in plane, car, or bar I was fascinated by his verbal riffs. I took notes. I thought my jottings might cramp him, but he never noticed. Being driven to a small Dutch town for a dinner in his honor, Lou told me about Nico. She was the most gorgeous creature he ever saw. And the craziest. One evening in a restaurant near the Chelsea Hotel, Nico thought a woman was laughing at her. She shattered a wine glass in the woman's face, red wine mixing with blood. Lou smuggled Nico from the bar and onto the next plane out of town. On that same car ride, Lou told me that he proposed to his third wife on twelve successive birthdays, until succeeding on the thirteenth. (Laurie denies this.)

When you hear of Lou Reed as photographer, you expect a certain something. You want a visual correlative of "Walk on the Wild Side" or "Dirty Boulevard" or "Heroin." You want sex, junk, drag, hustlers. There is none of that in Lou's photographs. Audiences were disappointed; I understood why.

The critics were disappointed too. They were not kind to Lou Reed the photographer. There can be disdain for a master in one medium who turns to another; it can seem like cadging a free ride. Two powerful reviewers, ones I respected, pounced on Lou. Roberta Smith in the *New York Times* and Vince Aletti in the *New Yorker*. Smith used her bully pulpit to lecture Lou on what makes a true artist. As if the writer of some of our greatest songs had no idea. I feared those reviews might hurt Lou's feelings, and hoped he wouldn't see them. When he did, he was unconcerned. His comment: "Warhol got worse reviews for his paintings; I've gotten worse for my music." That response taught me a lesson in equanimity I've never forgotten.

Those reviews taught me another lesson, about the maxim that all press is good press. When they came out, pending sales were canceled. If it weren't for Lou's friend Bono coming to the gallery—taking off his sunglasses for once, asking smart questions, buying seven or eight large pieces—I would have lost considerable money showing Lou.

Lou could be unkind. But to his friends he was giving. I asked him to gift me a picture from our first New York exhibition. He said "Of course." The picture I chose is titled *The Past*. We are above the West Side Highway seeing what Lou saw looking down from his apartment. We see a night pierced by lights. We see a rush of cars, see streetlights and headlights and lights on buildings. Beyond a black strip of river: the lights of Jersey. Rhythms of bright dots and dashes. A road flows in a blur. It hits the edge, bends up at an angle, rises to a new perspective. The horizon is askew. The night is reeling.

The show was called *Lou Reed: New York*. We laminated these lyrics to the gallery wall:

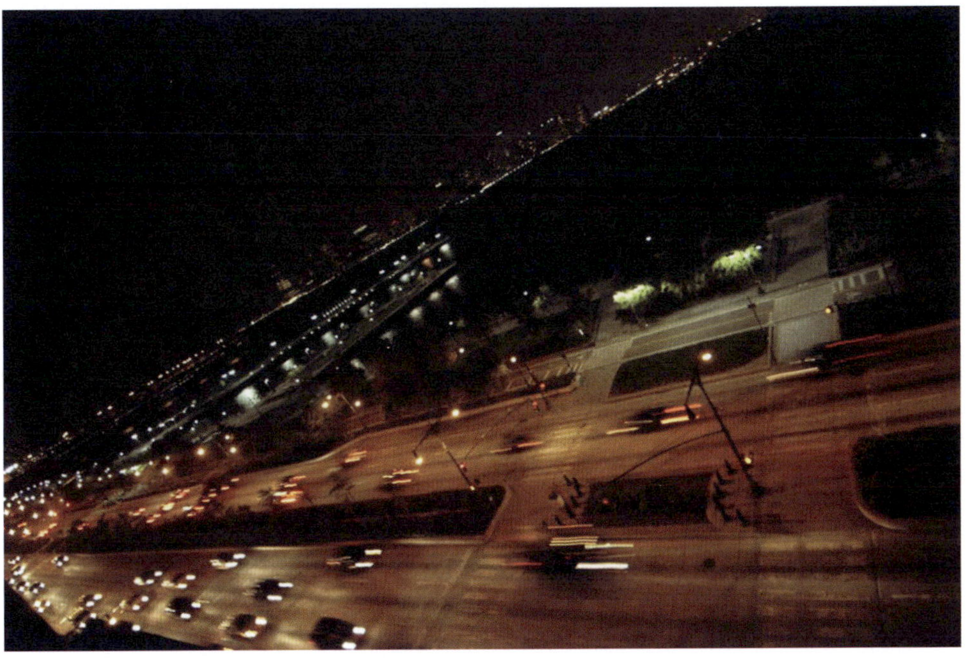

And you who accept in your soul and your head
What was misunderstood, what was thought of with dread
A new self is born, the other self dead
I accept the new found man, and set the twilight reeling.

Lou titled his pictures carefully. *The Past* is a rich title. What is seen when looking back: the past. What we flow past: the passed. Passing through obscurity, through blur, to illumination. Passing beyond. No present and no future without the past. Old selves passing into new selves.

The West Side Highway was a singularly important passageway when I was seven, eight years old. Weekdays I lived with my mother on the Upper West Side. On weekends I would stay with my father in the West Village. The route back and forth was the West Side Highway. In those days it was elevated on studded steel girders. Dad would drive us, my younger sister and me, driving as fast as the highway allowed. The highlight for us kids was "The Truck," an improbable Mack semitrailer mounted three stories up. It had illuminated spinning wheels. Week after week we glued our foreheads to the window;

when it rolled into view, we erupted with stupid glee: "The Truck! The Truck!"
It flew by as we passed it, a hulking magic carpet.

The West Side Highway shuttled us between worlds. The uptown world was
rule-bound, schooled, crowded with stepsiblings, haunted by a stepfather who
never seemed pleased. Downtown, we lived above a theater, Miles was on the
turntable, we rummaged the army-navy surplus stores on Canal Street, we ate
Chinese sausage at Wah Dor. Dad drank Scotch, splashed around Yiddishisms,
never got angry. The drive between uptown and downtown was a kind of ver-
tigo, like Lou's picture. It was like making the passage between wakefulness
and dream. Arriving at one end or the other, I was never sure which was real.

Who knows what *The Past* meant to Lou. I never asked him. If I had, he would
have flashed me his sidelong pseudo-sneer that meant "Are you kidding me?
What kind of question is that?" Or he would have talked camera tech, about
f-stop and shutter speed, how he made the headlights vibrate just so. Or Lou
would have kvelled about the beauty of the print. By David Adamson, with his
state-of-the-art inkjet studio, with his yellow Porsche that Lou drooled over.
Lou would pucker his lips, blow a kiss, and say "Adamson! Amazing!"

Lou—in his photography, in his music—sought out new collaborators and
new tools. He was a tech geek. He loved new toys. He was first to get the latest
gadget. The first time I saw a computer tablet was when he pulled out the latest
thing over dinner at Wallsé. Lou was on the prowl for new ways to make new
things—new and emotional.

The Lou I knew in his last seven years was sober. He wasn't thrilled when
people around him imbibed; evenings with Lou ended early. But not always.
The night *Lou Reed: New York* opened there was a two-part event. First, a
couple of hundred of Lou's friends crowded into the Hermès gallery on the
Upper East Side. David Bowie rushed over, gave Lou a big hug, said, "Great
show, Lou. Have to dash. The car is waiting." Then fifty invited guests repaired
to my Chelsea gallery. A long white table had been set. There were waiters in
white, fine wines, lovely food. The mood was celebratory and intimate. At the
end of a long night, just a smattering of guests remained. Lou's sobriety had
taken a break. He was tipsy. He made googly eyes at Laurie. I couldn't believe
I was watching the king and queen of downtown literally tête-à-tête, unboth-
ered, lovebirds. It was endearing. I grasped the devotion of Lou and Laurie.
Lou with Laurie was transformed. He was a new found man. He was no longer
afraid. The past was passed.

Janis

M arch 8, 1968, was a historic night for American music, the opening night of the Fillmore East. Janis Joplin topped the bill. I could have been there! I did buy her album *Cheap Thrills* when it came out that summer. I listened to it over and over. It shaped my notions of womanhood, of ardor, of summertime.

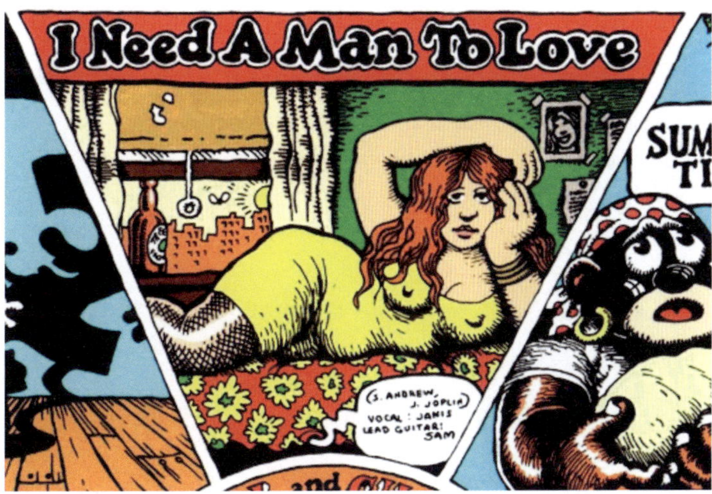

Janis Joplin was the first female rock star. To hear her was to be shaken. What words to conjure her voice? Gravel in molasses? Iron in cream? A tiger who swallowed a nightingale? Her singing soars like a Fokker and crashes like vanished love. She was our human sacrifice.

I have two pictures of Janis hanging at home. In the Jim Marshall picture she is offstage, off somewhere, spent. In the Francesco Scavullo picture she shimmies a performance of feeling good; she is exuberant, shyly joyful.

Jim Marshall was the lion of rock-and-roll photographers, none comparable. Jim loved to flourish a handgun. He pulled one on me the first time I met him, at his Castro home, just to show who was boss. He had only half a nose, the other half lost to cocaine. Jim was famous for keeping up with the bands on the inebriation score. His hard living earned him access to the musicians, their respect, their trust. No overload of pharmaceuticals or braggadocio could dull Jim's skills. His eye remained keen through every color of haze. He was master of his craft: shrewd lighting, dynamic compositions, a sharp eye for the milieu. Especially unsurpassed are his offstage pictures.

Here is Janis backstage at the Winterland, San Francisco, April of '68, after a concert, alone. A gashed vinyl couch leaks its guts. A roll of paper towels un-

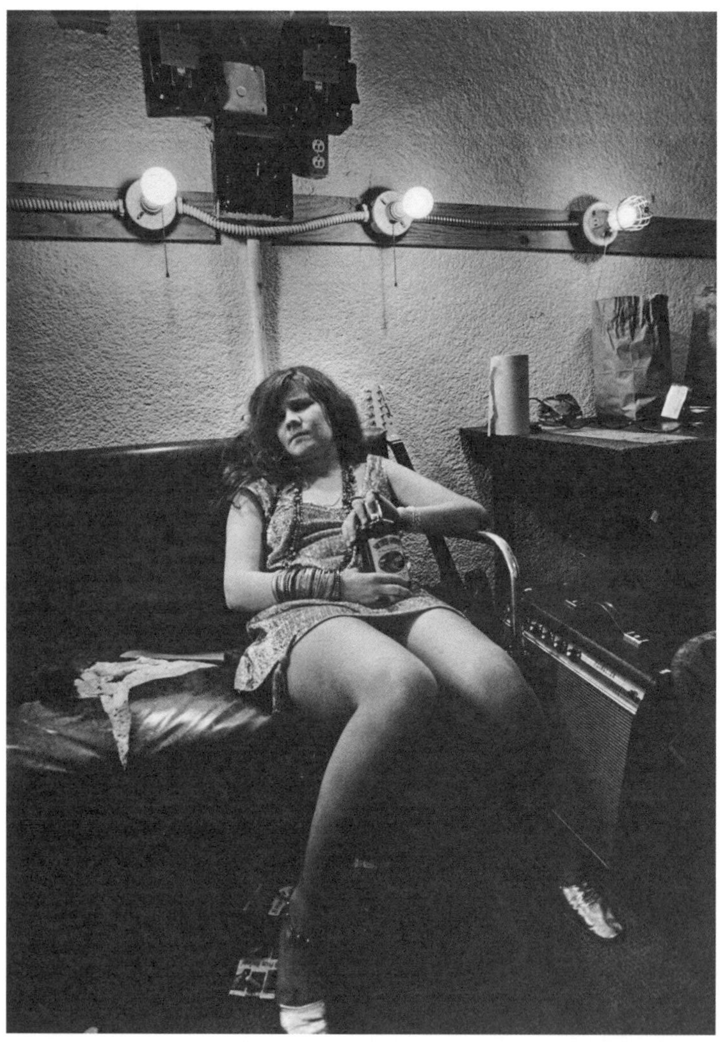

winds. Hanging above is a trinity of bare bulbs and a crucifixion of electrical boxes. Stockinged legs are full and fluid, bare arms pale. The bulbs are shining, the star's shoes and heavy bangles shine, her shiny gold minidress glistens. On her face is rank exhaustion; her lights are out. At her center: a black delta below a fat bottle of booze. This is the Janis who said, "Onstage I make love to 25,000 people—then I go home alone." With a bottle of Southern Comfort.

In this picture of Janis we can sense her humility. She had fled home on her twentieth birthday, fled the Texas town where she was dubbed The Ugliest Boy in School. She headed for San Francisco's Beat scene. She carried two books with her; one was *Lady Sings the Blues,* the autobiography of Billie Holiday. Janis said, "Billie Holiday, Aretha Franklin. Now, they are so subtle, they can milk you with two notes. They can make you feel like they told you the whole universe. But I don't know that yet. All I got now is strength. Maybe if I keep singing, maybe I'll get it." Janis understood herself as a wave in an ocean of female voices swelling up and breaking on the shore.

When I think of Janis I think of Leonard Cohen's great lugubrious song about their encounter. The song has two versions: "Chelsea Hotel #1," and "Chelsea Hotel #2." Number 1 has two stanzas that were later cut. One of those stanzas begins, "You got away, they can't pay you now / For making your sweet little song." Cohen means "sweet" and "little" ironically. The other stanza says, "You got away on your deepest dream / Racing the midnight train, babe." Six times Cohen repeats "racing the midnight train," each time more urgent and more dynamic. His Janis becomes a believable dynamo, a superwoman.

"Chelsea Hotel," both versions, starts with tawdry celebrity sex in graphic words that shock. It ends with sorrow for a woman and for a love cut short. But the song has a problem: it overexposes Janis; it is unkind. Two decades after recording it, after he had become a committed Buddhist, at a concert in 1994, Cohen apologized. He said he regretted his indiscretion; he said it was the only time he kissed and told. But the damage is done. We will never unhear Cohen telling Janis, "We are ugly, but we have the music." Janis will forever give head on that unmade bed.

In a 1969 interview, Janis told Doon Arbus that Cohen could not pull himself together enough to fuck her. "And then, all of a sudden about four o'clock in the morning you realize that, flat ass, this motherfucker's just lying there. He's not balling me. I mean, that really happened to me. Really heavy, like slam-in-the-face it happened." When thirty years later that interview was first published (in a book of Richard Avedon photographs), Janis gets some back-from-the-grave revenge on Cohen. But it's a little-read interview, small bore against the bombshell of a song we can't get out of our heads.

Janis died at age twenty-seven, when her dealer pushed extra potent heroin on her (and on other clients too, who also died.) Cohen's song and Marshall's picture point directly to her grave. They help us mourn the unnecessary, unexplainable fiat of her death. Doing so, they are beautiful. Yet these elegies for Janis also exploit her. Cohen sings mostly his own disappointments. Marshall's picture can be read as pinning the blame on a self-destructive drunk. Would a woman ever portray Janis the way Marshall or Cohen did?

An antidote to these mansplainings is to see Janis perform. In this Francesco Scavullo portrait, she performs ebulliently. She cants her hips and shakes her hair. She lifts her bangled arms in celebration. She makes fists of power. She closes her eyes for interiority and smiles to herself. She relishes her own style and grace, she owns her embodiment. Scavullo—whose best book of photographs is *Women*—delivers a woman in full.

"Mercedes Benz"—based on a lyric by Beat poet Michael McClure, cowritten by Janis and Bob Neuwirth over beers one afternoon at a Port Chester, New York, bar, verses jotted down on a napkin—was her last recording, captured in a single one-minute-forty-eight-second take on October 1, 1970. She says, "I'd like to do a song of great social and political import. It goes like this," then lays down a quavering, twanging a cappella accompanied only by her foot tap. She begs God for a Mercedes, for a color TV, and for a night on the town. We know she's kidding, since she had all of those things to the brim and was still an unhappy dope addict. She ends, "That's it." As basic a tape as she ever recorded, her cheapest thrill.

Janis died three days later. The take was released on the posthumous album *Pearl*, helping it become the number-one best-selling album in America a few months after her ashes were sifted over the Pacific. Her song's been covered by at least eighty artists; you can hear them on SecondHandSongs.com. The song remains startlingly alive because it teaches the perennial wisdom, stop running round on the consumerist wheel! "It's the want of something that gives you the blues," Janis said in an interview, "It's not what *isn't*, it's what you wish *was* that makes unhappiness." Freedom's just another word for nothing left to wish. The Buddha couldn't have said it better.

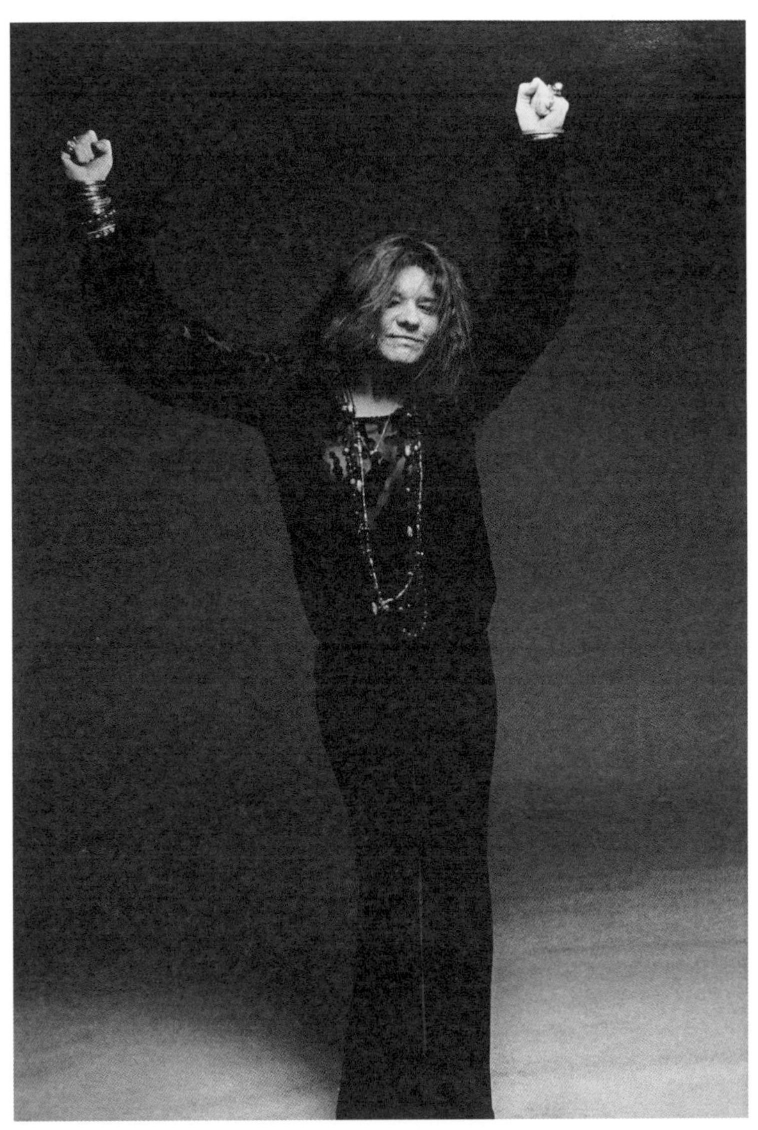

My Friend Ernest

In 2003, I was with the photographer Ernest Withers at the Pennsylvania Convention Center. Ernest was getting ready to present a slideshow; I was to introduce him to the audience. I made sure Ernest had the right slides for his talk, and handed them to a techie. Then I noticed a problem. Every time Ernest took a step, he used his hand to hitch up his pants. He had been ill and had lost a lot of weight. He needed a belt; I pulled mine off and handed it to him. He put it on and wrapped me in a big hug. I felt proud to have him as a friend.

I was nervous in Philly because of the last time we had shared a stage. It was a couple of years previous, at Duke University. I gave a slide lecture surveying the photography of the Civil Rights Movement; Ernest was to follow with a slide lecture about his photographs of the movement. He launched in with his picture of B. B. King on stage, boyish in short pants, then one of Aretha with that hairdo, then the one of Rufus Thomas dressed as an "Indian," standing next to Elvis in wide lapels. I whispered in Ernest's ear that maybe his intro was running long. "Wait a minute," he said. "I guess I brought the wrong slides." He apologized to the audience. Then he showed more slides and told more tales about Memphis and music and the 1960s. His listeners were charmed. He didn't need to show them pictures of the movement: he embodied the movement.

After the Philly lecture, we were invited to a dinner at the Curtis Institute of Music. There were a couple of big round table, a dozen diners at each, all gathered to celebrate Ernest. I sat at a table with mostly Philadelphians, mostly Black women. I was with my new girlfriend, Susan, a white Philadelphian. Susan brought us all together, making us laugh with conversation about food and place. I was wowed by her easy charm. I credit Ernest with helping make us a couple.

I first met Ernest in 1994, while I was writing a photographic history of the Civil Rights Movement. I had seen his astounding picture of demonstrators in Memphis holding signs saying I <u>AM</u> A MAN. (You can't see it here because of permissions issues, but if you search "Ernest Withers" at Google Images you'll see it right away.) The picture was not well known at the time, but I understood it was a key image for my last chapter. To learn more about it, I went to visit Ernest in Memphis. Why was it made? Where exactly was it made? Who were these demonstrators? Who made those signs—I <u>AM</u> A MAN, never before seen in the world, now so iconic? Why was Ernest there, with his camera? Who was Ernest?

Ernest had answers. We met in his studio, a storefront on Beale Street where he had been in business since the 1950s. Beale Street, "where the Blues began," had been the pumping heart of Black Memphis. Shredded by so-called urban renewal, Beale Street was now mainly tacky tourist bars. Ernest's studio was a maze of rooms with pictures spilling like Spanish moss from shelves and drawers. I asked how he could find anything in this mess. He said, "I can find what I need to find. My memory is strong." I asked to see the original negative of his soon-to-be-iconic picture. He rumbled his baritone laugh and told me, "It's long gone. I haven't seen it in years." He'd been printing from a copy negative.

I asked if we could head out to the site of the picture. Ernest drove; no more than five minutes away. We got to the intersection where Ernest had stood with his camera. We faced the way he had faced and held up a copy of the picture. "I knew all those guys," Ernest said, reeling off names like Jesse Epps, Taylor Rogers, Bill Lucy . . . I asked why the marchers had met up here. "It was because of Clayborn Temple. Rev. H. Ralph Jackson was head of COME, Community on the Move for Equality. He organized it. You see those sticks on the signs? I helped cut those. We were sawing and hammering in the Minimum Salary Building." That's the building seen in the picture. We went into it to have a look around. I asked Ernest who had come up with that genius motto, who had designed the signs, had them printed. He didn't know.

Then Ernest drove us eight blocks to the Lorraine Motel. From the courtyard, he pointed up to the balcony, to Room 306. One fine April day, Martin Luther King Jr. ate a catfish lunch, made a joshing phone call back home to his mom, stepped out of that room onto that balcony, and was shot in the head, shot dead. Ernest had been there earlier that day, meeting with King and his entourage. He was back within minutes of the shooting. He persuaded photographer Joseph Louw to give him the undeveloped film that recorded King's last moments, his bleeding out on the balcony as his friends pointed to where the rifle shots had rung out. Louw, from South Africa, happened to be in Memphis working on a documentary movie. He didn't understand the import of what he had photographed, Ernest told me. But Ernest did. He took the film back to his studio and developed it. The photographs were first published in Life magazine, have been published hundreds of times since, have become twentieth-century icons, as sad as any.

Heartrending as the Lorraine visit was, Ernest and I were hungry. We set off on a barbecue tour of Memphis. First stop the Rendezvous, a big red-leather-and-spotlights place frequented by tourists and fancier locals white and Black. The meat was good, the ambience tarted up. We were happier at a barbecue joint near Beale Street owned by Ernest's friend B. King. We ate barbecued shrimp—so simple and delicious that I've never ordered the dish again, for fear of a letdown.

Ernest was the single most important Black photographer covering the modern Civil Rights Movement. He was the only photographer, white or Black, who made significant work across the whole span of the movement, from 1954 through 1968. Over and over, he put himself on the spot, dealt with real threats and real dangers. He knew who to photograph, how to make telling images, how to get his pictures into print. Several images by Ernest have become iconic: I <u>AM</u> A MAN, Mose Wright pointing at Emmet Till's killers, King and Abernathy on the bus at the end of the Montgomery boycott. He was abused and threatened at the Till trial; he was beaten and arrested at the funeral of Medgar Evers. He made a treasury of images of King in Memphis, alive and dead.

Even if Ernest had not made his movement pictures, he would still be an important photographer of our times. He made three other singular bodies of work about Memphis: coverage of the city's Black baseball league, a deep dive into its Black music scene at midcentury, and in-depth documentation of Black daily life: nightlife, school life, family life, business life. Ernest Withers's images of the Black freedom struggles, of Black baseball, Black music, and Black life in Memphis constitute a photographic testimony important to our understanding of the United States in the twentieth century. The work's vigor, its beauty, its power to uplift is undeniable. It is a national treasure. It should be housed in museums and should be the subject of blockbuster museum exhibitions. That hasn't happened; I hope it will.

When Ernest died in 2007, the management of his estate was turned over to his eldest daughter, Rosalind Withers. Rosalind asked me to come down to Memphis to help with two things. First, Ernest's studio needed a preliminary sorting out. I supervised a crew of half a dozen volunteers in separating what needed to be secured from what was clearly trash. Second, I was invited to speak to the Withers family, convened in a lawyer's office, to discuss the future of their father's archive. I offered an outline of the various ways that photographic archives are appraised, protected, and moved out into the world. Since then, Ernest's work has been in the energetic and astute hands of Roz Withers.

So the first story ends, the story of Ernest Withers's photographic achievements. But in 2010, another side of Ernest came into focus. Federal Bureau of Investigation files were released documenting his work as a paid secret informant for the Bureau. His FBI work spanned 1958 to 1976, and earned him a considerable sum of money. He was run by the man who directed the FBI's Memphis operation, special agent William H. Lawrence. Lawrence befriended Withers; they listened to jazz together. Lawrence directed Withers to gather photographs and information on people the Bureau considered threats. Withers provided hundreds of reports on Civil Rights activists, antiwar activists, activist ministers, community organizers. He provided hundreds of his photographs to the FBI so that their subjects could be identified and surveilled. Some of these people considered Ernest an ally, a confidante, a friend. Withers may have considered himself an undercover federal lawman protecting people from local corruption.

The disclosure of Ernest Withers as a double agent was big news in Memphis, where Ernest was a local hero. And it was national news. In the *New York Times*, Randy Kennedy wrote: "The revelation that he spied on the very leaders who gave him unequaled access to the movement's inner workings, published this month by the *Commercial Appeal* in Memphis after a two-year investigation, has shocked many friends and admirers of Withers."

I was among those shocked. I reacted as Roz Withers did. Roz was quoted in the Times saying, "This is the first time I've heard of this in my life. My father's not here to defend himself. That is a very, very strong, strong accusation." Our initial reaction was disbelief. Then we tried to mitigate the revelations, to make excuses. The FBI must have entrapped him; he didn't give them anything harmful; he used the FBI for his own ends; he must have fed them false information; he needed the money for his family. Ernest had eight children by his wife Dorothy, and an additional daughter by another woman, a woman he met at a Beale Street movie house when he was a cop. He supported all of them, put most of them through college.

Roz and I were forgetting something. Ten years earlier, Ernest had revealed his FBI involvement, the tip of it, in an interview published in the first book about him, a book Roz and I—and everyone else interested in Ernest—had read. He said, "I always had FBI guys looking over my shoulder and wanting to question me. I never tried to learn any high-powered secrets. It would have just been trouble. . . . I was solicited to assist the FBI by Bill Lawrence. . . . He was a nice guy but what he was doing was pampering me to catch whatever leaks I dropped, so I was staying out of meetings where real decisions were being made." So, we knew Ernest had worked with the FBI; we knew he was providing low-powered secrets; we knew he was being "pampered." We knew quite a lot. But, following Ernest's lead, we minimized it all, we let it pass, we wiped it from our memories.

There are three books out that investigate Ernest's FBI involvement and what it means. One book consists entirely of 300 pages of the declassified documents that reporter Marc Perrusquia and attorneys at the *Commercial Appeal* obtained in 2012 by suing the government. The second book, Perrusquia's 2017 *A Spy in Canaan: How the FBI Used a Famous Photographer to Infiltrate the Civil Rights Movement*, details information and pictures that Withers gave to his handler Lawrence. Perrusquia interviews individuals Withers knew—Civil Rights organizers, Black ministers, Black Power activists, anti–Vietnam War protestors, Nation of Islam members, union members—asking how they feel about his betrayals. In *Bluff City: The Secret Life of Photographer Ernest Withers*, Preston Lauterbach looks at generations of the Withers family in the context of Tennessee history, in the context of Boss Crump's brutal and treacherous segregated Memphis. Grandson of a CIA agent, Lauterbach sees Withers as a manipulative and manipulated law-and-order guy, understandable.

Ernest's work for the FBI was not the first time he worked in law enforcement. The first time connects directly back to Boss Crump. E. H. Crump was elected mayor of Memphis in 1909; over the next half-century Crump took control of every public job in western Tennessee. It is doubtful that any other US region ever had as strong a dictator as Boss Crump. Crump patronized Black voters—paid their poll taxes, organized registration drives—so long as they voted for his picked candidates. "I've dealt with niggers my whole life, and I know how to treat them," he said. Ernest's father was a Crump organizer; he was awarded a job in the post office. In 1948, after a Memphis policeman killed an unarmed Black man, Crump conscripted a first few Black officers to join the force. Ernest was one of them.

But the Memphis police department remained segregated. The Black officers carried no guns and were not allowed to arrest whites. Ernest's beat was Beale Street, where the pecking order was complex. There were white and Black clubs, but Crump allowed liquor licenses only to the white ones, leaving the Black ones to all kinds of chicanery and graft. White cops took a cut of the liquor trade, but when Ernest tried the same, he was busted out of the force. He returned to operating a photography studio, located now on Beale Street.

Ernest's second job in law enforcement was as FBI Confidential Informant (CI). He was informant "ME 338-R (Ghetto)" (ME for Memphis, R for Race) and later "ME 338-E" (E for Extremist). His job was to identify subjects with his camera and by written report, marking them for FBI surveillance, marking them for files still attached to their names today. The marked didn't know they were marked by Ernest. He surveilled leaders such as MLK, Andrew Young, James Forman, Rev. James Bevel, and Rev. James Lawson, as well as hundreds of other movement soldiers.

Fifty years later, when his subjects learned about his undercover role, many of them, especially the Black ones, declined to condemn Ernest. They knew the FBI had been on their tails, and knew the pressures Withers was under. Ernest had cultivated friendships with white subjects as well, spying on their peace movement activities, for instance. Some were harassed by the FBI, were fired from jobs, acquired permanent damaging stains on their employment records that stunted their success ever after. These folks were bewildered to hear of their friend Ernest's role in their persecution; they felt hurt and betrayed. They did not forgive him.

Look back at Ernest's famous picture of the sanitation workers lined up with their signs. There is a press print by another photographer that shows the same workers and signs wedged into the rear of a crowd waiting to march. To make the now-iconic image, Ernest must have pushed the crowd aside, leaving the workers as if at the front rank of a march. We see them lined up so that at least twenty-five of them are clearly identifiable.

When Ernest reeled off those names to me, he did it by rote. It was obvious he had named those names before. Had he reeled them off to others of his new patrons in art and publishing, to show off his insider status? For sure. But earlier on, had it been to the FBI? Perhaps. The subject files that Ernest helped create were anchored by his photographs. Sometimes the photos attached to the files were just the faces, cut out with scissors from a larger scene. Using Ernest's later-to-become-famous picture and the names he could have matched up, these men could have been marked for surveillance.

I <u>AM</u> A MAN. Who designed those now-iconic signs, who coined the resounding phrase? I haven't been able to answer those questions. I would like to know, so I could salute them. They summed up in a singular phrase and a powerful graphic centuries of struggle for human dignity.

More is known about the sticks that held the signs, the sticks Ernest helped cut. After the March 28, 1968, march, when rioting broke out, they were used to smash Beale Street windows. To deal with the aftermath of that rioting is what brought Dr. King back to Memphis a few days later; that is when he was assassinated. In 1976, when the House Select Committee on Assassinations investigated the Memphis events, they investigated the sticks, asking if they had been planted with malice aforethought. They investigated what role the FBI might have played in the protests, the rioting, the assassination. They investigated Ernest, and brought him in to testify. The final report of the Committee noted that conflicting testimony "tarnished the evidence given by both the Bureau [Lawrence] and the informant [Withers], and it left the committee with a measure of uncertainty about the scope of the FBI involvement."

Ernest worked for the Memphis Police Department in the 1950s, then for the FBI, and in the 1970s he was a paid law officer one more time. He was an agent of the Tennessee Alcoholic Beverage Commission, wearing a badge and carrying a gun. And once again, Ernest was a double agent. His shadow employer was Tennessee governor Ray Blanton. Among Blanton's many schemes, his most notorious was cash for clemency: selling pardons. These get-out-of-jail cards were on the market for $10,000 to $80,000. Blanton had a network of operatives scoping out customers and cutting deals. Ernest was one of them. But Ernest was set up—in a sting by the FBI! He was taped cutting a deal. That tape helped bring Blanton and his cronies down, ending their corrupt reign, sending them to jail. Ernest served a five-month term, a lighter sentence in exchange for testifying.

Those are some of the facts about Ernest. They are troubling. On the one hand, we have Ernest the eminent photographer, Ernest the Civil Rights hero, Ernest friend of the blues, Ernest the (not quite) faithful family man, Ernest my colleague and friend. He was kind to my daughter, shown here in 1997, who has two beautiful photographs by Ernest hanging in her living room. We can say Ernest did good. We can say his pictures fostered goodwill toward the Civil Rights Movement. We can say that as a cop on Beale Street he cast his lot with embattled Black bootleggers, worked with them so they could support their families and he his. We can say that as an FBI informant he added little burden to the people he betrayed. We can say that in the Blanton scheme he was helping buy the freedom of a Black man who was unjustly jailed. We

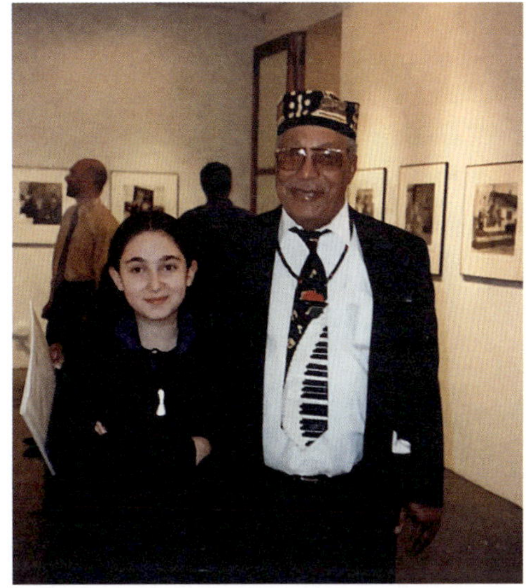

can say he was deftly running the maze of the white man's law, the law that segregated him and paid his living, that betrayed him and that he betrayed. We can understand and excuse Ernest.

On the other hand, we can find that Ernest betrayed the trust of his friends and colleagues, he abetted power unchecked, he furthered corruption, he undermined independent journalism, he undermined freedom of speech. He undermined the Civil Rights, peace, and labor movements. He undermined rule of law, undermined history, undermined democracy, undermined the truth.

Ernest did all of those things. He crossed all those moral thresholds, back and forth. His actions and their effects are indelible. What should we do? Should we cancel Ernest, turn him from hero into devil? What about his pictures, are they now inadmissible? Are they canceled? Are they contaminated? Shouldn't we continue to give them credence—though with new, more nuanced readings, more complicated contexts?

Buddhists don't speak of betrayal. We speak of craving, anger, and delusion that bring suffering. We speak of a path of right attitude, right speech, right action. As we seek enlightenment, we walk twin paths, of suffering and of wisdom. We seek not to hurt, not to harm, though we know that we frequently do. There are precepts to guide us; we follow them and we fail to follow them. We aspire to relieve the suffering of those around us and in ourselves. We revere those who succeed in these aspirations. We cultivate compassion for those of us—all of us—who fall short. We don't judge the failures. That would be like the butterfly judging the butterfly for fluttering.

A sign appears mysteriously on March 28, 1968. I <u>AM</u> A MAN. The emphasis is on the verb. It's an act of refutation of humanity denied. It harks back to the eighteenth-century Abolitionist credo "Am I not a man and a brother?" It echoes Sojourner Truth's nineteenth-century speech "Ain't I a Woman?" and this from Martin Luther King's book *Where Do We Go From Here: Chaos or Community?*, published June 1967: "I am somebody. I am a person. I am a man with dignity and honor."

A few weeks before this picture was made, Echol Cole and Robert Walker, two Memphis sanitation workers, were grabbing their lunch break at the only place permitted, on the back of their truck. The compactor switched on and they were eaten alive. The remaining sanitation workers went on strike: for safety on the job, for living wages, for the right to a union. But mainly they went on strike to be MEN.

I <u>AM</u> A MAN. I will not be eaten alive. I will walk in dignity and honor.

Let's let Ernest walk.

The Fire That Won't Go Out

The Black protest movement in Birmingham, Alabama, in the spring of 1963 was a high-water mark of the modern Civil Rights Movement. Its organizers dubbed it "Project C," for confrontation with the city's power holders, but the campaign was determinedly nonviolent. It dismantled Birmingham's segregation laws. It fostered the March on Washington, the biggest protest in US history to that date. It led to the Civil Rights Act of 1964. The Birmingham movement's primary spokesperson, the Rev. Martin Luther King Jr., became a national political and spiritual force, an interlocutor of Presidents, an international dignitary—and a scapegoat. Backlash against the movement was relentless; white Birmingham responded with violence, murder. Then that backlash stirred up a renewed Black agency and anger that was called "Black Power." We live on the road from Birmingham.

In Birmingham, on a single day, May 3, 1963, photographer Charles Moore made several of the most iconic images of the Civil Rights Movement. They show the "water hoses and police dogs" of racist oppression. They have been referenced thousands of times since, reproduced in countless publications. President Kennedy saw such pictures on the front pages of his daily newspapers and said they made him sick. Andy Warhol's silkscreened paintings of those photographs are featured in museums worldwide. They have become iconic images because they both embody a specific time and place and transcend those moments, rising up to depict a bigger perspective.

In 1963, *Life* magazine reached more Americans than any TV show, reached half of the adult population of the United States. *Life* showcased these images in their featured story of the week. This picture leads off that eleven-page article, titled "They Fight a Fire That Won't Go Out." It is printed two pages wide, a wingspread of a full fourteen inches, unmissable. It is packed with signs of mid-twentieth century America: the block letters on the jacket, the faux-stucco wall, the chrome fenders of the sedans, the casual wear of the protestors, the streamlined helmets not unlike those worn by Nazi stormtroopers. And the picture evokes combat more ancient: jousting from a medieval tapestry or a battlefield scene from the Bhagavad Gita, the battlefield poem that Gandhi called his "spiritual dictionary."

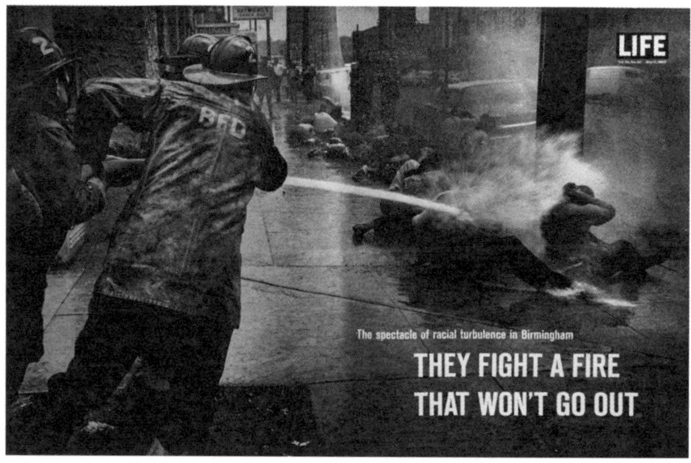

You see here protesters sitting on the sidewalk, lined up in formation, hands protecting their heads. They had trained for this moment, trained to withstand bravely all that authority could mete out. They trained in the ways of the Shanti Sena, the Peace Army, the nonviolent army organized by Gandhi. Following Gandhi, the Reverends James Bevel, James Lawson, Fred Shuttlesworth, and Martin Luther King Jr. organized a new Peace Army in Birmingham. They trained to confront violence with militant nonviolence. They trained to fight by not fighting back.

Charles Moore too had trained for his Birmingham moment. Charles was from small-town northwest Alabama, son of a white Baptist preacher. He became a photographer working in Montgomery for Alabama's leading daily newspapers, papers that were far from antiracist. In 1958 Moore recorded an arrest of Martin Luther King. He followed King, snapping pictures, as he was arm-twisted into the police station and shoved against the booking desk. Moore jumped behind the booking sergeant to photograph the captive from the viewpoint of power. He implicated himself and us, the other viewers, in the aggression. King's gentle eyes and pursed mouth appeal to the booking sergeant, and to us. When it was published in *Life*, this extraordinary photograph

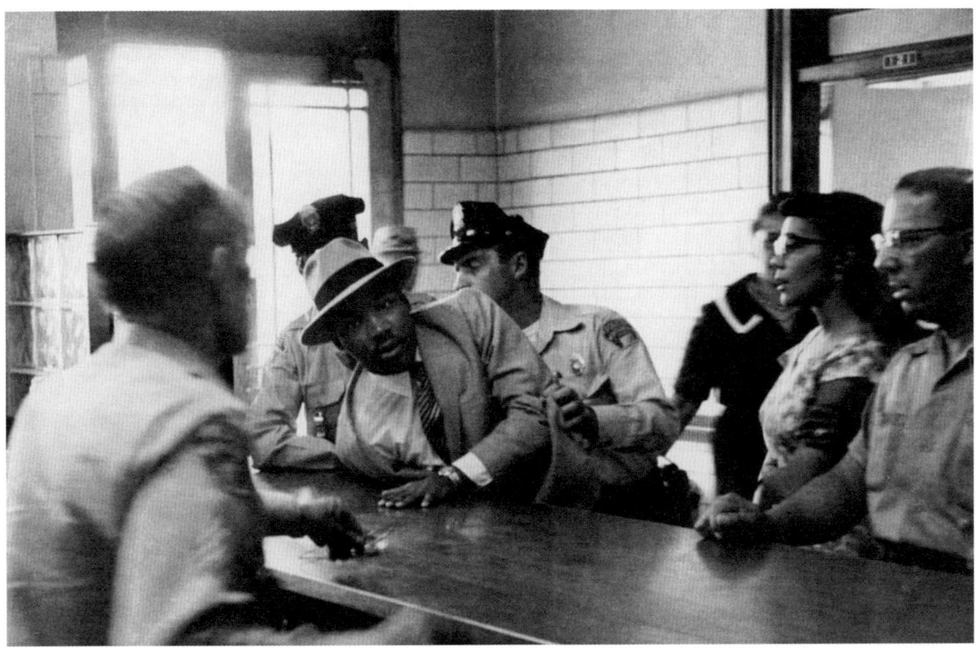

launched Moore's national career. And it taught him how to make a picture that speaks to the entire nation and is morally expansive.

In Moore's Birmingham picture, the fire hose we see has been fitted with a special high-pressure water cannon designed to inflict pain and terror. Moore again positioned himself, and us, on the side of the oppressors. We lift the water-cannon up, we aim at the human target, we make the liquid lance shatter against unsurrendering Black bodies, pummeling them down the sidewalk. By this fierce image they are tumbled into history.

If the militant resisters are soldiers in a Peace Army, then who are the attackers under the insignia BFD? The Birmingham Fire Department trained its members to fight fires for the benefit of their fellow citizens. But here we see a horrible inversion. Their fellows have become a fire to extinguish. In what world could the protectors of the citizenry be twisted into attacking their fellows? How could these civil servants have become enforcers of such a dehumanizing law? We know the answer. This is the realm and the logic of racism.

We see two faceless armies clashing across a gray void. They are connected by an arc of water. The arc connects oppressed and oppressor, right and wrong, justice and injustice. It is the arc of the moral universe. Martin Luther King famously proclaimed that this arc bends towards justice. If it does, it must bend into a circle of community, a circle of common humanity. Or the fire won't go out.

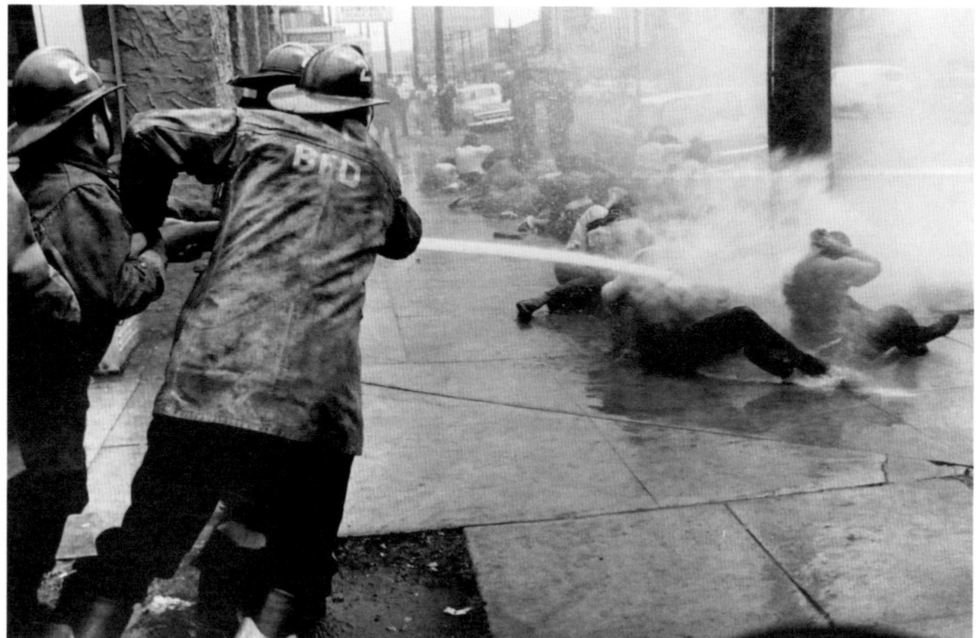

Death War Protest Love

Some years ago I was invited to inspect a trove of photographs stashed in a chilly storage unit in Chicago. A photographer named Henry Schaefer had rescued 50,000 press prints from a dumpster. I organized an exhibition of 120 of those 8 × 10 inch black and whites selected to spotlight the predominant themes of twentieth-century American photojournalism. I called the show "Death War Protest Love." The *Hindenburg* exploding, Lee Harvey Oswald shot, Malcolm X shot, mushroom clouds, burning monks, Kent State . . . The "Love" pictures were bitter: Marilyn Monroe's suicide, Bonnie and Clyde. The show was dark, drenched in blood. I wanted to demonstrate how crazy we become with such images tattooed on our brains.

This "Protest" photograph from the show hangs framed in my office. It is an unknown picture, perhaps never published before. To me, this picture acts as an antidote to the horror of the "Death," "War," and bitter "Love" pictures.

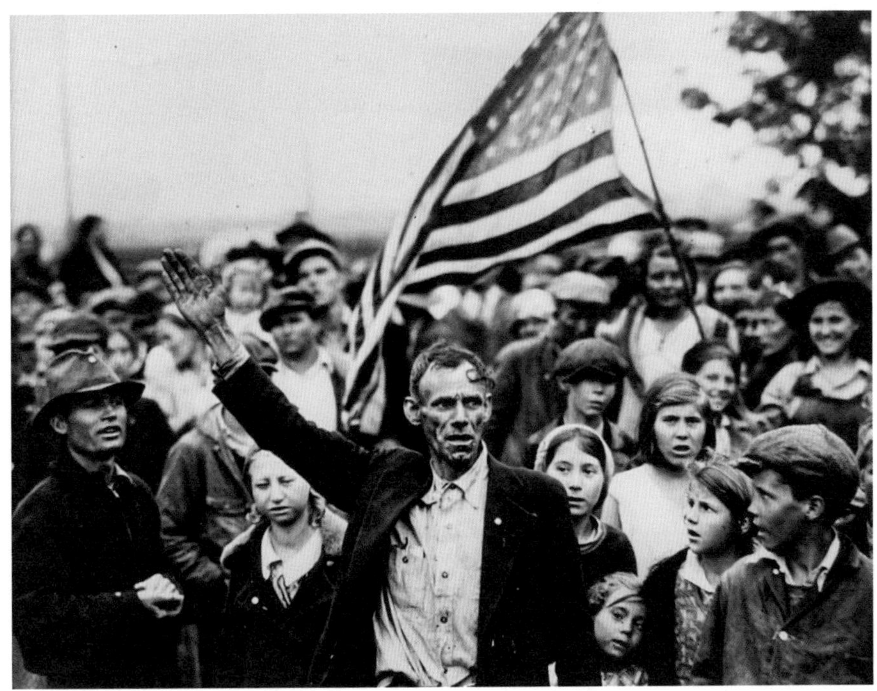

Protest pictures are medicine for the soul because of the optimism at their core.

One could almost believe this picture is a still from a movie about the Depression. It seems perfectly framed, lit, cast, costumed, propped. But it's not a movie still. It's photojournalism of a high order, iconic, encapsulating in a small rectangle a wide world in contention.

The American flag is at top center, backwards, sagging. It suggests a nation weary. Crowding children react with attentiveness, curiosity, bemusement, admiration. The protagonist is dead center, in sharp focus. He is hatless, his broad forehead graced with a tempestuous curl. He turns forward, his head twists, his eyes are transfixed by some vision terrible. From the sinews of his jaw a cry issues forth. He raises arm and calloused hand in a commanding gesture. It is a gesture we can recognize: Christ's right arm raising the dead in Michelangelo's *Last Judgment,* the raised fists of Black Panthers, the call to attention of Roman orator statues, a rock star quieting a stadium, the supplication linking Earth and Spirit realms in Dogon statuary. The leader in this photograph gestures both forwards and back. To his people behind he says: Stop! Stand fast! We are seen! To the powers that be, he says: We are here! See us! Listen! His gesture is the embodiment and epitome of protest.

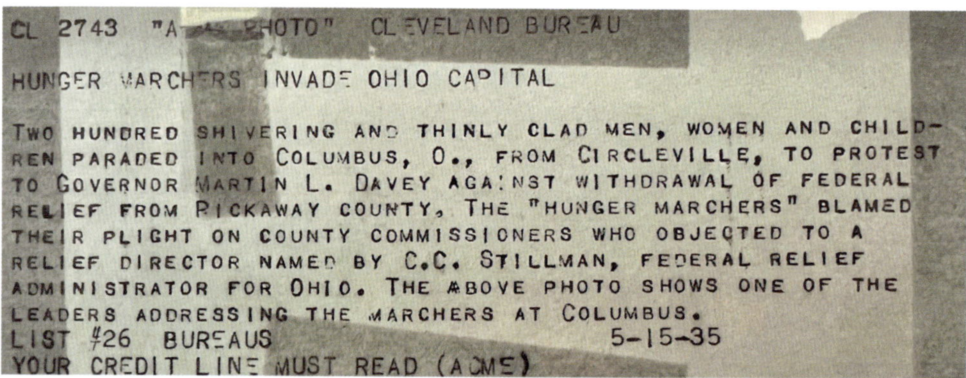

This picture is titled *Hunger Marchers Invade Ohio Capital,* and dated May 15, 1935. I have not been able to find these Hunger Marchers in any history book. (Even Wikipedia has no mention of American hunger marches.) But, luckily, the vintage press print has a caption taped on back that allows us to contextualize this image. It explains how during the Great Depression these marchers walked from Circleville in Pickaway County to the Ohio capital to demand from Governor Martin Luther Davey the reinstatement of direct "federal relief": money for food and rent. That money had been cut off by clashes between Davey and national officials. Was the governor moved, was direct relief restored? The historical record indicates no.

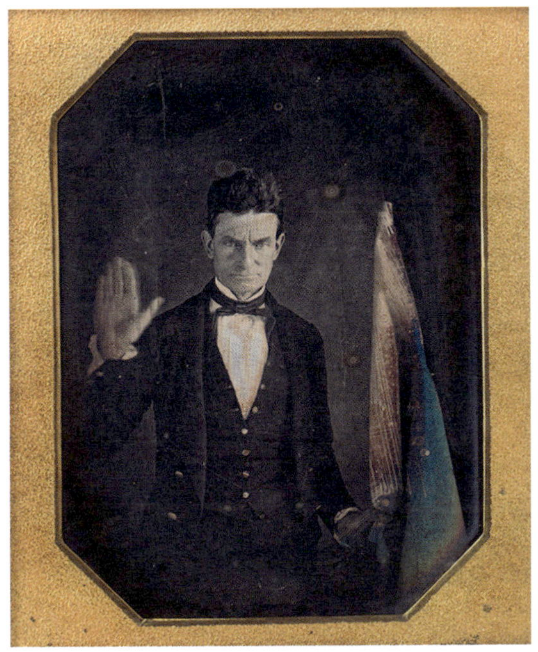

Here is a protest photograph from ninety years earlier, the National Portrait Gallery's daguerreotype of John Brown, the famous Radical Abolitionist. The flag is believed to be that of the Subterranean Pass-Way, Brown's planned vast expansion of the Underground Railroad. In 1859 Brown led an attack on the federal armory at Harper's Ferry, Virginia, an insurrection credited with helping drive the Southern states toward secession. Brown's gesture signifies a sole command: Stop Slavery!

Brown's photograph was created by a fellow abolitionist, the Black daguerreotypist Augustus Washington. Washington was born a free person of color (ineligible to vote) in New Jersey in 1820. He was brought up by a father and stepmother who had been slaves. Washington created a flourishing photographic studio in Hartford, Connecticut. In 1852 he decided to move to Liberia to escape the racism of the United States, joining thousands of other African Americans building a new nation in Africa where they would enjoy equal rights. In Liberia he again opened a portrait studio. He again became disillusioned, realizing that despite his positive intentions his images were serving the colonial subjugation of native Africans. He turned to politics in his new country; he rose to become Speaker of the Liberian House of Representatives from 1865 to 1869.

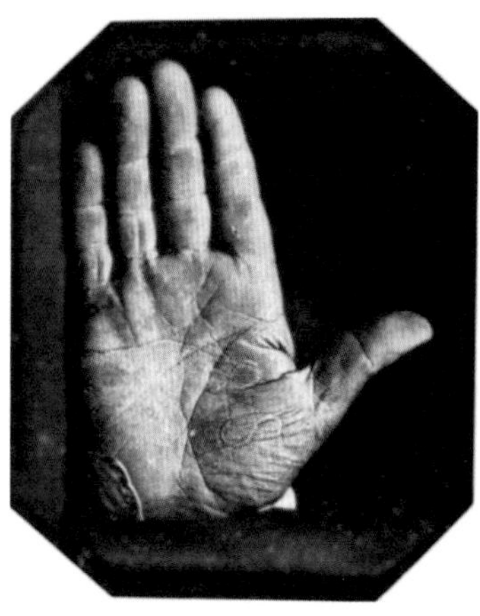

Here is another abolitionist's hand photographed, Southworth and Hall's 1845 daguerreotype *The Branded Hand of Captain Jonathan Walker*. Walker was captured attempting to ferry seven escaped slaves to freedom. After a year in torturous solitary confinement, he was sentenced to have his right hand branded with the letters SS, Slave Stealer. This picture has been called the earliest conceptual photograph—for letting a fragment stand in for a whole society. The recaptured slaves were not photographed. They were returned to slavery and who-knows-what tortures. None of the several biographies of Walker, neither contemporaneous nor later, mention their names or fates.

Thirty years after the Depression hunger marches, in the early spring of 1965, hundreds of protestors trudged from Selma, Alabama, through the Black Belt to a different state capital, Montgomery. Another Martin Luther led that three-day march, to petition another governor, George Wallace, for the right to vote. This was a hunger march too, the hunger of Black citizens of the United States to be counted equally in the political contests of their counties, states, and nation. This picture of the march by James Karales is a singularly iconic protest march image, the most widely disseminated of its kind. The Black-led integrated multitude, the jaunty rhythm, the ominous sky, the perspective stretching to infinity produce feelings ranging from alarm to political and spiritual exhilaration. All of it spirals around a central American flag.

Every American flag at a protest is a challenge to that flag, a challenge for it to tell us who it represents. We wave the flag to end our internal exile. We wave our flag to become integral to America. We wave it to claim centrality in America.

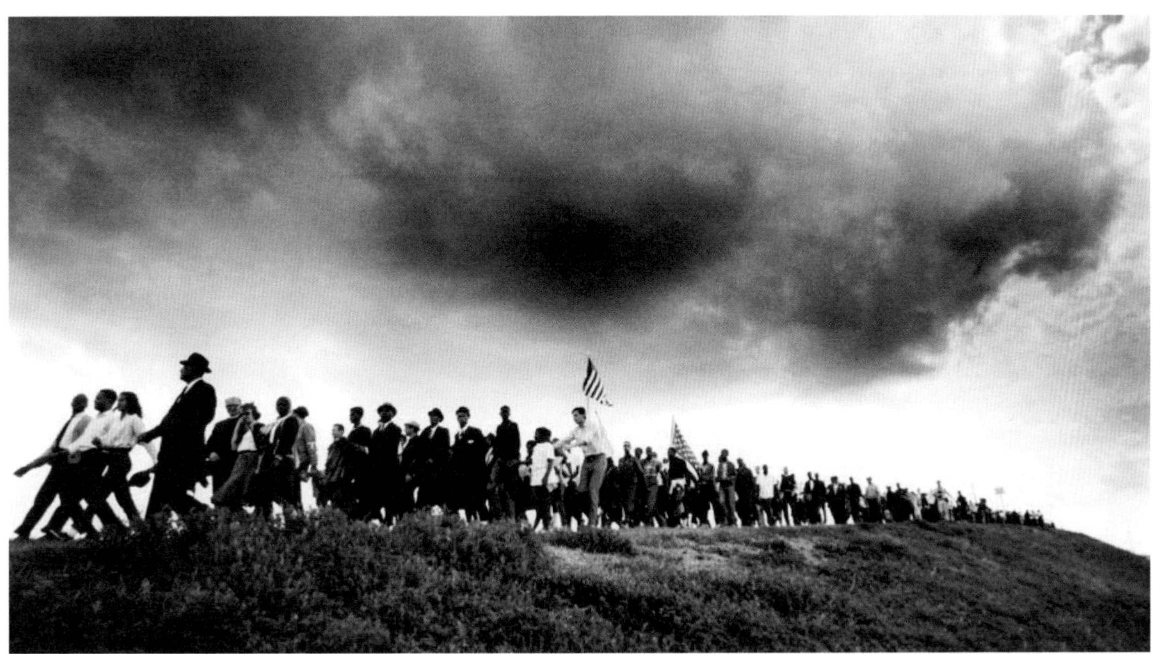

In an image captured May 28, 2020, in Minneapolis, a store called Minne-haha Lake Wine and Spirits has been set afire; the flames backlight a Black Lives Matter protester streaming the American flag upside down. On January 6th, 2021, insurrectionists at the US Capitol wrapped themselves in American flags—and Confederate battle flags and Trump banners. The American flag in 2020–21 was a war flag taken into battle in a country at war with itself.

Forty years prior to the Circleville hunger march, the first-ever march on Washington had set out from nearby Massillon, Ohio. "Coxey's Army" of 6,000 unemployed marched to the Capital to deliver a petition demanding bodily and spiritual relief:

We have come here through toil and weary marches, through storms and tempests, over mountains, and amid the trials of poverty and distress, to lay our grievances at the doors of our National Legislature and ask them . . . that they should consider the conditions of the starving unemployed of our land, and enact such laws as will give them employment,

bring happier conditions to the people, and the smile of contentment to
our citizens.

Death War Protest Love. Every day, images of death and war and bitter love
enter our homes. Let us not be crazed by them. Every day, flags and protests
are raised on our byways, at our horizons. Let them be in the spirit of Jonathan
Walker and John Brown, of Coxey's Army, of the Hunger March, of Selma, of
Black Lives Matter. We need more protest. We need more direct relief. We
need more love.

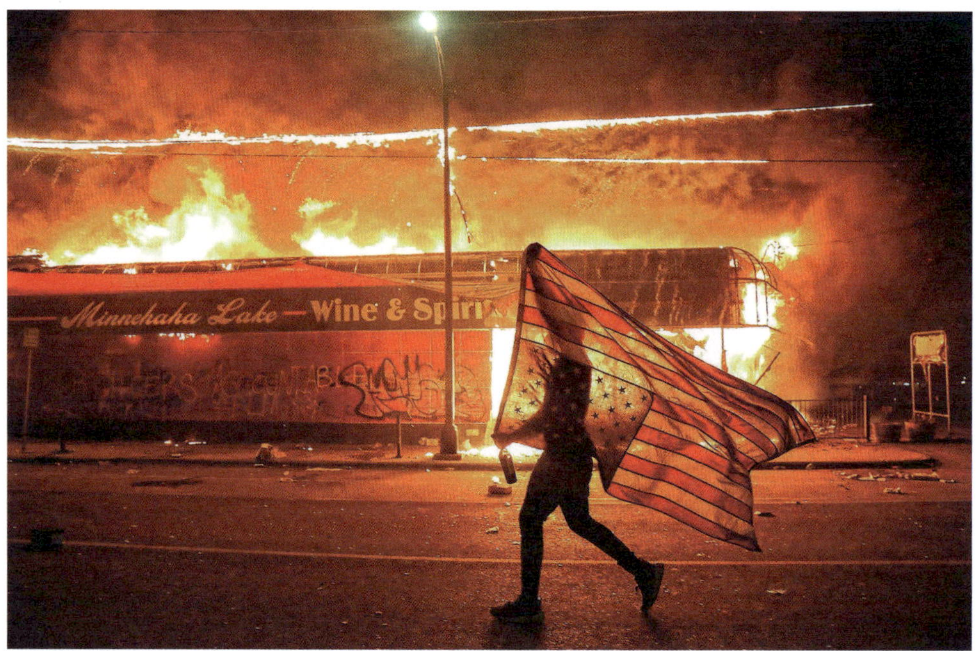

A Clayoquot Woman

My favorite book before I could read was *The Golden Book of Indian Crafts and Lore.* It was published in 1954, the year of my birth. I loved its instructions for building rawhide teepees, for drying fish, for beading war shirts. I imagined a life where I made everything I needed to be free. I asked my dad and my uncle to help me make a war bonnet storage case. But they were inept compared to the Indians. I decided my bourgeois culture was deficient.

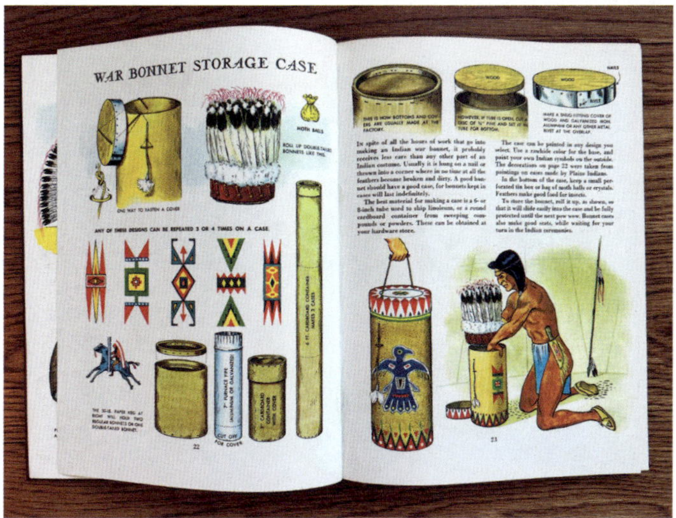

I wanted to be a cowboy too, of course. I would gallop through tumbleweed landscapes flashing double-barreled domination. I would never back down. The Lone Ranger was my number-one TV hero. I felt pride when he and his steed Silver rode into some wooden town swirling dust and bringing justice. I aspired to the Ranger's emotionless masked face. I was fascinated by his side-kick Tonto and a bit scared of him. I could see that Tonto's motives were complicated. Did the underdog's teeth have some purchase on the overdog's balls?

The revisionist Western *Little Big Man* hit the screens just after the My Lai massacre came to light. I watched it through tears and shame—shame at the massacres committed in my name—in the West, in Vietnam. The movie helped me understand how much of who we are and what we have in America depends on the murder and subjugation that birthed our nation. I was learning how the victors write and rewrite, film and refilm history. We kill the vanquished, we wipe away their bodies, we wipe away their histories, we wipe away the wiping away. Rinse and repeat. We, the perpetrators and heirs, do not pay for the crimes. We do not make amends. Responsibility is evaded.

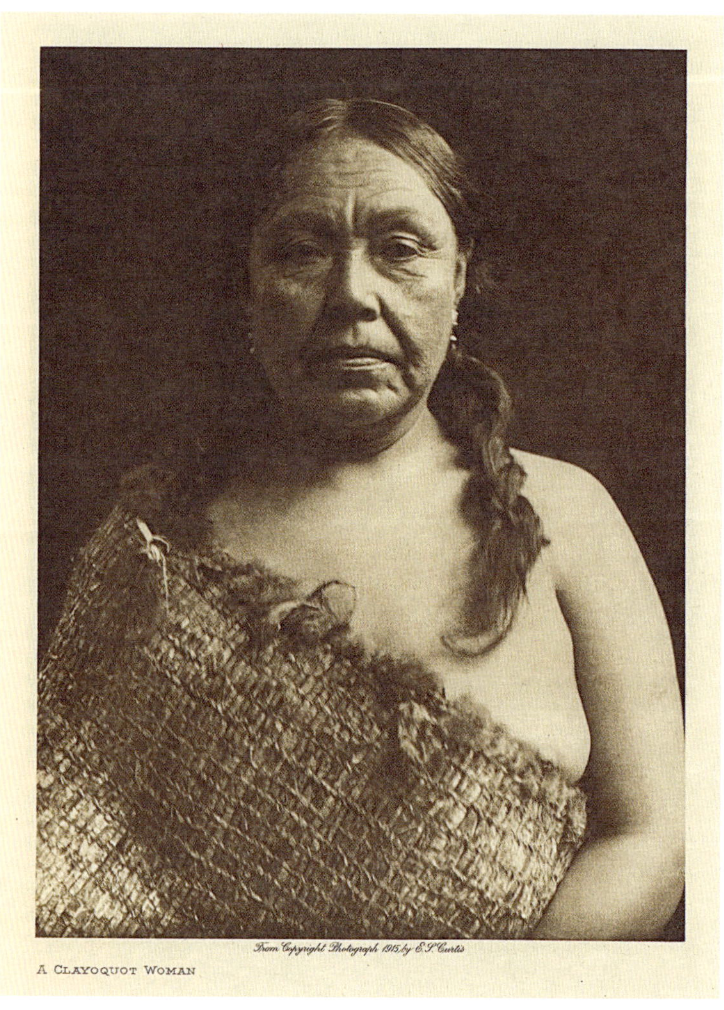

A couple of decades after watching *Little Big Man*, I would buy this picture at a Sunday morning tabletop photography sale. *A Clayoquot Woman*, printed in 1916 by Edward Curtis. Have a look. What do you feel for this woman? What do you think the photographer felt about her? Don't think too hard, go with your first feelings. Keep those in mind as you read on.

When I stumbled on this picture, I immediately wanted this woman in my life. I fell for her staunch gaze set in a tournament of creases hacked by the weather of her life. Fortitude holds her erect. She is centered in equanimity. Her gaze says, "I know what to do. I am a leader of men." Her gaze says, "Don't fuck with me." I saw the rough wool shawl, I felt on my skin the scratchy fronds grating on hers.

I noticed the nipple half-revealed. That nipple is a fine example of Roland Barthes's idea of the photographic *punctum*, the central point of a photograph, the telling detail around which the viewer's personal meaning revolves. For me, when I first saw it, this picture revolved around the friction of its elements, fecundity and age rubbing against each other, sensuality rubbing up against magisterial composure. Here is a hard life well survived. She reminded me of my Grandma Rose, who escaped Nazi Germany to live a long life of solitary dignity.

In the late 1980s, I made an installation called *The Art of Hitler*, a pseudo-museum of real documents such as this 1930s German photograph. I drew

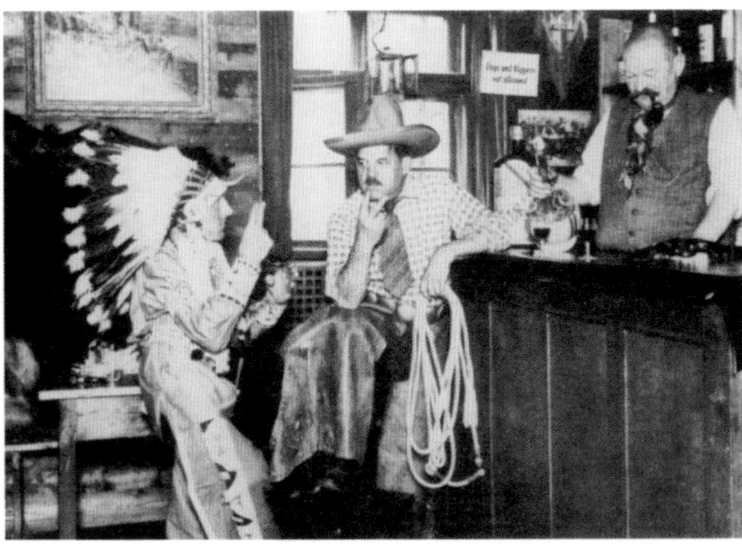

connections between the Nazi genocide and the earlier American genocide. I pointed to Hitler's admiration of America's colonialism, our Manifest Destiny that gave us license to kill. The Nazis studied our Jim Crow laws and our "Indian" reservations while devising their cruel anti-Semitic laws and their murderous concentration camps. The exhibition asked: Who are we to judge the Nazis? Isn't it just so easy for us to cast blame? Aren't we turning away from looking inward? When will we clean up our own charnel houses, liberate our own camps?

From 1907 through 1930, photographer and ethnographer Edward Curtis created his twenty-volume magnum opus *The North American Indian*. It encompassed more than 3000 pages of his writing and over 1400 of his photographs. *A Clayoquot Woman* is included in Volume 11, which documents the "Nootka" of Vancouver Island, now known as the Nuu-chah-nulth First Nations. The Clayoquot, now known as the Tla-o-qui-aht, are one of those Nations. Curtis wrote:

> The physical characteristics of the Nootka cannot be better described than in the words of Cook, or perhaps we should say the ethnologist who accompanied him. . . . "Upon the whole, a very remarkable sameness seems to characterize the countenances of the whole nation; a dull phlegmatic want of expression, with very little variation, being strongly marked in all of them. The women are nearly of the same size, color, and form, with the men; from whom it is not easy to distinguish them, as they possess no natural delicacies sufficient to render their persons agreeable; and hardly any one was seen, even amongst those who were in the prime of life, who had the least pretensions to be called handsome." . . . As to their mentality it is sufficient to say that it ranks no higher than their physical attractiveness."

Note that the final racist aspersion, to Nootka mentality, is not from Cook writing in 1789, but from Curtis in 1915.

The Nuu-chah-nulth were over one hundred thousand souls when the European invaders arrived. Ninety percent of those children, women, and men were wiped out, mostly by germs the Europeans transmitted. Those few who survived into the twentieth century were subject to kidnap into residential schools designed to extinguish their native language and culture. Sexual abuse was endemic in the schools. Needless to say, these traumas resound in the surviving communities to this day.

The charming town of Tofino on Clayoquot Sound is the premiere tourist destination on Vancouver Island. It was the destination Susan and I chose for our honeymoon. Our suite overlooked a craggy rise of wind-twisted pines. Evenings we took in the full moon rising blood-red over Chesterman Beach, thinking its face never seemed so human. On a kayak trip to Meares Island, our First Nations guide led us to the tree named Hanging Garden, a thousand years old, reputedly the largest tree in the Northwest. What that tree had lived through! We enjoyed ourselves untroubled by the history of that land.

Clayoquot Sound and Meares Island have been home to the Tla-o-qui-aht people for thousands of years. The trees that tourists and locals enjoy would not exist save for local First Nations activists battling the logging industry. Their coordinated acts of civil disobedience against the clear-cutting of forests were known as the Clayoquot Protests and as the War in the Woods. In 1993, nine hundred people were arrested for blocking logging roads. These actions led to a complete cessation of logging on Meares Island. The Clayoquot Protests remain to this day acts of civil disobedience seminal in Canadian history. They are widely credited with kick-starting the Canadian environmental movement. They received widespread attention via mass media; they sparked anti-logging movements around the world.

Since the 1970s, the Nuu-chah-nulth Tribal Council (NTC) has played the lead role in Canada for reclaiming indigenous autonomy. The NTC was the first delegated aboriginal agency in British Columbia; they received the first block funding given by the Canadian government. It was the first tribal council to take over responsibility for health care, and its Department of Family and Child Services became the first aboriginal agency in Canada to exercise full delegated authority for child welfare.

Today the NTC serves and supports fourteen Nuu-chah-nulth First Nations with approximately ten thousand members. The website of the NTC is headed by two Curtis portraits. The Wikipedia page for the Tla-o-qui-aht First Nations, written by members of the Nation, bears a single illustration: Curtis's *A Clayoquot Woman*. Despite the racist, cruel, destructive language Cook and Curtis used to describe her, her majesty survives.

Tintypes and Disfarmers

The tintype photograph was invented in America just prior to the Civil War. Before the tintype, unless we were wealthy we had no pictures of our mothers or daughters, and they had none of us; no beloved person was kept in our wallet or album or frame. Before the tintype, unless we had lots of money only a mirror could show ourselves how we looked. Before the tintype we couldn't stand in front of a camera to make a picture of ourselves; there were no selfies.

These men—brothers, judging by their matching cheekbones and eye sockets—showed up at a rustic tintype photographer's studio in their battered outfits and dusty boots. They chose to make this image—they posed for it, paid for it, kept it. In that makeshift studio, probably a tent, they were steadied by cast-iron posts called posing stands. They faced the camera purposefully, forthrightly. One brother sported his pipe, a signifier of relaxation, of time off, of a small surplus of cash to burn. His brother made the extraordinary gesture of empty pockets. He said: Something is wrong here! Not even enough for a smoke! He did not shy away from whatever bankruptcy or depression he was facing down. He told his truth. He put it out there.

This image of these two men is fixed to a metal plate that continues to tell their truths. What an extraordinary notion! To make an image of oneself! And to do it not just standing there, not just with whatever face on, but to craft a scene, a tableau! In this case about poverty and ease, about struggle and survival. And how remarkable that this picture, a century later, should up-anchor from some private place to sail into the wider world. These brothers have left their home and become history. We don't know their names, but we can know something about them and relate to them. They have joined the family of mankind, become brothers to us all.

In the summer and fall of 1872, a fierce epidemic spread, sickening and killing many of the eight million horses and mules in North America. Garbage rotted in the streets, fuel could not be delivered, fire engines could not reach

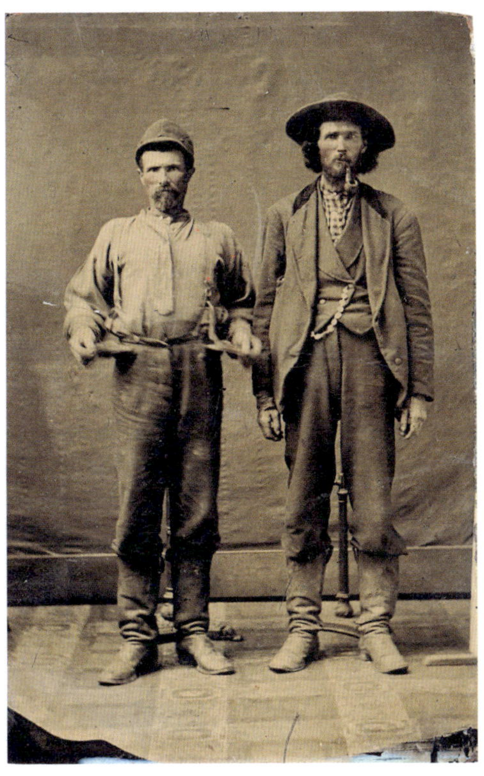

the blaze. Delivery carts were hitched to humans. That Great Epizootic of 1872 led to the Panic of 1873 and then to the financial collapse known as the (first) Great Depression—or the Long Depression because it lasted longer than the Great Depression of the 1930s. Eighty-nine railroad companies, hundreds of banks and ten states went bankrupt. This economic monsoon ravaged the globe for over two decades.

In the 1870s and '80s, in the panic and depression, the tintype was wildly popular in the United States. Americans made millions of these pictures of themselves. Getting your tintype made was cheap entertainment, available to all of us, even the poorest. Tintype studios sprung up on every main street and boardwalk, at every resort and fair, in wagons that wended to the smallest hamlets. Your tintype cost the equivalent of a movie, no popcorn. It was quick, wrapped up and ready to go in minutes.

But tintypes were more than cheap quick diversions. They were our documents, records of our precarious lives in that long depression. We wanted to capture some of that, wanted some evidence of our short joys and hardships, something to help us witness ourselves. And we made these images to share with family and friends. They were links in chains of affection. Preserved in albums, sleeves, and frames, tintypes told our stories across generations. They cojoined the living and the dead. Your tintype was your now and ever social medium. It mediated across space and time.

This earliest type of people's pictures has always been neglected. Tintypes are mostly banished from photo history and from most photography collections private and public. A prejudice against tintypes started immediately at their invention. It was said that anybody could learn to make them, therefore nobody of worth should bother. Anybody could afford them, so obviously they are worthless. This prejudice, looking down on the lower class of tintype makers and subjects, is still alive today.

But a cosmopolitan perspective on people's pictures also lives. Walter Benjamin, photography's greatest philosopher, wrote: "In photography one encounters something strange and new: in that fishwife from Newhaven who looks at the ground with such relaxed and seductive shame something remains that does not testify merely to the art of the photographer Hill, something that is not to be silenced, something demanding the name of the person who had lived then, who even now is still real and will never entirely perish into art."

Though just a metal plate, an artifact you can hold in your hand, a tintype invites our attention not as art, but by remaining a person, a person who stood in front of that plate. In the tintype camera there was no negative; the plate that we now hold was in the camera. Through the camera lens the plate gathered the light that radiated off of unique beings. The plate holds that light like a frozen mirror. That mirror crossed the bridge between past and present. People cross over; they reveal themselves. People to whom we can attend, people to whom we can be open—now, in the present moment. We can ask them: What do you want to tell us? We can listen to them, our ancestors, our brothers and sisters across time. We can care about them.

In roughly the same year that the two brothers were posing in the (first) Great Depression, Mike Meyer was born in Indiana. He came to believe that a tornado had swept him up and deposited him with the wrong parents. He left home and changed his name to Mike Disfarmer, dissing the farmers who claimed to be his forbears. During the Depression and World War II, he made portrait photographs for the rural clients that walked into his Main Street storefront studio in Heber Springs, Cleburne County, Arkansas. After he died, his negatives were discovered in dusty boxes in the abandoned studio. His images were published, shown in galleries, admired as revealing and idiosyncratic portraits of common folk of the era.

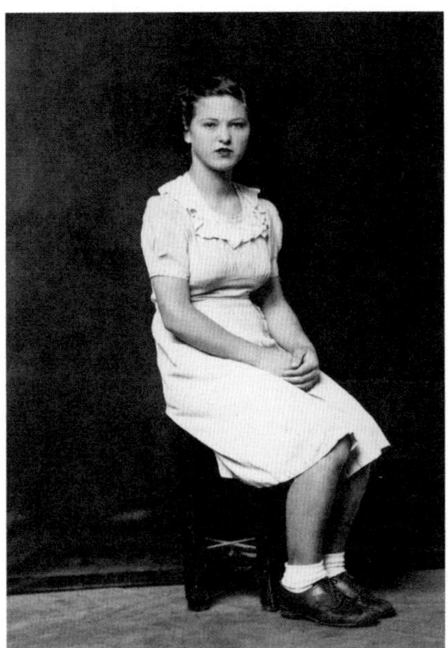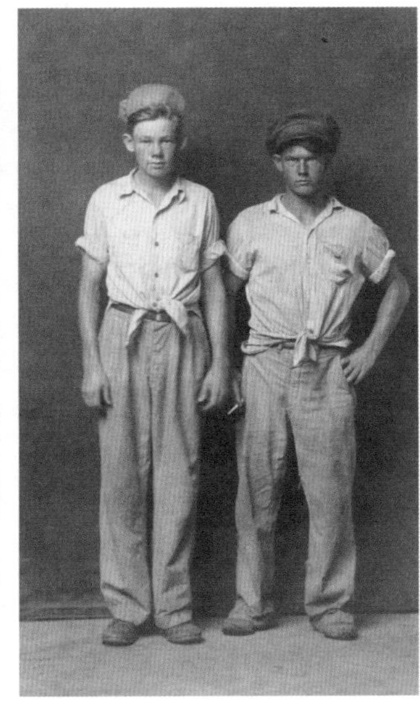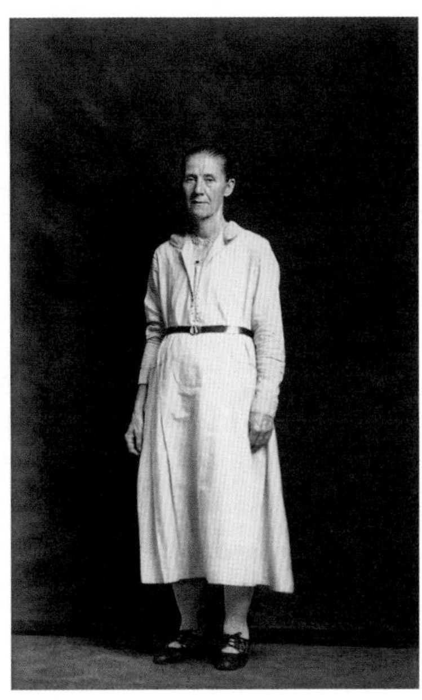

Disfarmer dismissed the basic tenet of his business: make the client look good. He discarded prettifying poses and trite smiles; he gruffly ordered his subjects to be direct, don't pose. He displaced decorum with uncompromising plainness. He took a minor craft—small-town pleasing studio portraiture—and turned it on its head.

Disfarmer was a loner, a recluse holed up in his studio. He had no intimate relationships. He made of portraiture a surrogate for touching and being touched. He set up to touch people through his lens, and for that he needed them to be real. The psychological frictions evoked by Disfarmer's method are intense. Though postcard-sized and without color, the best Disfarmer portraits rival in sheer thereness the painted portraits of Rembrandt or Van Gogh.

Collaborating with Disfarmer were the people of Cleburne County. Ex-

pressing their lives through these images, they produced powerful drama—
and some comedy as well. We see souls honest-faced and dressed for action.
We recognize one child's boldness, another's confusion. We share a youth's
confidence in his big-handed power, a maiden's pride in her new beauty. We
feel the dust and dishevelment of work, the exhaustion of loneliness. We feel
the communion of nine sisters gathering to represent their common root and
individual shoots. Through their images, their stories come into our lives.
Disfarmer's people matter to us.

We learn something through these encounters. When we look at Disfarmer's
characters performing themselves—so present, so vivid in their scenes—when
we applaud them, we applaud ourselves too. When we attend to them, we too
are confirmed and enlarged.

Capture

There was a time when eBay was paradise for collectors. Alone at our computers, we seemed to enter an Ali Baba's cave of riches beyond our wildest dreams. Strangers invited us into their attics, opened their bedside drawers; we rummaged shamelessly. I got hooked on one category of offerings: people's pictures, everyday images of everyday people—snapshots, tintypes, autochromes, Polaroids. Pictures of people wrested from the stream of history, drenched in its turmoil and its luminescence. Mostly people dead,

but not dead to me. As a dealer, I bought and sold these pictures, these people. As a collector I kept my favorites, the ones I found most heartrending.

This picture hangs at home near the front door. It tells a tale of captive and capturers, of cage and freedom. The gorilla's expression is foreboding, intelligent, complex—as intense as any painted portrait in a museum. It makes me think of Rembrandt's late self-portraits, or Van Gogh's. This small photo packs a big punch. It hits me in my guts.

I go to the zoo rarely, but sometimes I'll take my grandsons. We go to see the animals, to enjoy them, to learn about them, to commune with them. But I always feel ashamed, ashamed to be free

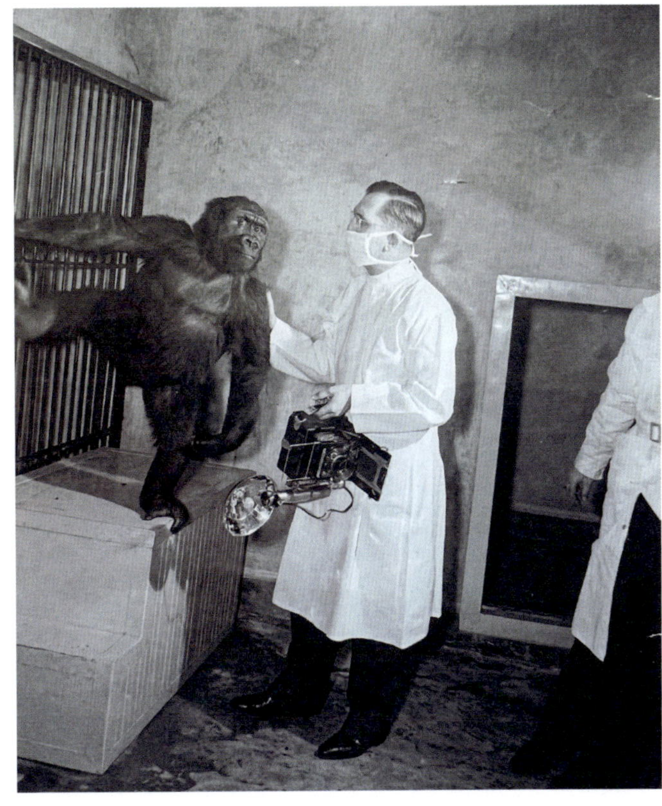

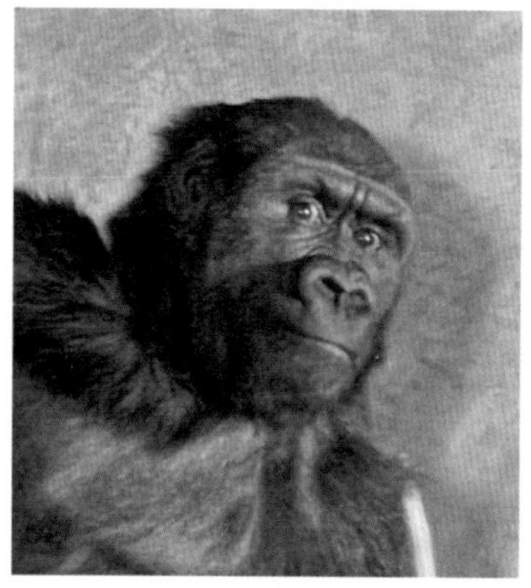

and easy. And I'm pained for the imprisoned. I imagine myself behind those bars. Pacing or swinging back and forth. Day in, day out. Far from home. Anger burning inside. No hope of escape.

No wonder this great ape is upset. Caged in a small, hard space. Men there not to give but to take away. Take away what little remains. Space. Privacy. He's outnumbered three against one. What enrages our friend the most is the third human there, the one we don't see, the one capturing this picture, the one detonating the flash in the subject's face, the one who stood where we stand now. The second cameraman reaches out to reassure. He is not successful. How reassuring can a masked intruder with an explosive flashbulb be?

Every year in the United States we use 65,000 nonhuman primates for experiments. We lock them up one by one, we infect them with disease, study them, let them die. Or we feed them toxic drugs, study them, let them die.

Great apes and humans share 98 percent of the same DNA. Apes don't build prisons or zoos or laboratories. Apes don't build police forces or build wars. That other 2 percent must be our cruelty genes.

Photographs of captives are a special category of image. We see suffering beings stunned in their capture. Cruelly, we have stolen their privacy, thrust them unwilling into the public eye, our eye, where we subject them to our surveillance.

One night on eBay, I came across the offering of a heavy canvas-covered ledger with photographs glued in, photographs taken in 1942 by the San Francisco police department. I bid fervently for this album, and paid extravagantly to win it. These mug shots capture women accused of "vagrancy," a euphemism for prostitution. San Francisco during World War II was a major Navy port where sailors needed outlets. In that ledger are hundreds of women each caught in the pathos of a specific life lived, each caught at a moment of raw vulnerability. A similar collection, from Minneapolis in the 1960s, also fell into my hands. The accumulation of these captive portraits is overwhelming.

The San Francisco album, now housed in the Smithsonian Museum of American Art, challenges our capacity to care about the suffering of others.

But we can try. We can see in these photographs a special distinctness that shines through the entrapment. We can bond with these captives. We can love these beings that are so frantically alive. We can love them for their sheer sadness and bravado. We can offer them camaraderie. We can offer them recognition—redemption even—in the chambers of our imaginations. Because we know that we too are caught—looking sideways, looking straight ahead— between birth and death. None of us escapes our number.

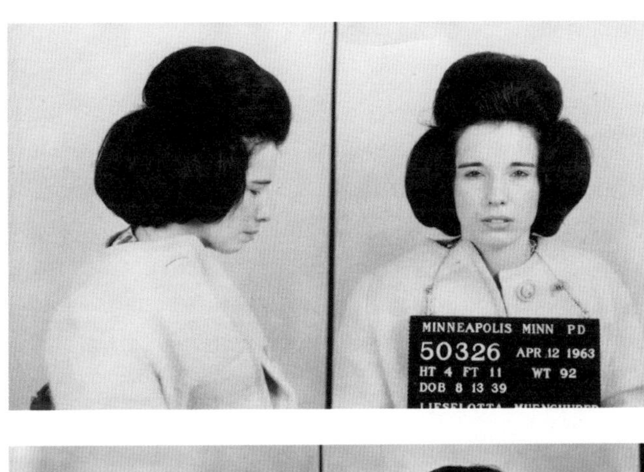

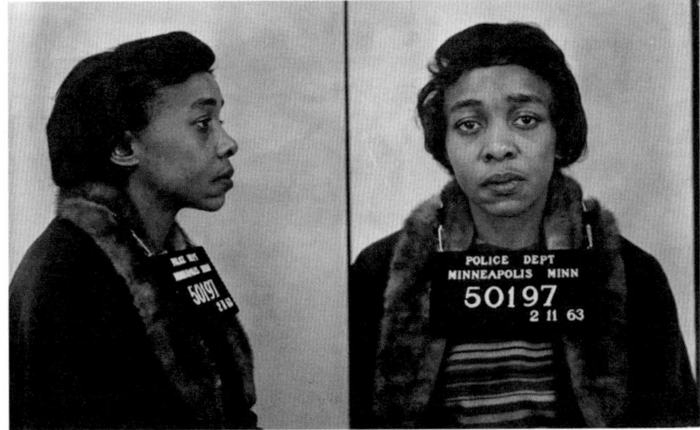

Love Melts Ice and Steel

I met Gulnara Samoilova, my second wife, in Ufa, a city in central Russia known for its oil and chemical industries and its catastrophic pollution. We were an English speaker and a Russian speaker, a Jew and a Muslim, a capitalist and a communist, an intellectual and an instinctual. We fell in love quickly.

Gula was a photographer. In New York, she went to work for the Associated Press, the large American news agency. Among our friends was the head of the New York office of TASS, the official Russian news agency. He was a short, dark man with a tall, beautiful wife. At a party one night in their Riverdale apartment, he challenged me to a drinking contest. Some quantity of vodka later, I stood proudly above him as he snored under a glass table. One day, this apparatchik mentioned a New York picture agency called Sovfoto. My photo dealer's ears perked up. It turned out that in a Midtown office, Sovfoto housed about 25,000 vintage prints made in the Soviet Union before, during, and after World War II. I sold that archive to a Canadian museum. But not before I pulled this photograph. It remains one of my most beloved pictures.

The photographs in the Sovfoto office had been mailed to New York by the propaganda agency of the Soviets to be distributed to the North American press. To make them useful, each print had a typed caption glued to the back that provided dates, location, other info, even the name of the photographer, all in English. This print, however, has nothing on its verso. Everything we can guess about it must be gleaned from the visual cues on the front.

A steely tank with snow-encrusted treads and opened hatch is parked beside a wooden house with hand-carved windowsills. We see a snowcapped roof with icicles. In burnished sheepskins a family gathers by the tank. A young kerchiefed woman hugs the helmeted young man, kisses him. He smiles and kisses back. He cradles the head of a four- or five-year-old boy whose sheepskin is belted with twine. The boy presses against the young soldier and looks down, emotional. A thinner figure, a bit hunched, seemingly an older woman,

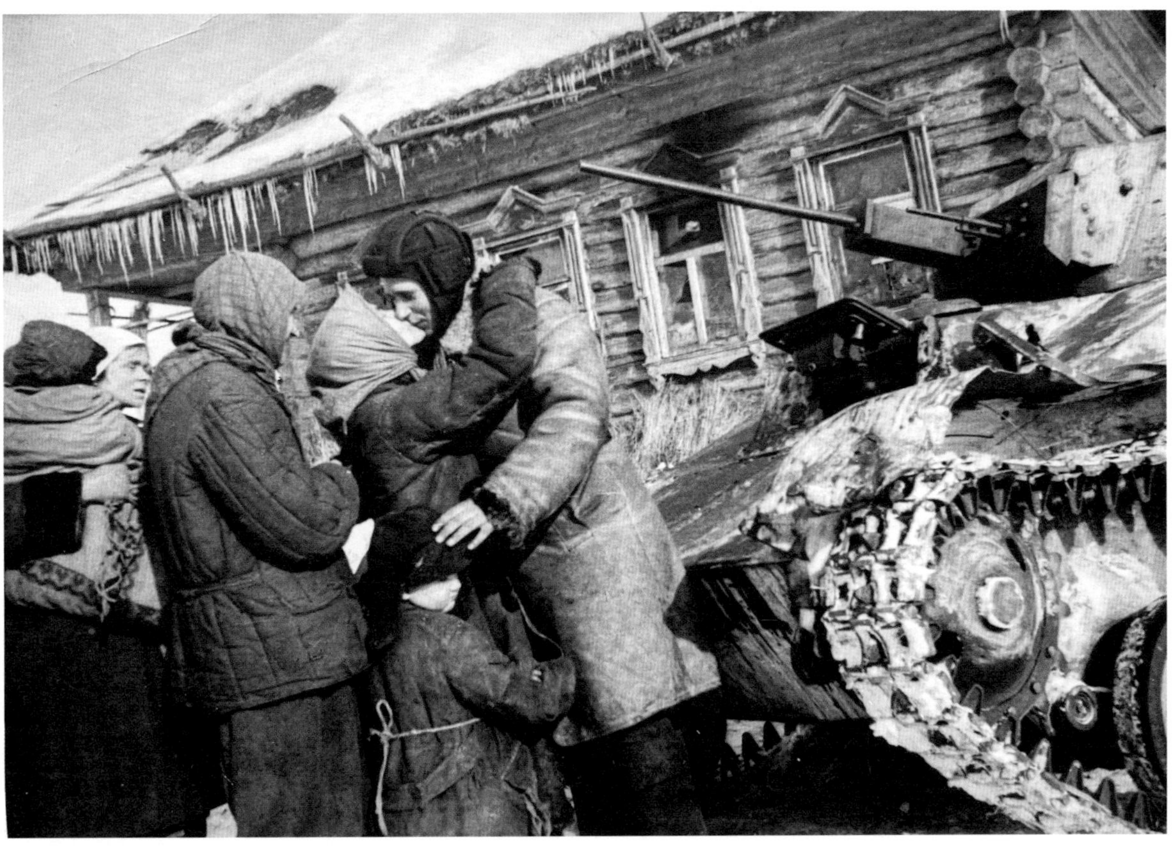

pushes into the huddle. Farther back, a young woman seems to rush forward, carrying a wrapped and hooded baby.

There is much to unpuzzle here. We can be quite sure the youth is the tankist and the others are his family. Are those his wife and son in his tender embrace? Is the hunched woman waiting in line his mother? Is that his sister behind, with niece or nephew? Is this his home? How did his tank come to be at his home? Is this a detour on the way to the front? Or maybe he's back to the motherland, alive, survived. Whether coming or going, is the visit so rushed that there is no time to go indoors, no time for even one cup of tea from the samovar? And who is the photographer? Why is he or she there?

And what happened after? Perhaps the youth returned home to his family and drank tea safely for decades. Perhaps he died in the tank, one of 8.8 million—or is it 10.7 million?—Soviet military killed in the Great Patriotic War against the Nazis. As Stalin said: "Each position, each metre of the Soviet territory must be stubbornly defended, to the last drop of blood."

The unknown photographer has compressed a great deal into this fragile rectangle. This uncaptioned picture calls our hearts out to the questions it poses. It moves us with its density of emotion sandwiched between the tenderly handcrafted home and the menacing tank, its density of peril and love. Love is unmistakable in the family's body language. Love resonates in the soldier's gently delighted smile. It is a love that ignores the icicle teeth above and the tank-tread teeth below. Love is that movement of the heart which opens and includes. Love can melt ice and steel.

Weegee's Celestial Echoes

My desert-island photographer would be Weegee. I love Weegee because I am a New Yorker and Weegee is the indispensable photographer of our multitudes, the chronicler of our fears and desires. What Weegee teaches me about our town makes me love it all the more.

Weegee was born as Usher Fellig in 1899 in what is now Ukraine. In New York, Usher's father was a street vendor on the Lower East Side, the super of a building on Jackson Street, a millinery worker on Wooster Street. He gave bar-mitzvah lessons and wanted to be a rabbi. Usher, become Arthur, stayed clear of temple. At fourteen, he went into business taking tintype street portraits of kids posing on a rented pony, foisting the pictures on ambushed parents. He hawked candy in the aisles at burlesque shows. He played fiddle to accompany silent movies. ("I could move them to either happiness or sorrow.") He delivered bootleg whiskey. In his twenties he worked in the darkrooms of the *New York Times* and Acme Newspictures. He started at the bottom, with menial jobs like drying wet photographs with a squeegee (one source of his name).

By 1935 Weegee had established himself as a rare bird: a freelance photographer flying above the scrum of staff news photographers. His stalking ground was the New York night; he preyed on the meat of local news: car crash, fire, murder. He lived out of a room not much bigger than a bed on Centre Street next to Police Headquarters. He tooled around in a sedan outfitted with a police radio so he could tune into the emergency calls and arrive early at the scene. Arriving before the cops, he claimed to have a sixth sense, like a Ouija board (the other source of his name). After hours, he barhopped looking to get laid for free, but most nights finished up at a whorehouse. Waking at dawn, he would develop film, make prints, make a daily round of news editors, hawk his catch. He chain-smoked fat cigars, spinning tales of his escapades, murdering the King's English with a toity-toid-and-toid New York accent that's a perfect crime. Treat yourself: check out the Weegee audio recording on the ICP website. And don't miss on YouTube Steve Allen's interview with Peter Sellers. Sellers explains how director Stanley Kubrick, himself a former NYC news photographer, hired Weegee to be the stills photographer on the set of *Dr. Strangelove*. Hearing Weegee's voice, Sellers lifted it to create Dr. Strangelove's strange accent.

Weegee's first book, *Naked City,* was published in 1945. It was dedicated "To You, the People of New York." Langston Hughes, writing for the *Chicago Defender,* called *Naked City* a "wonderful, wonderful book . . . It's just about the most dramatic and, at times, amusing collection of photographs ever put together." Alfred Stieglitz, the godfather of photography as art, sent Weegee a couplet: "A copy of your 'Naked City' was given to me. My laurel wreath I hand to thee." Promoting *Naked City* every which way, Weegee made himself a media personality. The book was a hit. He dubbed himself "Weegee the Famous." *Naked City* inspired a long-running TV show and more than one movie. It was the prototype for the ambitiously raw photography monographs that followed: William Klein's *New York*, Robert Frank's *Americans*, Roy De-Carava's *Sweet Flypaper of Life*. It has been reprinted many times and remains a classic.

Naked City is made up entirely of pictures of New Yorkers; the naked city is New York. The naked city is exposed, flaunting its bare truths. The naked city is ready to frolic. It's a naked city that makes you think bad thoughts; it excites longing, hunger, lust. Weegee's naked New York has no modesty; it spreads its overcoat wide to show us its flasher's glory below, while above it wears a big toothy grin. Weegee exposes New York without apology.

Weegee aches to see it all. Give me tenement fires, give me gang murders, give me car wrecks with gore! Give me pliable strippers, give me brazen neon, give me falling-down drunks! Give me Coney Island glazed in sweat, give me high-hatted Harlem queens and kings! Give me melancholy music on night-time streets. Weegee shows and tells it all.

Weegee is special to us New Yorkers. We hired Weegee to creep around, look around thirstily, show us what we dared not see on our own. Weegee was our sanctioned Peeping Tom. We scarfed up his pictures in the dailies and week-lies of the Depression, the war, the postwar. We made his books best sellers. We brought him into our foremost museums. Weegee even became MoMA's darling. Nancy Newhall, MoMA's curator of photography, embraced him (at a certain distance). MoMA featured him in a number of shows; his great picture

The Critic was an audience favorite. In the late 1960s, Diane Arbus, curating the seminal MoMA show *From the Picture Press*, included more pictures by Weegee than by anyone else. The cover of the catalog featured a Weegee murder scene. Arbus was working on a Weegee retrospective for MoMA when she killed herself. (The show was canceled.)

Weegee's special grace is that he doesn't judge. He doesn't look down his nose at the down-and-outs, he doesn't gaze up with envy at the rich. Weegee is not racist in his work—an astounding feat for his time and place. His creed was equality: everyone equal in their birthday suits, everyone equally fallible. Especially himself. He inserts his big personality into the shenanigans, the mishigas, the tomfoolery. He puts himself at the scenes of crimes as compromised, as an accomplice. He's desperate for money, for fame (attention, recognition), and for escape from pain. He's just one of us.

Weegee could ignore the niceties because of his special innocence, his childlikeness. From his childlike incorruptibility we learn to confront ourselves without judgment. Because he has no shame or pride, our shame and pride are banished. Weegee can rub our faces in the dirty, but because he accepts dirty, we are left feeling clean. In Weegee's world there is no Evil—no Good either. We are in Paradise Garden. Or what Buddhists call the Pure Land.

Here is a Weegee picture I love. Not Weegee pursuing murder, fire, or the scandal of the day, not the satiric or macabre Weegee. This is Weegee gentle, lyrical. It is a picture about music, about night, about tenderness. Delivered by Weegee's flashbulb light, three figures strain into visibility. Two men dressed for a chilly evening, nicely dressed, play saxophones in unison. They buttress a bright-coated, bashful young lady. She has the hands of a baby. She sings out into chilly space. Each figure is tilted diversely askew; each pair of eyes gazes in a different direction. If you look carefully, you can detect a fourth figure in the background, a spectator, looking at the photographer, at the other spectators, at us. We can only guess what kind of music this is. Jazz? A show tune? A hymn? And where are they? In a park, on a pier, or some street pitch-black? Are they buskers scaring up spare change, are they raising funds for a church, are they entertaining a political rally? We are left wondering. The picture creates wonder.

This picture was not shot in New York. Weegee made it during his four-year sojourn in Los Angeles. In 1947 Weegee moved to Hollywood to seek fame and

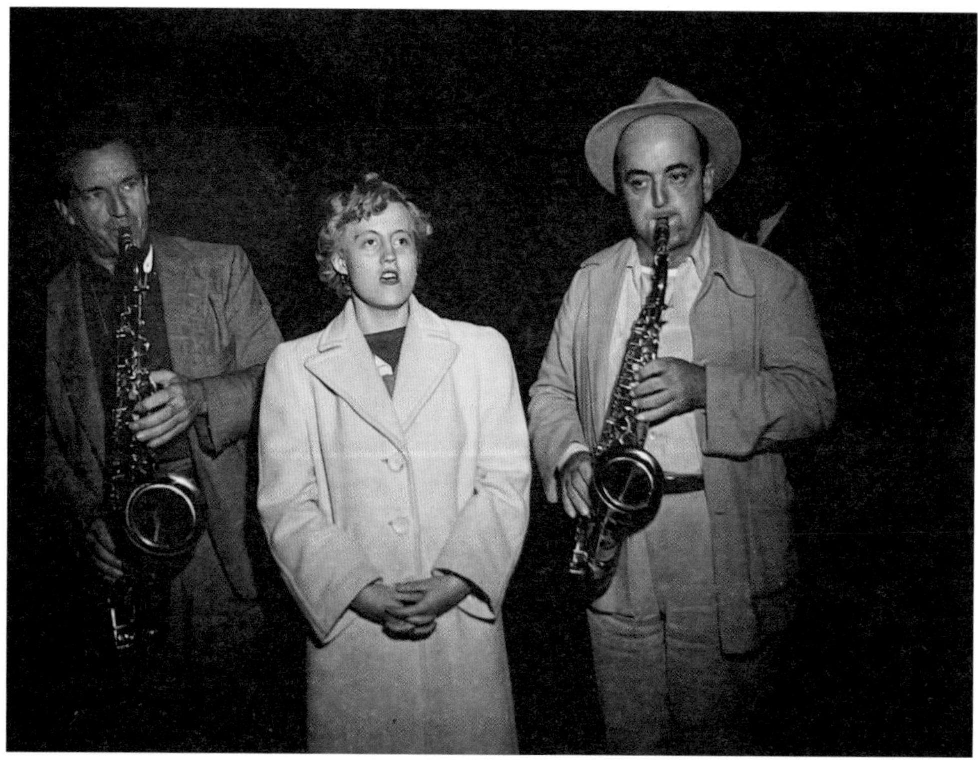

fortune in the movies. He didn't love it there. He found little work and was thrown off his game. "Land of the Zombies" was how he titled the LA chapter of his autobiography. "Of course, since the natives were zombies, there were no rest-rooms in the Hollywood restaurants. (They drink formaldehyde instead of coffee, and have no sex organs.)" The book of pictures he made there is called *Naked Hollywood*. It is an unpleasant book. It is full of trick-camera celebrity caricatures, bad puns, lame innuendoes. And lots of buttocks: those of Jane Russell, of Trigger the movie horse, of Oscar the statuette. The book puts Weegee's skeevy side on full display. Writer Miles Orvell sums it up nicely: "In *Naked City,* naked means a revelation of the real city. In *Naked Hollywood*, it's just bare behinds." Excerpts were published in the brand-new men's magazine *Playboy. Naked Hollywood* has the stench of an exhausted era.

But the double-page spread that includes a variant of my picture is an exception. These pictures relate to Weegee's working on the movie *Journey into Light*; the producers hired Weegee as location scout and "technical adviser."

It's the story of a minister (played by Sterling Hayden) reduced to a Skid Row bum who finds redemption through his love for a missionary's blind daughter (Viveca Lindfors). Weegee explained: "I did a lot of RESEARCH for the movie 'JOURNEY INTO LIGHT' and some of my photographs were duplicated in the movie. I went down to SKID ROW in LOS ANGELES & in one of the MISSIONS this POOR HOMELESS WOMAN WAS FINDING PEACE IN HER SOUL, as she followed the HYMN SINGING ON HER HARMONICA.... You might say that Weegee brought REALITY into Hollywood—the reality I thought I'd left behind in NEW YORK CITY."

This spread is placed at the conclusion of *Naked Hollywood* as a kind of antidote to the rest of the book. It is put there to show that, at least on Skid Row, "[Hollywood] differs little from other communities." Nowhere else in this cruel book does Weegee show warmth; only on these two pages is grace portrayed. In the center of the layout we see a hymnal in the hand of a Black man, no face, just a cross and "Celestial Echoes." "Celestial Echoes" becomes

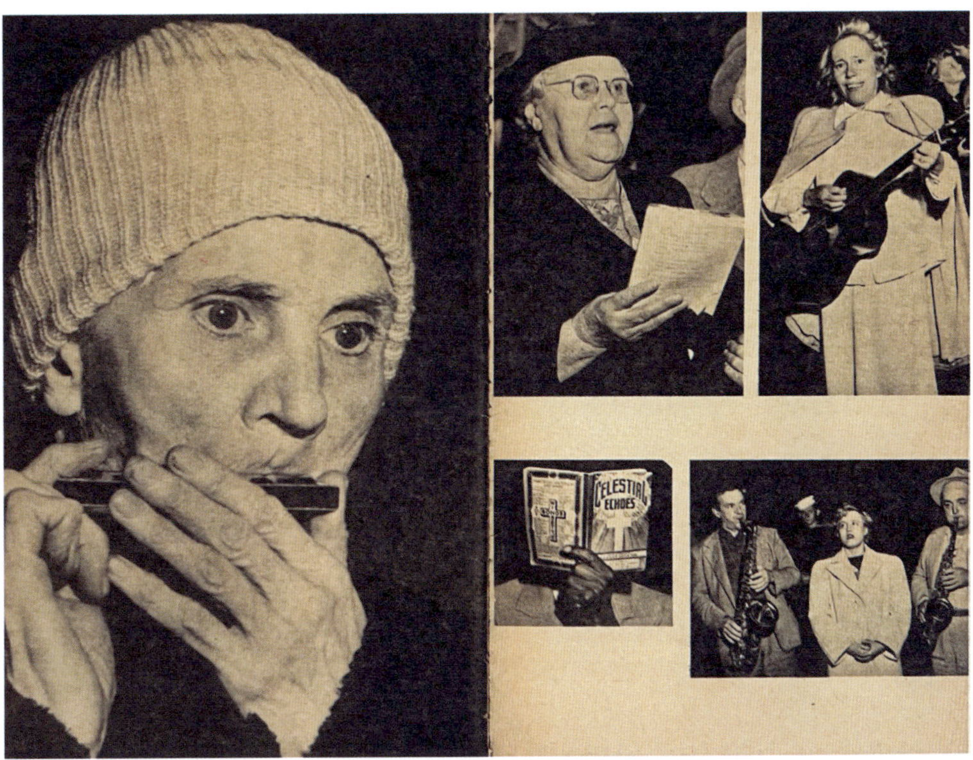

the caption for the spread. Weegee offers us the sincere if goofy spirituality of these Skid Row musicians. He is not mocking them; he is joining them, joining their spiritualized interiority.

When I was a kid, I loved those cartoons about snake charmers. A turbaned, bare-chested man would blow a flute at a basket. Out would pop a poisonous cobra; it would hiss a threat. But then the serpent would hear the piping, would begin to sway rhythmically, would relax: tamed, tranquil. Like every kid, I longed for that kind of power over what I feared. I knew I didn't have the power of force to overpower force; that's not the kind of power a kid could have. I sought a magical power that could waft through the air, beguiling by invisible force. That kind of power a kid might find, the power of the underdog's secret knowledge. As a kid in New York, I sought those powers, looking for them in fairy tales, in TV cartoons, in comic books. I still look for that secret knowledge.

What is visible in Weegee's picture is born from nothing. The dim light that radiates out of pitch black pays tribute to invisibility. What we hear, the music, emerges from a well of silence, is born from nothing. These emanations, the weak light, the faint sound, have a struggling, underdog energy. That energy is embodied in the singer's plaintive face, her moonlike, cross-eyed visage. From that face she inches her voice into the void, tentatively. Despite shyness and fear, she opens herself up, lets herself become undefended. She is vulnerable, she is generous. Her tentative, generous vulnerability entices Weegee. He recognizes it. He recognizes her magical underdog tune. It has the power to tame the zombies. It can enchant the snakes that lurk in the naked city. It enchants us. It awakens celestial echoes in our hearts.

Gabrielle Bell's Avatars

J ust before the pandemic struck, I started work on a documentary about autobiographical comics artists. My producing partner, Andrew Mer, brought in autobiographical film director Caveh Zahedi. Caveh was friends with renowned comics artist Gabrielle Bell; he proposed her as the lead subject and as codirector. Caveh invited us to an evening meeting at his Brooklyn apartment. Caveh's eyes were mostly on Gabrielle. He was trying to seduce her to sign onto the project—trying to seduce her in general. The more Caveh stroked her, the sharper her retorts; she was like static electricity, crackling with reactivity and wit.

Gabrielle soon withdrew from the film project. By then I had read her books and become a devotee. Her mournful, sardonic stories with their deadpan antiheroes reminded me of master sad sack Buster Keaton. They should be falling flat, but they stay on their feet, fly even. They do it frowning.

Gabrielle draws her friends, family, pets, and mostly herself. They are drawn with a modest virtuosity, and drawn from real life. They sit or stand stiffly in small rooms, they walk city streets or country roads, they are always talking. They wear basic street fashions. The "Gabrielle" character is the most disheveled and most slumped of all—except for her mom. The speech and thought bubbles trace "Gabrielle's" merciless ruminations. Her expressive vulnerability, her willingness to tell on herself with alarming specificity, garners her friends and lovers. She works hard to push them away. She often feels helpless and hopeless. There are stories where she can't get out of bed. But then she rises to face another day of self-analysis and self-help, of big anxiety and small solace.

In a typical Bell story nothing out of the ordinary happens. "Gabrielle" talks and walks, eats with friends. She makes art about not wanting to make art, or about doing it unsatisfactorily. She travels to comics conventions and has an okay time. She visits her mom in her shack in the Oregon woods, which is not fun because her mom needs constant mothering. She practices yoga: Bikram yoga in a tent in her Brooklyn apartment rigged with two electric heaters that short out her whole building in the dead of winter, causing her neighbors and her landlord to . . . She has relationships with assorted dweeby or oblivious guys. She practices under various self-satisfied gurus. A classic Gabrielle Bell line: "Cruel mind, playing malicious tricks on myself." This is from her small 2016 book *Get Out Your Hankies (Because You're Gonna Be Bored to Tears)*.

Sometimes Gabrielle directs her anger outward. Her stepfather is portrayed hugging the young Gabrielle inappropriately, if not worse. His violence looms over her stories.

Harsh as Gabrielle's scenarios are, they make me laugh out loud. I might laugh at the punch line, but more often it's at some foible minutely detailed that sparks delighted/ embarrassed recognition. Her streams of consciousness while sitting in meditation are particularly poignant and hilarious to me. She knows how funny it is to ardently desire not desiring, how funny and tender it is to be on a warpath for peace. One hand clapping slaps her upside her head.

I made an appointment to visit Gabrielle, to see her original drawings, to choose one for my collection. During the visit she sheathed her orneriness. I got her caring, soothing side. She made us tea. She (semi)patiently showed me all the drawings she could dig up. I chose this unpublished, atypical four-page story:

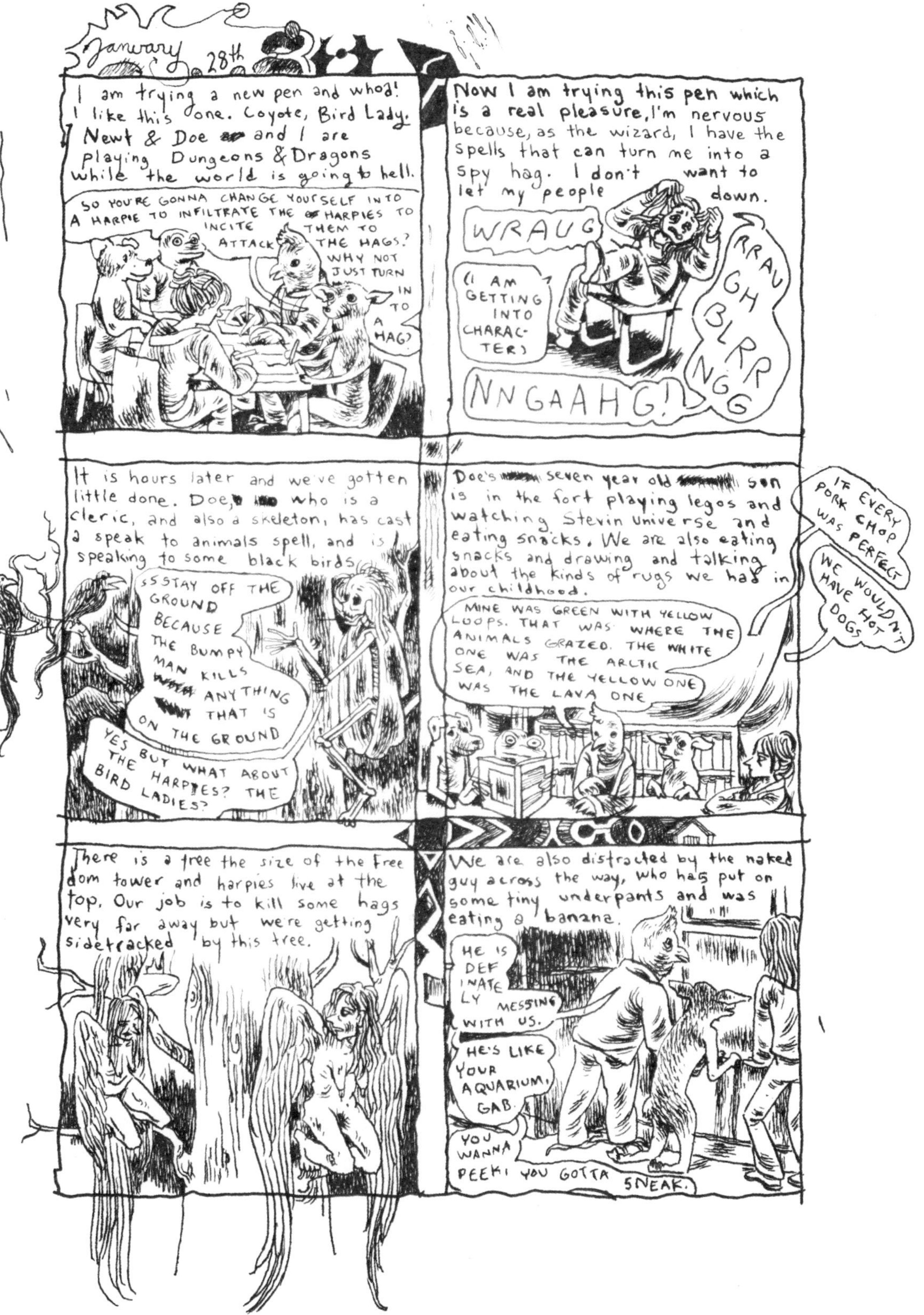

January 28th

I am trying a new pen and whoa! I like this one. Coyote, Bird Lady, Newt & Doe and I are playing Dungeons & Dragons while the world is going to hell.

SO YOU'RE GONNA CHANGE YOURSELF INTO A HARPIE TO INFILTRATE THE HARPIES TO INCITE THEM TO ATTACK THE HAGS? WHY NOT JUST TURN INTO A HAG?

Now I am trying this pen which is a real pleasure, I'm nervous because, as the wizard, I have the spells that can turn me into a spy hag. I don't want to let my people down.

WRAUG

(I AM GETTING INTO CHARACTER)

RRAUGH BLRRNGG

NNGAAHG!

It is hours later and we've gotten little done. Doe, who is a cleric, and also a skeleton, has cast a speak to animals spell, and is speaking to some black birds

SSSTAY OFF THE GROUND BECAUSE THE BUMPY MAN KILLS ANYTHING THAT IS ON THE GROUND

YES BUT WHAT ABOUT THE HARPIES? THE BIRD LADIES?

Doe's seven year old son is in the fort playing legos and watching Steven Universe and eating snacks. We are also eating snacks and drawing and talking about the kinds of rugs we had in our childhood.

MINE WAS GREEN WITH YELLOW LOOPS. THAT WAS WHERE THE ANIMALS GRAZED. THE WHITE ONE WAS THE ARCTIC SEA, AND THE YELLOW ONE WAS THE LAVA ONE

IF EVERY PORK CHOP WAS PERFECT

WE WOULDN'T HAVE HOT DOGS

There is a tree the size of the Freedom tower and harpies live at the top. Our job is to kill some hags very far away but we're getting sidetracked by this tree.

We are also distracted by the naked guy across the way, who has put on some tiny underpants and was eating a banana.

HE IS DEFINATELY MESSING WITH US.

HE'S LIKE YOUR AQUARIUM, GAB.

YOU WANNA PEEK? YOU GOTTA SNEAK.

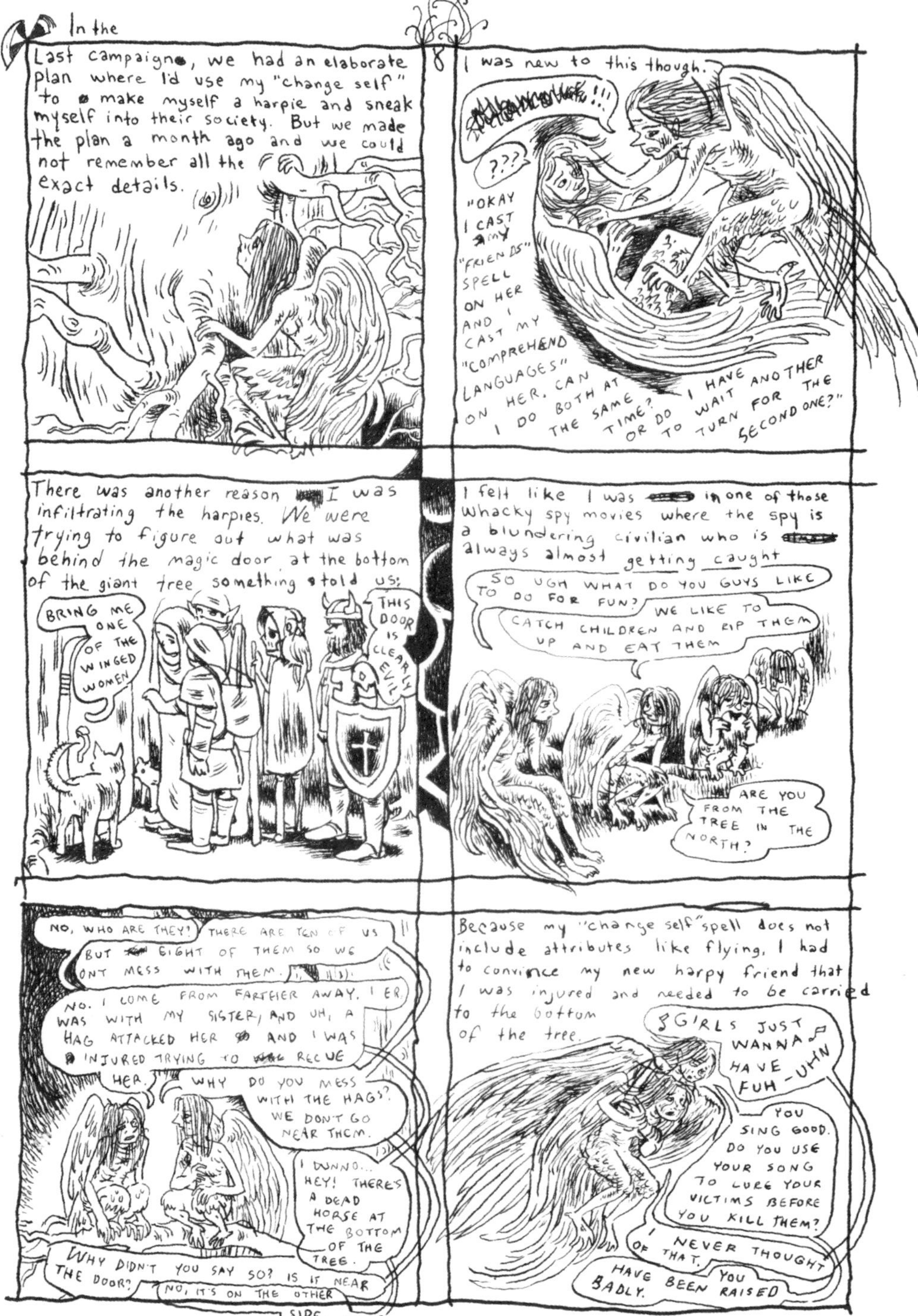
In the
Last campaign, we had an elaborate
plan where I'd use my "change self"
to make myself a harpie and sneak
myself into their society. But we made
the plan a month ago and we could
not remember all the
exact details.

I was new to this though.
!!!
???
"OKAY I CAST MY "FRIENDS" SPELL ON HER AND I CAST MY "COMPREHEND LANGUAGES" ON HER. CAN I DO BOTH AT THE SAME TIME? OR DO I HAVE ANOTHER TO WAIT FOR THE TO TURN FOR THE SECOND ONE?"

There was another reason I was
infiltrating the harpies. We were
trying to figure out what was
behind the magic door at the bottom
of the giant tree something told us:
BRING ME ONE OF THE WINGED WOMEN
THIS DOOR IS CLEARLY EVIL

I felt like I was in one of those
whacky spy movies where the spy is
a blundering civilian who is
always almost getting caught
SO UGH WHAT DO YOU GUYS LIKE TO DO FOR FUN?
WE LIKE TO CATCH CHILDREN AND RIP THEM UP AND EAT THEM
ARE YOU FROM THE TREE IN THE NORTH?

NO, WHO ARE THEY? THERE ARE TEN OF US BUT EIGHT OF THEM SO WE ONT MESS WITH THEM.
NO. I COME FROM FARTHER AWAY. I ER WAS WITH MY SISTER, AND UH, A HAG ATTACKED HER AND I WAS INJURED TRYING TO RECUE HER.
WHY DO YOU MESS WITH THE HAGS? WE DONT GO NEAR THEM.
I DUNNO... HEY! THERES A DEAD HORSE AT THE BOTTOM OF THE TREE.
WHY DIDN'T YOU SAY SO? IS IT NEAR THE DOOR?
NO, IT'S ON THE OTHER SIDE.

Because my "change self" spell does not
include attributes like flying, I had
to convince my new harpy friend that
I was injured and needed to be carried
to the bottom
of the tree.
GIRLS JUST WANNA HAVE FUH-UHN
YOU SING GOOD. DO YOU USE YOUR SONG TO LURE YOUR VICTIMS BEFORE YOU KILL THEM?
I NEVER THOUGHT OF THAT. YOU HAVE BEEN RAISED BADLY.

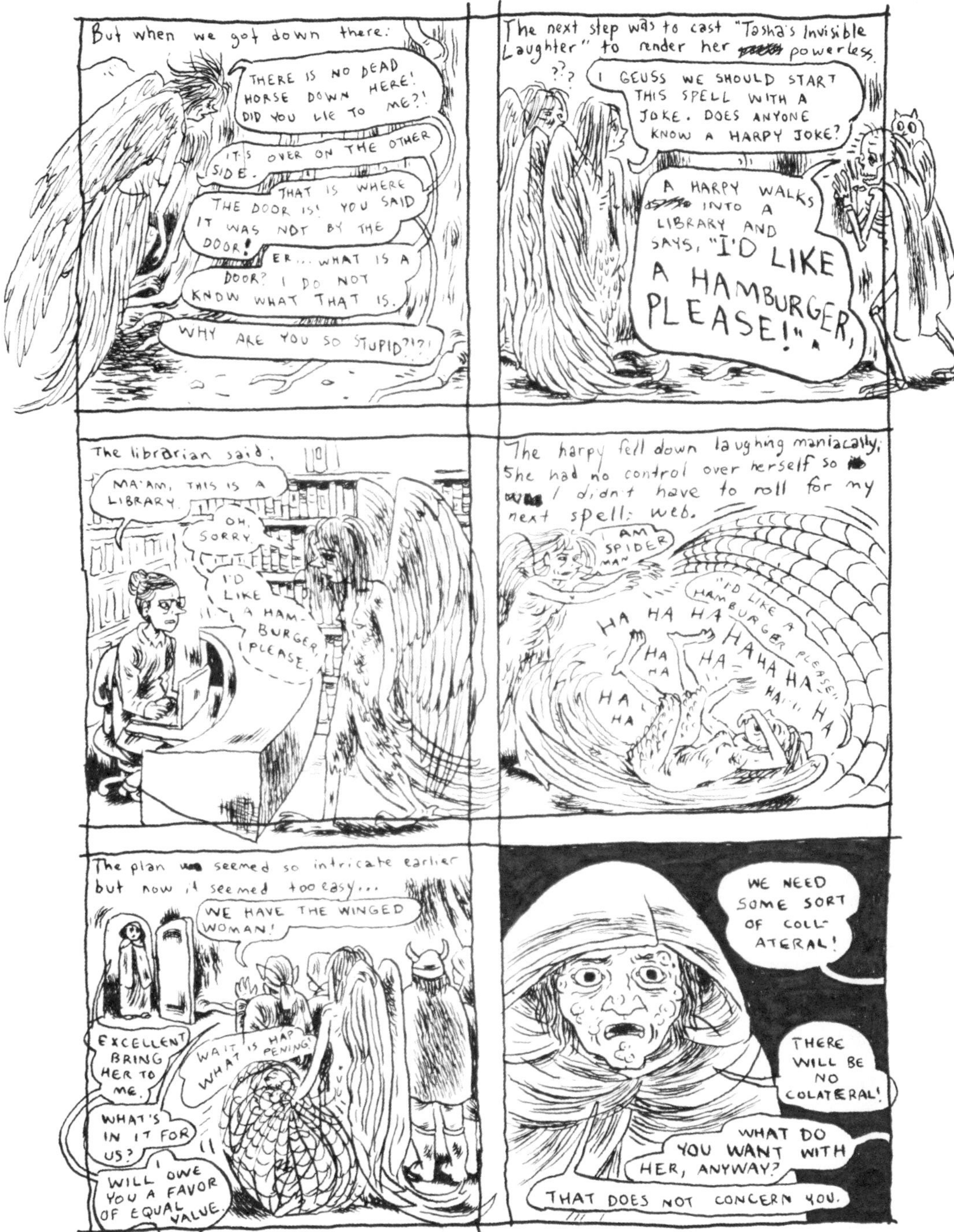

But when we got down there:
THERE IS NO DEAD HORSE DOWN HERE! DID YOU LIE TO ME?!
IT'S OVER ON THE OTHER SIDE.
THAT IS WHERE THE DOOR IS! YOU SAID IT WAS NOT BY THE DOOR!
ER... WHAT IS A DOOR? I DO NOT KNOW WHAT THAT IS.
WHY ARE YOU SO STUPID?!?!

The next step was to cast "Tasha's Invisible Laughter" to render her powerless.
??
I GEUSS WE SHOULD START THIS SPELL WITH A JOKE. DOES ANYONE KNOW A HARPY JOKE?
A HARPY WALKS INTO A LIBRARY AND SAYS, "I'D LIKE A HAMBURGER, PLEASE!"

The librarian said:
MA'AM, THIS IS A LIBRARY.
OH, SORRY.
I'D LIKE A HAMBURGER, PLEASE.

The harpy fell down laughing maniacally, she had no control over herself so I didn't have to roll for my next spell: web.
I AM SPIDER MAN
"I'D LIKE A HAMBURGER PLEASE"
HA HA HA
HA HA
HA HA
HA HA HA HA
HA HA
HA HA

The plan seemed so intricate earlier but now it seemed too easy...
WE HAVE THE WINGED WOMAN!
EXCELLENT BRING HER TO ME.
WAIT IS HAPPENING. WHAT IS
WHAT'S IN IT FOR US?
I WILL OWE YOU A FAVOR OF EQUAL VALUE.

WE NEED SOME SORT OF COLLATERAL!
THERE WILL BE NO COLATERAL!
WHAT DO YOU WANT WITH HER, ANYWAY?
THAT DOES NOT CONCERN YOU.

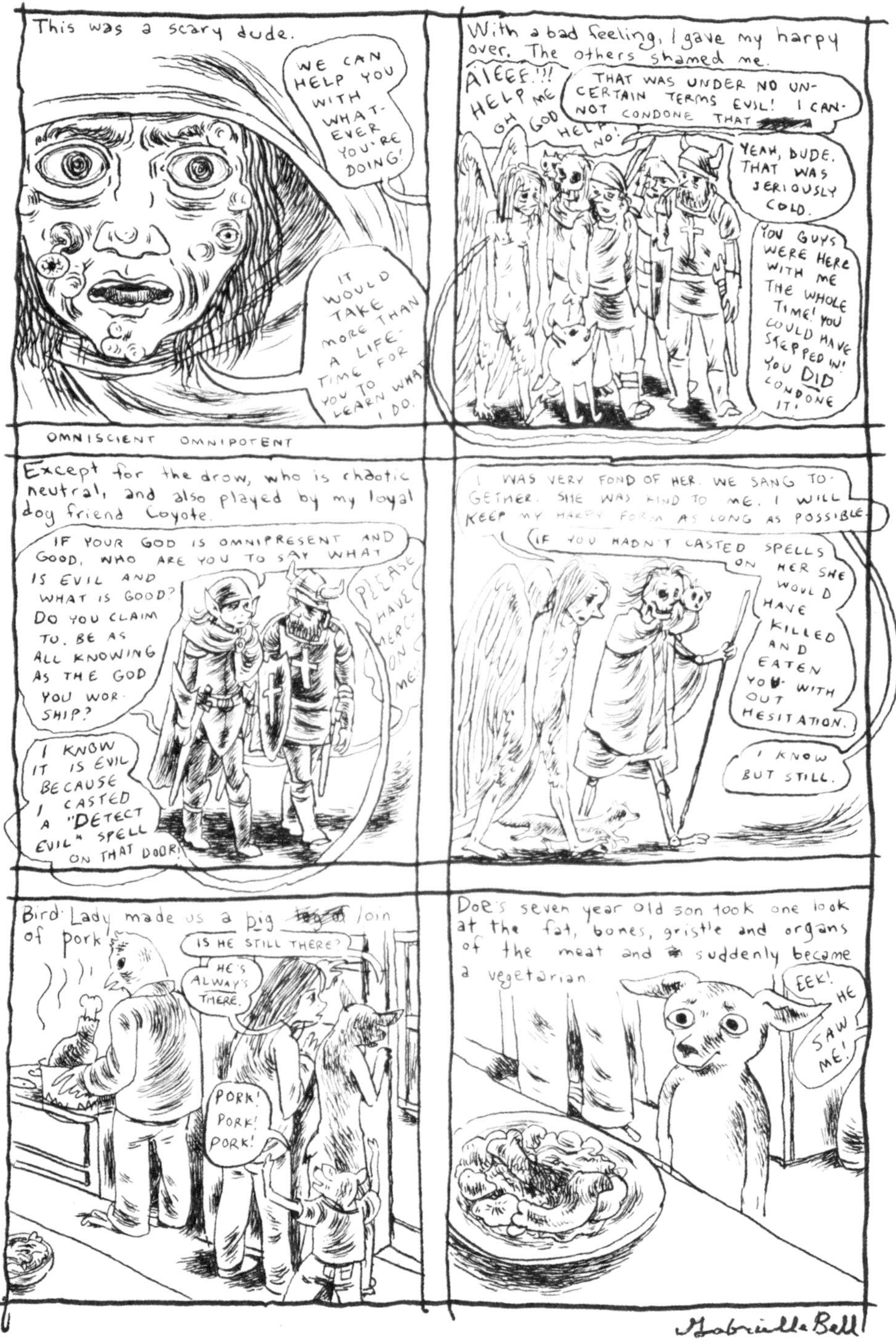

This was a scary dude.
WE CAN HELP YOU WITH WHATEVER YOU'RE DOING!
IT WOULD TAKE MORE THAN A LIFETIME FOR YOU TO LEARN WHAT I DO.
OMNISCIENT OMNIPOTENT
With a bad feeling, I gave my harpy over. The others shamed me.
AIEEE!!! HELP ME OH GOD HELP NO!
THAT WAS UNDER NO UNCERTAIN TERMS EVIL! I CANNOT CONDONE THAT
YEAH, DUDE. THAT WAS SERIOUSLY COLD.
YOU GUYS WERE HERE WITH ME THE WHOLE TIME! YOU COULD HAVE STEPPED IN! YOU DID CONDONE IT!
Except for the drow, who is chaotic neutral, and also played by my loyal dog friend Coyote.
IF YOUR GOD IS OMNIPRESENT AND GOOD, WHO ARE YOU TO SAY WHAT IS EVIL AND WHAT IS GOOD? DO YOU CLAIM TO BE AS ALL KNOWING AS THE GOD YOU WORSHIP?
PLEASE HAVE MERCY ON ME!
I KNOW IT IS EVIL BECAUSE I CASTED A "DETECT EVIL" SPELL ON THAT DOOR!
I WAS VERY FOND OF HER. WE SANG TOGETHER. SHE WAS KIND TO ME. I WILL KEEP MY HARPY FORM AS LONG AS POSSIBLE.
IF YOU HADN'T CASTED SPELLS ON HER SHE WOULD HAVE KILLED AND EATEN YOU WITHOUT HESITATION.
I KNOW BUT STILL.
Bird Lady made us a big loin of pork
IS HE STILL THERE?
HE'S ALWAYS THERE.
PORK! PORK! PORK!
Doe's seven year old son took one look at the fat, bones, gristle and organs of the meat and suddenly became a vegetarian.
EEK! HE SAW ME!
Gabrielle Bell

This story is about a Dungeons & Dragons party. Even though it features fantastical creatures, it is still a "diary story," a retelling of real events. Gabrielle portrays her friends as animals and avatars; she portrays herself as her usual frumpy human self and as a harpy. They play the game, they snack, they cook, they make small talk. They spy across the backyard at an exhibitionist diddling his manhood.

The D and D story line is dominated by a character identified only as "a scary dude." He is the archvillain. His abode is called "clearly evil." He has wide maniacal eyes. His pustules sport extra eyeballs. He commands Gabrielle-the-harpy to deliver him a captured woman. Though fearing the worst, Gabrielle submits and gives him the human sacrifice. She is condemned by her friends; they "cannot condone" her act, which is "under no uncertain terms evil" and "seriously cold." The story traces the harpy's/Gabrielle's defensiveness, insecurity, nerves, distraction, ineptitude, fear, feelings of betrayal, lame jokes, shame, anger at friends, guilt, feelings of defeat. Despite the fantasy trimmings, this is a typical Gabrielle Bell tale after all, what she usually harps on.

I discovered this work in October 2020, just days before the election victory of President Joe Biden. It was drawn on January 28, 2017, just days after the inauguration of President Donald Trump. It starts with Gabrielle saying she is "playing Dungeons & Dragons while the world is going to hell." She's already seen what Trump would be, the improbable tyrant who would swarm our psyches with dragons and dungeons, tricksters and traitors, harpies and hags, pizza-parlor pedophile cannibals and other nightmare characters. The clearly evil scary dude who looms over this story, who makes friends turn on each other, who demands obedience, who is as ugly as can be, who tortures women, who declares "There will be no collateral!" is an avatar of Trump—not to mention her stepfather and his ilk.

At the beginning of the story, Gabrielle introduces us to a seven-year-old boy, Doe's son, drawn as a cute dog. He has built himself a makeshift tent—one of many small enclosures that pop up regularly in Bell stories, little spaces of safety and healing. In his tent he hears Steven Universe telling the despotic White Diamond that for hot dogs we need imperfect pork chops. In the very last frame, the boy is served a plate of "fat, bones, gristle and organs" that the adults have cooked up. He turns away in disgust. He's not having it. He "suddenly became a vegetarian."

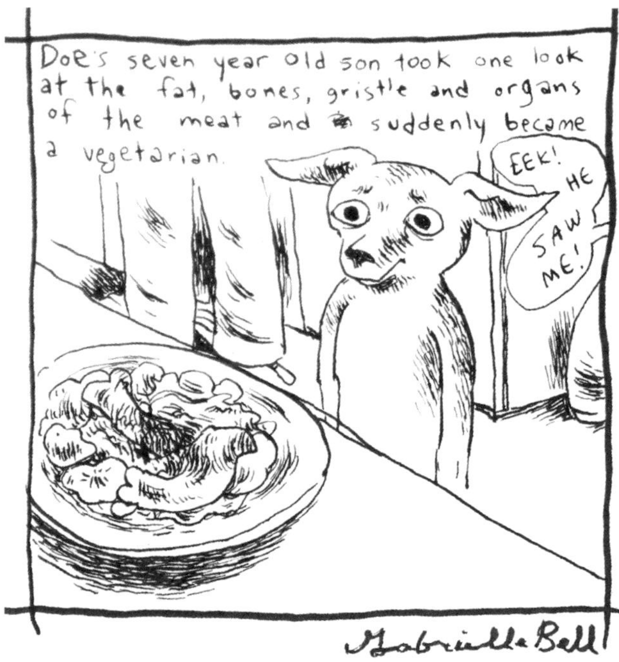

Gabrielle's characters, starting with herself, have high moral standards. They strive to be not evil but good. Gabrielle draws them in boxes and gives them speech so that we can relate to them, learn from them, take comfort from them. We can learn, for instance, like Doe's son, to turn away in disgust from the abattoir; we can learn to seek less devouring ways of life. We can learn to turn away from the masturbatory spectacles that entice our eyeballs. We can learn to resist those dudes, within us and without, who demand human sacrifice. We can live our better avatars.

The Wound That Never Heals

I asked Leela Corman to send me a self-portrait for my gallery's website. She sent herself standing by a tree, a poorly focused snapshot. I laughed; she had forgotten all those beautifully rendered self-portraits that fill her comics. Or she thought them too arty. Maybe she thought they were too scary. Maybe they are.

Leela Corman was brought up on the isle of Manahatta (Lenape land). She spends much of her imagination dwelling in the Old World, in the Europe of World War II. Her ancestors' departure from that world cut her a wound that never heals.

Leela has a second wound that never heals, even deeper. Her first daughter, her only child, at two years old, for no apparent reason, died in bed.

Leela would rather have died herself. Parents understand that. I understood it in my every cell the moment I was pushing my daughter's stroller and a truck bore down on us and I knew I would instinctively die if that would save her. In those moments, as they value that other life above their own, parents die to themselves.

Corman's first graphic novel, *Unterzakhn*, 2012, is an entwinement of twin sisters. They are first-generation New Yorkers who grow up kneaded by the shtetl of the Lower East Side. Esther shakes free as a dancer, then a prostitute, then a blasé penthoused diva. Fanya, stuck downtown, cares for their harsh mother, fights off men's frantic fingers, apprentices to an abortionist, dies in childbirth on her sister's silken bed. Here is the novel's last panel. The surviving twin sister cradles the daughter of the dead twin sister. "Fanya doesn't live here anymore."

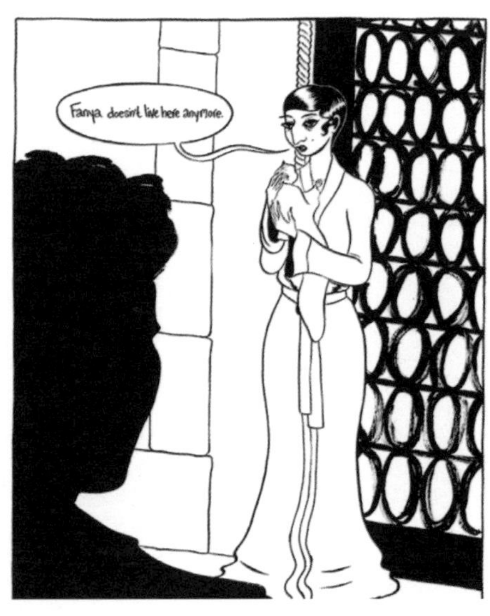

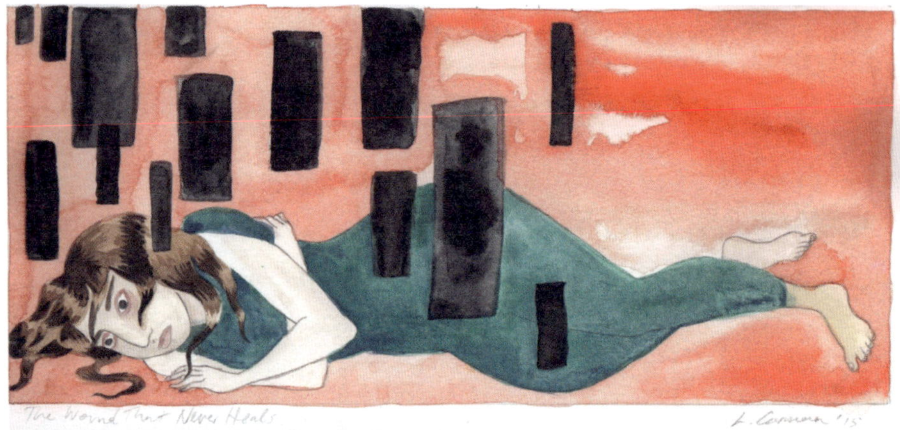

In 2015 Corman published the graphic story *PTSD: The Wound That Never Heals*. She paints the pain of loss in images that stumble from the everyday to the diagrammatic to the mystic. Her words mimic the cold language of psychology primers, or drag bloody metaphors up from her viscera. Her images and words draw us into the convolutions of her pain. We are with her as she hugs the pain, won't let it go, won't medicate it or meditate it away. She offers us her story as an inoculation against our own pain. Then, in the last panel, she offers some symptomatic relief, a cradling. "Eventually, very gentle yoga, gentler than I'd ever given myself permission to do before, helped me get to a base level of functioning."

Life is an Ambush: My Two Birth Stories came out a year later. The drawings are shot with black and red, the language is enraged and discouraged, there is more death than life. At the center of the story are two paintings: a forest

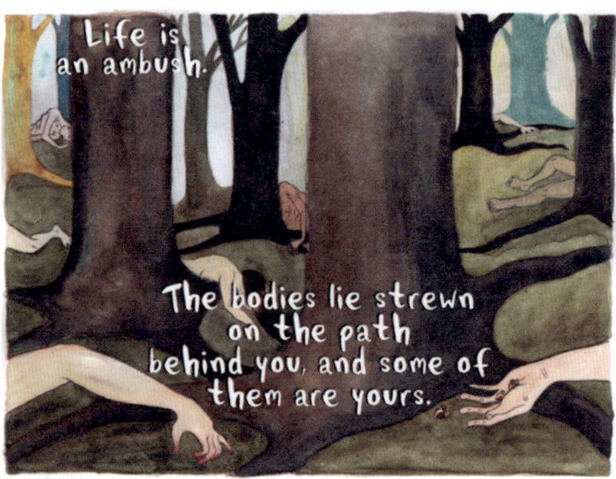

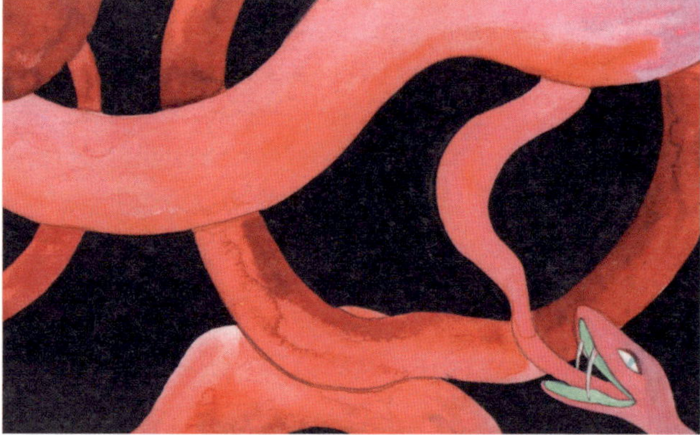

of corpses and an ocean of ash and bones. It is a tale of Corman's two child-births and a tale of two deaths, the death of her firstborn child and the death of mid-century Europe. The last frame is a beautiful painting of a blood-red umbilical snake biting its tail, shown here before the text was inscribed: "You can't control what happens at the gates of life and death."

The next year, 2017, Corman published *It Only Masquerades as Entertainment*, a story about her connection to musician Nick Cave. Cave's son, at age fifteen, died in an accident. In the story hands touch across death and life, across memory and presence. In describing Cave's music, Corman describes her own work:

If anything, his new songs have even more power. Coming as they do from the place beyond reach. Each one is like a gigantic lullaby for people whose grief is exhausting. A cave to crawl into, where our sorrow is seen, and we are allowed to rest.

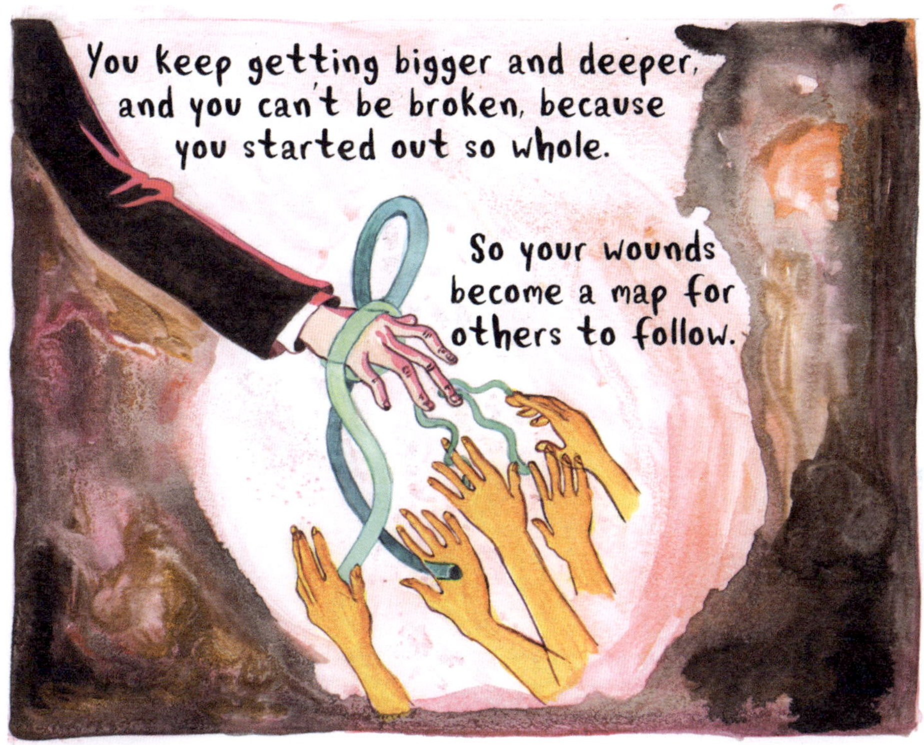

Like *Life is an Ambush*, the 2021 story *You Are Not a* Guest spirals around a forest. This Polish forest is a killing ground. It is a burial ground. It is a memorial. This is a story of "multigenerational trauma." It is also a story of rediscovery and reunion. The watercolor panels are lush, sensual. The text is conversational, full of Yiddish. We are served a proper borscht and correct pierogi. Corman concludes: "I floated above her history, along the river of my own blood, back to Poland, to where my living memories are safe." It is a tale of healing, of repatriation and rebirth.

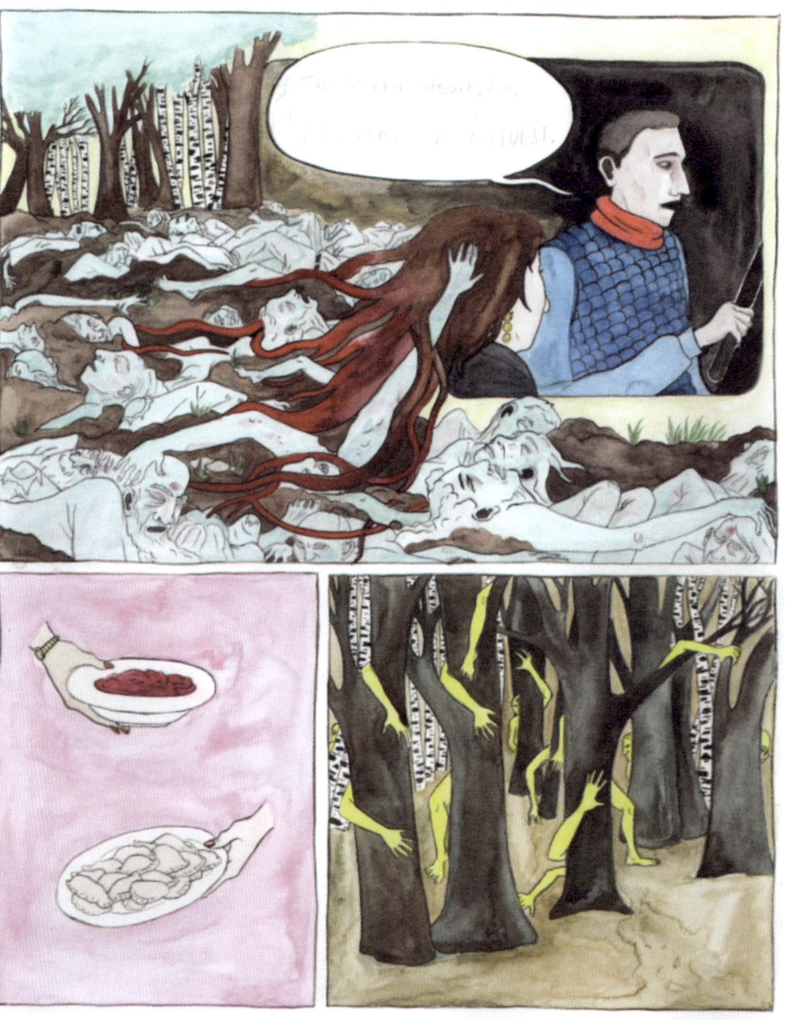

Victory Parade, published in 2024, is an Expressionist graphic novel of war and love. We pass through battlefields of the heart and through the genocide of World War II. *Part I* is set in Brooklyn, in the Navy Yards, by the East River, at Coney Island, in a tenement, a cafeteria, a wrestling arena. The German/Jewish emigre Rifke becomes Ruthie, then becomes Ruthless Ruby the Killer Kraut, a wrestler who crushes her opponents with malice. There is a flashback to Ruthie's feral childhood in Weimar Berlin. Rifke/Ruthie/Ruby is devastated by a nightmare encounter with her dead mother. Ruby's friend Rose, a riveter, tenderly beds a neighbor, guiltily, while her husband Sam is overseas liberating Buchenwald.

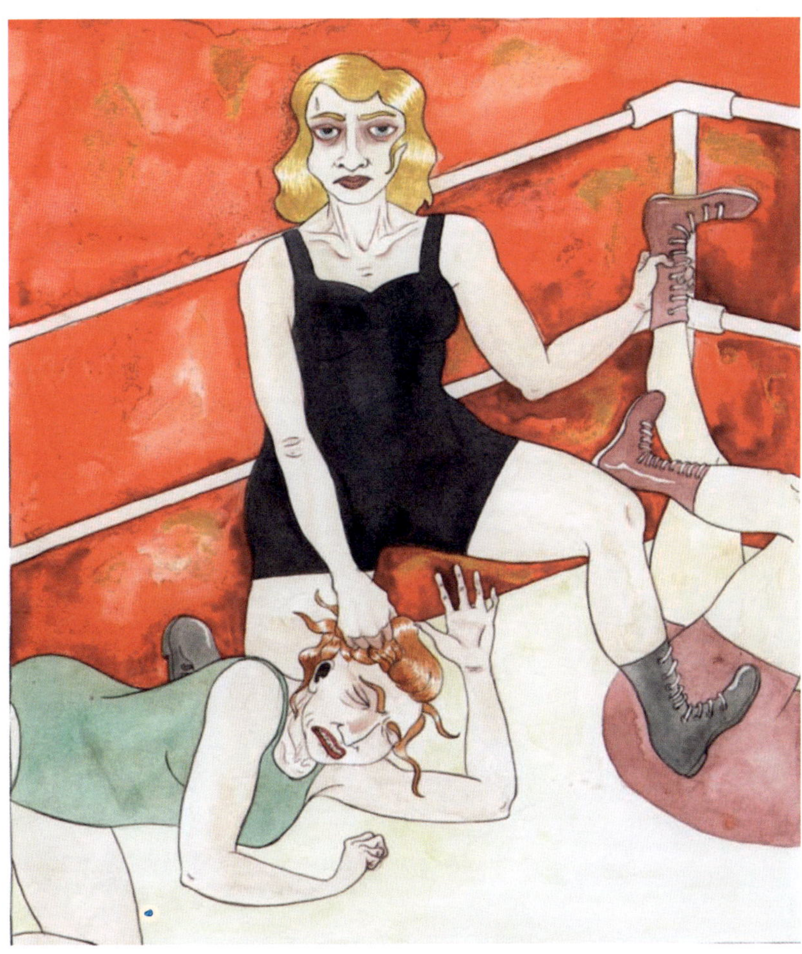

For the emotional complexity she needs to tell this tale, Corman draws inspiration from movie close-ups. She gives her dramatic personae overripe eyes. Look at the emotions Rifke/Ruthie/Ruby feels over the course of five pages:

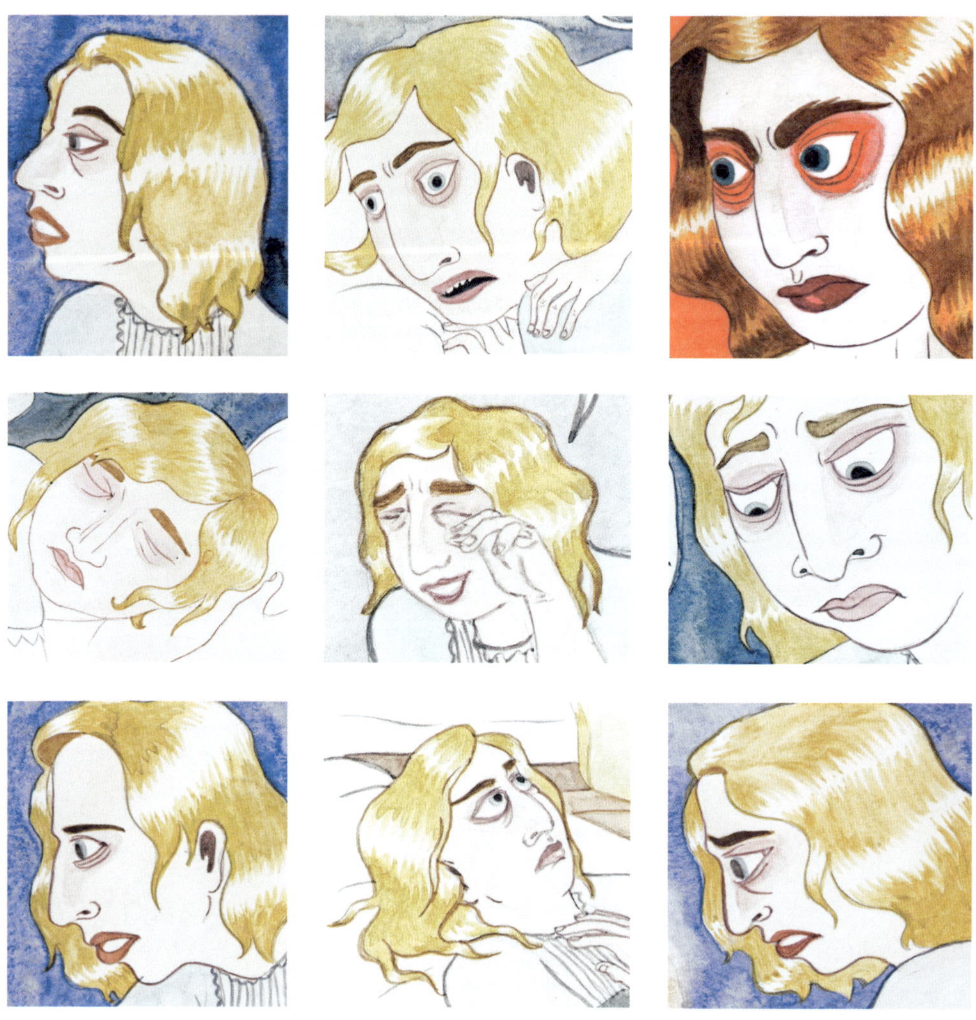

And let's take a close look at some hands on those same pages. They are
poems of kindness:

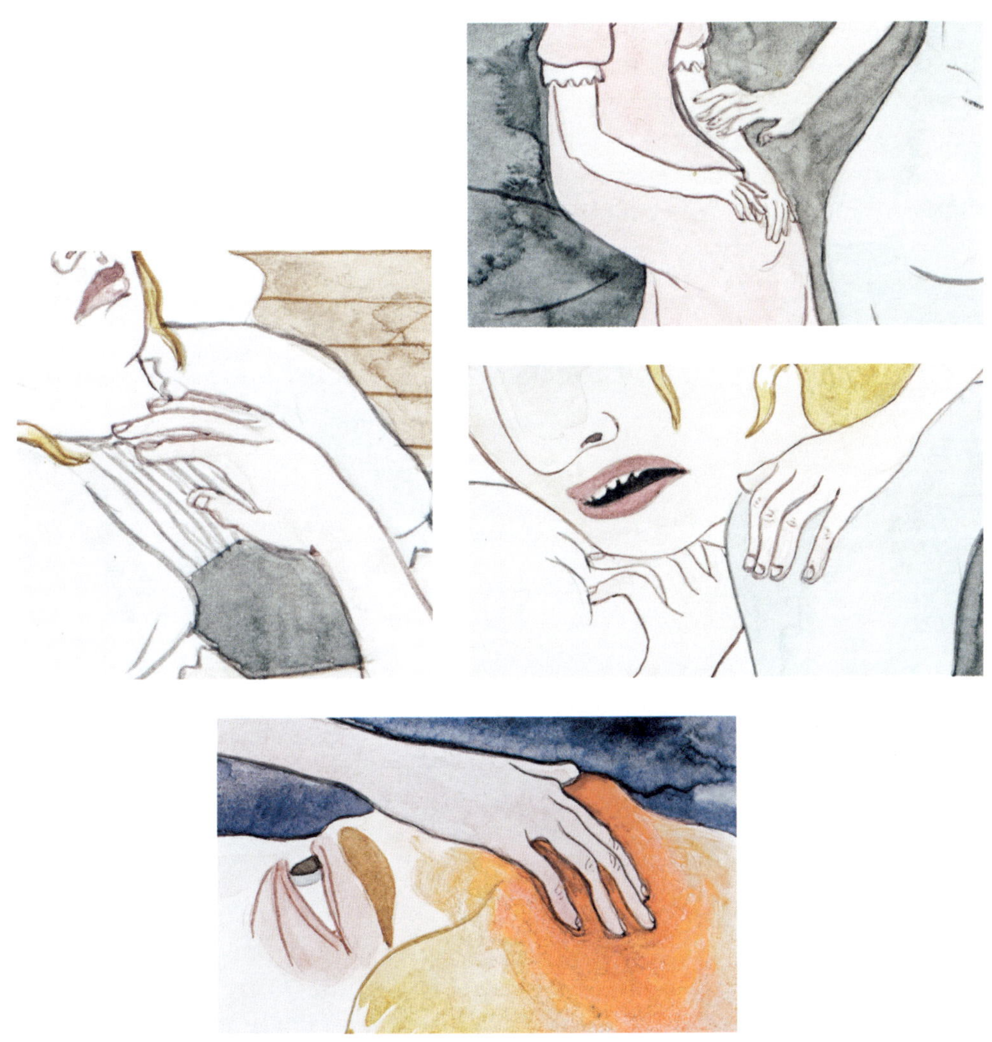

Corman's audacity tightens the screws in the book's later chapters, con-centration camp scenes. Rising to the challenges of Resnais, Lanzmann, Wertmüller, Spielberg, she directs an extraordinary cast of original Holocaust characters. A Black GI who learned good Yiddish from his Boston neighbors. A German who vomits at the pile of corpses she is forced to smell, begs for a cig-arette, has smoke blown in her blond face. A commandant put to the gallows: in fourteen mystic drawings he is dissolved into the black shards of a Malevich painting of pure abstraction. "Liberated" prisoners—are they alive? are they dead?—are ghosts. The ghosts have sea-green eyes without pupils. They see differently. They see the living and the dead as twins.

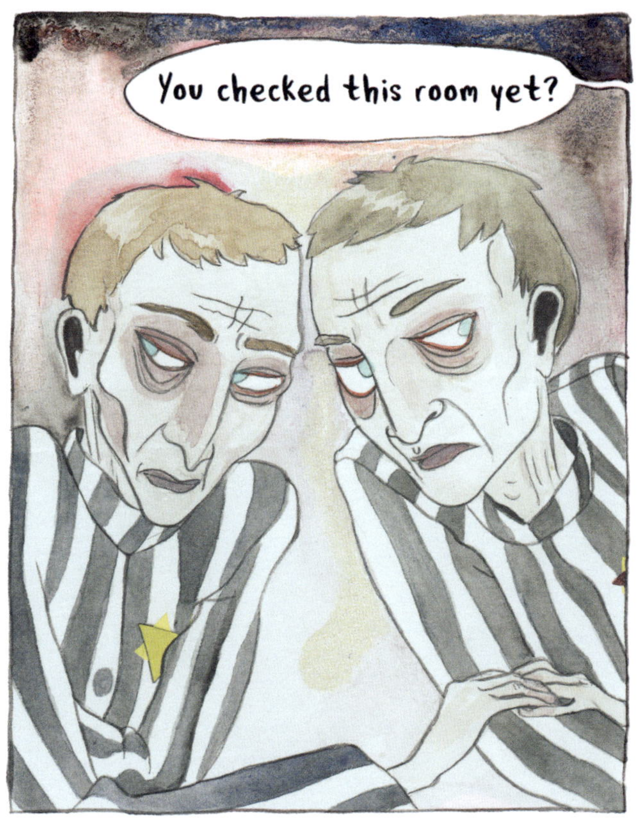

Preposterous Pictures
of Peculiar People

In 2009 I stumbled upon a Basil Wolverton exhibition at Gladstone gallery in Chelsea. Wolverton's mid-twentieth century drawings—zany nerds tying themselves in knots, *meshuggeneh* heads half dissected—looked familiar. They jolted me back to grade school, to bubble-gum cards and *MAD* magazine.

Alongside the familiar grotesques, the show featured Wolverton works even more disturbing. He had made intricate drawings of apocalyptic nightmares, mash-ups of zombie films, Hiroshima, the Holocaust, the Bible. Half the show, the gross-out noggins for maladjusted kids, made me laugh, nervously. The second half, the horrific visions of the End of Days, left me queasy and scared. The show as a whole bewildered me. How had one guy at the same time made such antithetical bodies of work? Were they two sides of a coin? What coin?

Wolverton's shadow looms over comics artists of several generations. When I was working at David Zwirner gallery, which represents Robert Crumb, the certified genius of underground comics, I realized how much he had been influenced by Wolverton. Crumb: "The first time I ever saw the work of Basil Wolverton . . . it changed forever the way I looked at the world." S. Clay Wilson: "His influence on myself and lots of my fellow cartoonist/artist friends cannot be overestimated." Dan Clowes: "Wolverton is one of the greatest of the greats, a never-duplicated one-of-a-kind comic-book genius whose work holds the same visceral impact today as it did 50 years ago." We can see Wolverton's influence on Gary Panter, Peter Saul, Mike Kelley, Jim Shaw, Charles Burns, Art Spiegelman—bad-boy catastrophizing artists who are in the limelight now.

At Zwirner I proposed an exhibition tracing the influence of Wolverton. To start, I asked the redoubtable comic-art dealer Scott Eder to bring in his Wolverton drawings for consideration. Scott showed up with a dozen grandly

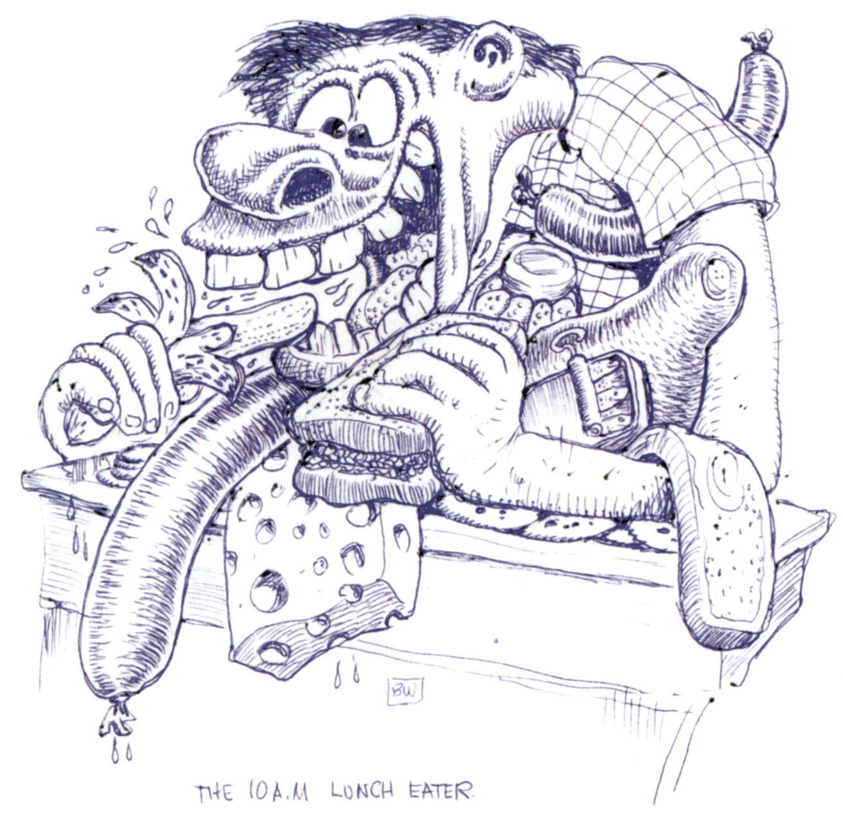

obnoxious Wolverton heads meticulously dismembered in India ink. Though the exhibition never happened, I remained haunted by one of Eder's drawings, this atypical Wolverton sketch in blue ink titled *The 10 a.m. Lunch Eater*. I was amazed by its ballpoint-pen immediacy drawn without corrections. I loved its cornucopia of gastronomical, gastrointestinal intensity. The drawing reminded me of the later work of Philip Guston.

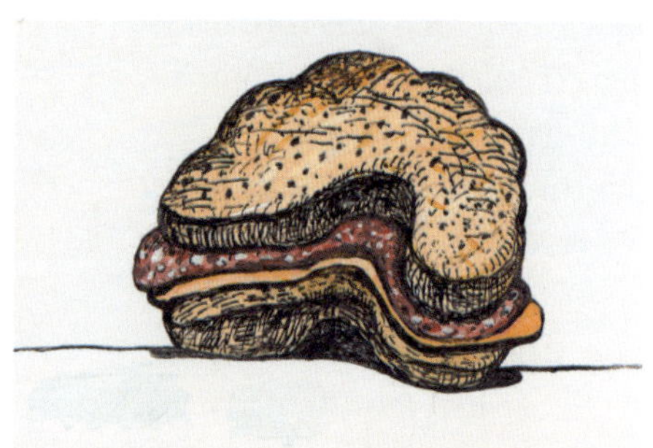

The raw right angle of the eater's hairy arm was like one of Guston's nightmare legs; Wolverton's fat slices were like Guston's fat books and clocks, or like this Guston painting of an animated salami and cheese on rye. When I bought the Wolverton drawing from Eder I felt like I was also getting a bargain-basement Guston.

Whenever I look at it, I greet *The 10 a.m. Lunch Eater* with a smile of recognition. It's a portrait of my insatiability. Every morning I eat a hearty breakfast. Around 10 or 11 a.m., I am ready for Second Breakfast. I'll brew a Nespresso and rummage up one of the snacks Wolverton illustrates so fulsomely. I'll grab a banana, some ham or Swiss cheese or salami, maybe a pickle and some sardines, perhaps a small sandwich of meatloaf or headcheese. The word *fresser* comes to mind, Yiddish for "big eater," "glutton." In Yiddish and German, *essen* is to eat like a human, *fressen* to eat like an animal. This drawing depicts the way I look to my wife when I'm gnashing gleefully on a sparerib or chicken carcass. She says I'm like a dog.

You'll notice the lunch eater chows down first on a banana. I love bananas too, to eat and as metaphor. Bananas featured in my book *America and the Tintype,* a book about the world's first selfies. In America in the 1880s, bananas caught on as a snack, became a craze. Here you see four young ladies who sat down in a tintypist's studio to memorialize the banana craze in a picture. In

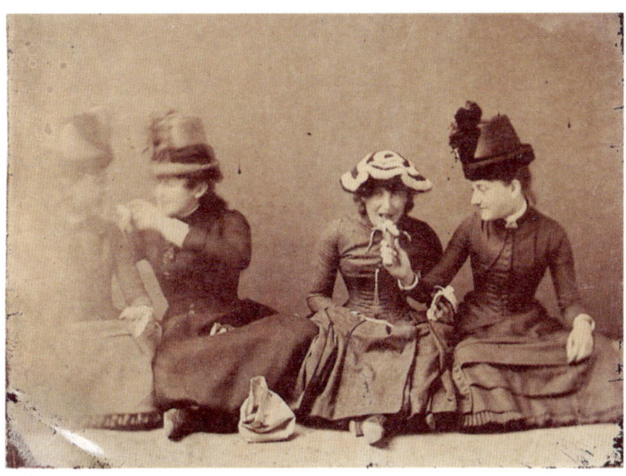

the book, the picture's caption quotes an 1885 article titled "De Banane," from a popular Anglo-American magazine: "After all, a food-stuff which supports hundreds of millions among our beloved tropical fellow-creatures ought to be very dear to the heart of a nation which governs (and annually kills) more black people taken in the mass than all other European powers put together.... It is high time we should begin in return to learn somewhat about fetishes and fustic, Jamaica and jaggery, bananas and Buddhism. We know too little still about our colonies and dependencies." In other words, a snack eaten obtusely is colonialist; we forget, at the cost of our humanity, where it came from, forget those who struggle there to pleasure us. Wolverton's boy is not only gluttonous and gross but also oblivious.

The drawing's sausage front and center also has special meaning for me. My Grandma Rose was a woman of dogged habits. Every morning she ate the same breakfast: coffee and a toasted Thomas's English Muffin piled with Breakstone Sour Cream and Dundee Orange Marmalade. Every week she visited us grandkids bearing a treat. In season she brought a couple of navel oranges "from Israel, the best." Most weeks she brought a salami. Only one Broadway butcher sold it. It was a kosher *cervelatwurst,* a fatty, moist salami that had the exact shape and heft of the of the lunch eater's sausage. We ate it in thick slices. Grandma Rose left behind so much when she was driven from her homeland by the Nazis. She would never return, and refused to buy German goods. But she maintained this culinary contact with her homeland, enjoyed passing that bit of heritage on to us. We understood her salami was a Jewish-German taste of the old country. Sometimes a sausage is a link to a grandmother's kosher upbringing. Sometimes a salami is a history lesson.

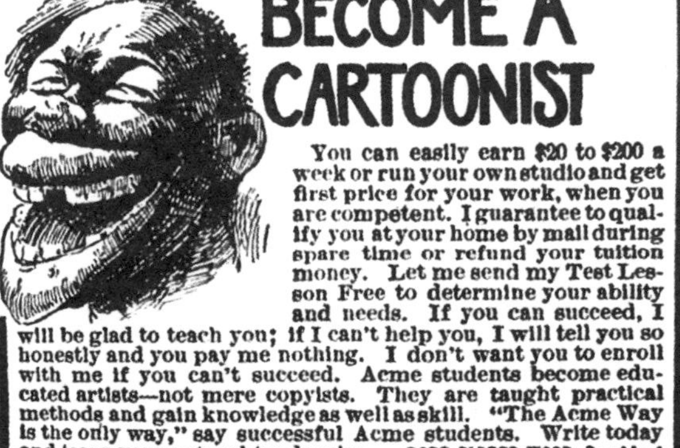

Basil Wolverton was born in 1909 (a year after Grandma Rose) in Oregon. He married his high school sweetheart, a girl with the comic-book name Honor Lovette; he honored and loved her until his death in 1978. His first profession was playing ukulele and tap-dancing in local vaudeville shows. Vaudeville was then the most popular entertainment in America, having supplanted its wildly popular forebear, blackface minstrelsy. At the end of the 1920s, as the Great Depression began, Wolverton became a professional cartoonist. He drew characters like Marco of Mars, Mystic Moot, Scoop Scuttle, struggling to find his foothold in the trade.

In April 1942, right after Pearl Harbor, Wolverton launched his character Powerhouse Pepper. Pepper is a roughhouse all-American hero who stands up to bullies with a do-gooder spirit and, when necessary, overwhelming force. When nose to pickle-nose with swarthy Cutthroat McBloat's monstrous

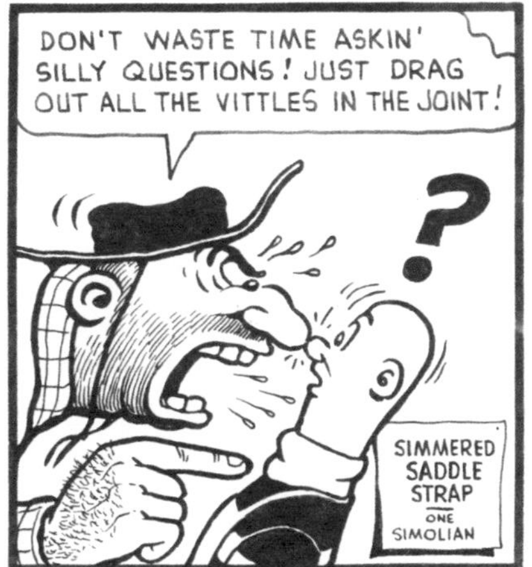

DON'T WASTE TIME ASKIN' SILLY QUESTIONS! JUST DRAG OUT ALL THE VITTLES IN THE JOINT!
?
SIMMERED SADDLE STRAP
ONE SIMOLIAN

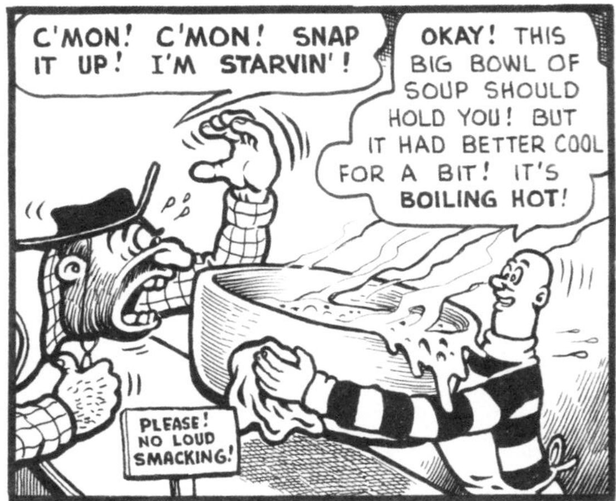

C'MON! C'MON! SNAP IT UP! I'M STARVIN'!
OKAY! THIS BIG BOWL OF SOUP SHOULD HOLD YOU! BUT IT HAD BETTER COOL FOR A BIT! IT'S BOILING HOT!
PLEASE! NO LOUD SMACKING!

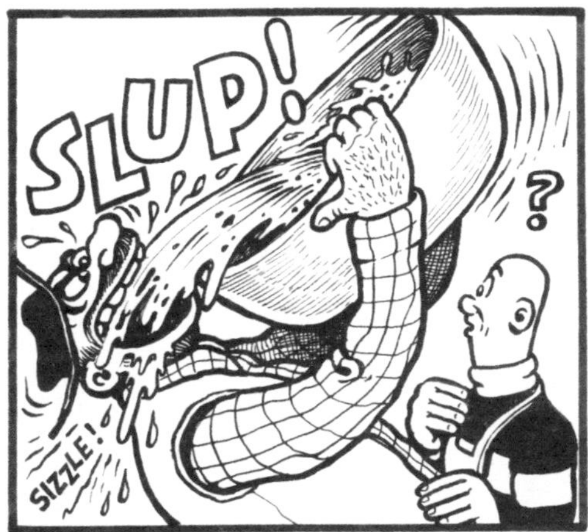

SLUP!
SIZZLE!
?

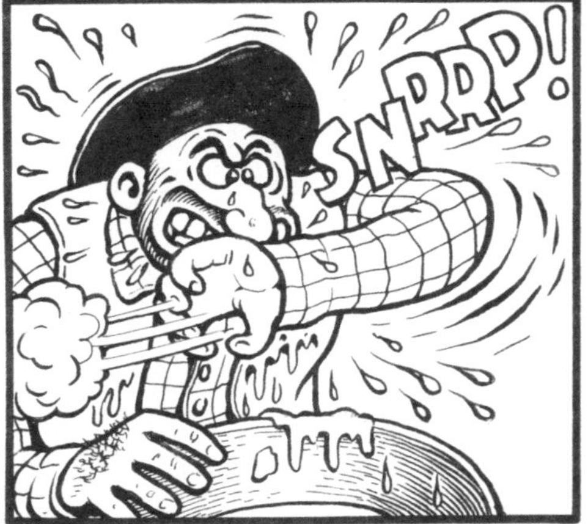

SNRRP!

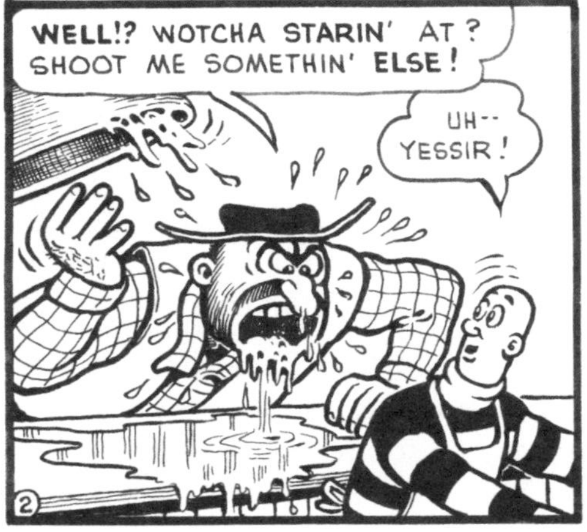

WELL!? WOTCHA STARIN' AT? SHOOT ME SOMETHIN' ELSE!
UH-- YESSIR!
2

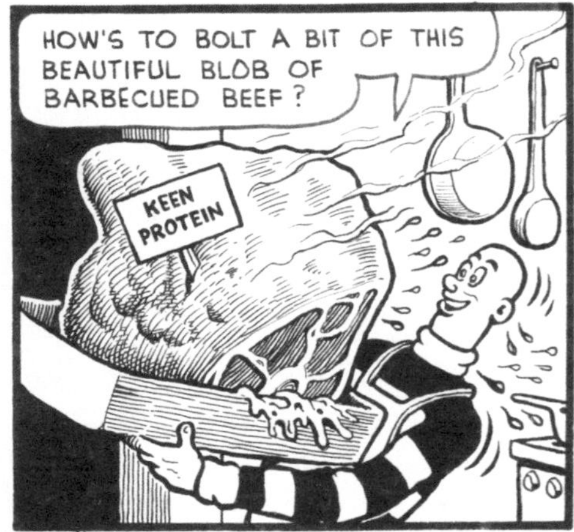

HOW'S TO BOLT A BIT OF THIS BEAUTIFUL BLOB OF BARBECUED BEEF?
KEEN PROTEIN

appetite, he proffers "How's to bolt a bit of this beautiful blob of barbecued beef?" But appeasement doesn't pay; in the end Pepper has to strongarm the slob and speed him to the slammer. Pepper's alliterative lines were shtick much admired by his readers. Pepper cemented Wolverton's career.

Wolverton was, by all accounts, a hardworking man and affable. He styled his letterhead "Producer of Preposterous Pictures of Peculiar People." His son Monte, who became a cartoonist too, remembers his father spending his Sabbaths enjoying boxing and wrestling on TV.

Wolverton's career took another turn in the aftermath of the war. The culture industries needed to come to terms with the new horizons of human-on-human butchery that had opened. Horror had to be mainstreamed. In 1946, the hugely popular syndicated comic strip *L'il Abner* staged an inverted beauty contest. The prize would go to the ugliest drawing of "Lena the Hyena, Lower Slobovia's ugliest woman." The (fictive) judges would be three celebrated lady-killers: flesh-melting Surrealist Salvador Dalí, horror icon Boris Karloff, and Frank Sinatra, Ol' Blue Eyes, who made the girls scream. Marketing copy claimed five hundred thousand drawings were submitted. Wolverton's brand of horror was just what was needed. His (real) winning drawing won the contest and brought him national fame. Even *Life* magazine, America's most read publication, commissioned Wolverton drawings.

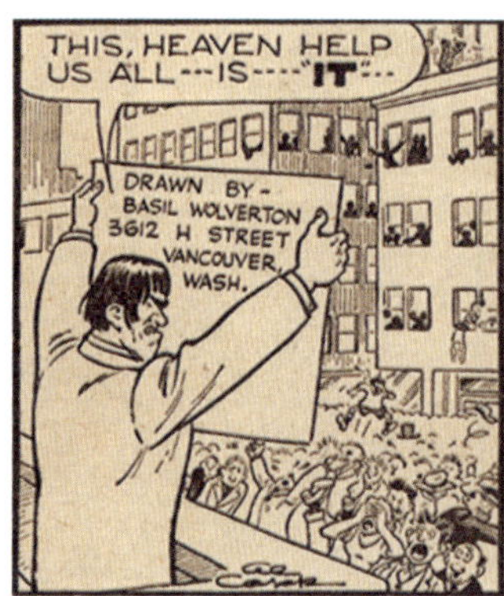

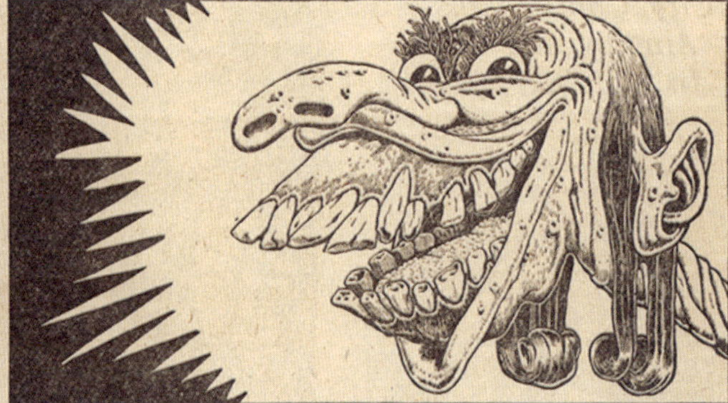

In 1954, *MAD* magazine hired Wolverton to draw a parody of *Life*'s popular Beautiful Girl of the Month. Nothing like this Wolverton drawing had been seen on the cover of a magazine before. To call the Girl a grotesque insults the most fetid grotto. She has stalactite teeth, spaghetti hair, Cheerio skin pores, a penis nose, a scrotum tongue. She leers at us with bedroom eyes. She is our

Holocaust Mona Lisa. She hovers over the city like a statue of ill-literacy. The subtitle says she reads *MAD*. She is you, dear reader, or your girlfriend.

MAD joined the Beats, bebop, Brando in *The Wild One*, Baldwin's *Giovanni's Room* as a counterculture voice yawping at American postwar triumphalism. *MAD* was founded by William M. Gaines—son of Maxwell Gaines, né Max Ginzberg. It was edited by Harvey Kurtzman—until he demanded 51 percent of the stock, was fired, replaced by Al Feldstein. Leading contributors included Mort Drucker, Dave Berg, Larry Siegel, Lou Silverstone, and Will Elder, born Wolf Eisenberg. Art Spiegelman has called *MAD* his Talmud.

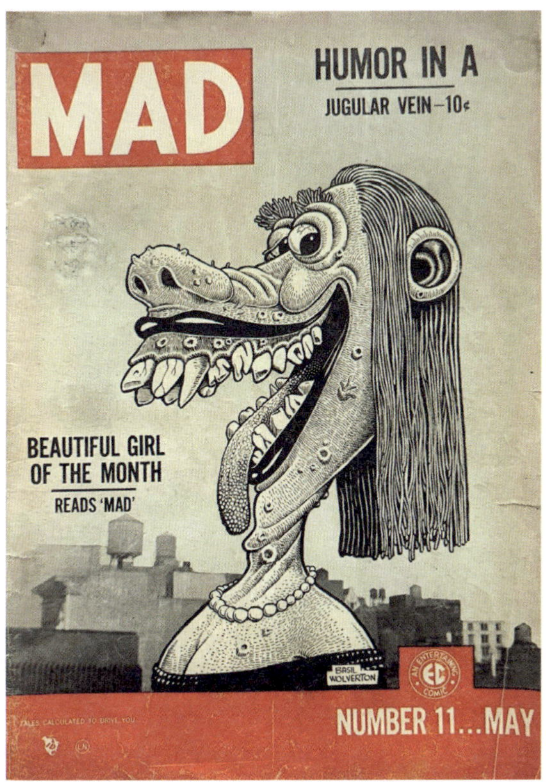

Wolverton was not Jewish. On the contrary. Wolverton was raised a devout Christian. By his twenties he had turned atheist. In 1941, as he was launching Powerhouse Pepper in the midst of the war, Wolverton began tuning into the radio sermons of Herbert W. Armstrong, a former adman, founder of the Radio Church of God. In 1943 Wolverton was ordained an elder of the church.

The Radio Church of God, later called the Worldwide Church of God, and also known as Armstrongism, was a Christian Adventist sect. At its height, it had millions of followers in hundreds of congregations in over ninety countries. The church observed Saturday Sabbaths and forbade non-kosher meat. They proscribed medical interventions. They instituted obligatory triple tithing—a 30 percent tax on the congregants' incomes. This made the church—and Armstrong personally—extremely wealthy. In 1946, Armstrong moved the church from Eugene, Oregon, to Pasadena. There he founded Ambassador College and built Ambassador Auditorium, which flaunted exterior walls of emerald onyx, a lobby of rare pink onyx, a concert hall with rosewood acoustic paneling, chandeliers from the Shah of Iran. Wolverton sat on the six-member board of trustees that incorporated the church in California. But he remained in Oregon, assigned to take over Armstrong's ministry.

Nineteen fifty-four (year of my birth) was a busy one for Wolverton. He drew his *MAD* Beautiful Girl of the Month. He drew the large apocalyptic drawings I had seen at Gladstone. And he started work on *The Bible Story*, an illustrated Old Testament. Armstrong had noticed Wolverton's success in the media; he commissioned a Bible retold "for children five to a hundred and five." Wolverton would work on the project for two decades, producing seven hundred illustrations and a thousand pages of text. He worked on salary for the church's publishing company, which serialized 156 installments in their two magazines, *The Plain Truth* and *Tomorrow's World*. They also published *The Bible Story* in book format: six volumes, not for sale, given free to members at church gatherings, to encourage donations and as propaganda.

Like other charismatic leaders—Jesus, Hitler, Trump for instance—Armstrong claimed special understanding of the world's corruptions, claimed that he alone knew how to fix them. From his introduction to *The Bible Story*: "The truth emerged of the diabolical master-conspiracy for deceiving the whole world . . . through the system of education. . . . Today's children are born into a confused, mixed-up, divided religious Babylon. . . . Children need, as they need life itself, an awareness of the basic TRUTHS of the Bible . . . of the invisible yet inexorable spiritual laws He set in motion . . . of the knowledge that the Bible definition of sin is simply the transgression of these laws."

Here Wolverton illustrates a signal transgression in his retelling of Numbers 11. Moses has lead the Israelites out of Egypt and across the Sinai. The Lord has given them a daily diet of manna, a grain that springs miraculously each morning from the dew. But the people crave meat. The Lord is incensed. I "will give you flesh and ye shall eat . . . until it come out at your nostrils, and it be loathsome unto you." He materializes flocks of quail; the Israelites catch and eat vast quantities. And choke on them. "And while the flesh was yet between their teeth, ere it was chewed, the wrath of the LORD was kindled against the people, and the LORD smote the people with a very great plague. And he called the name of that place Kibrothhattaavah [Graves of Greediness]."

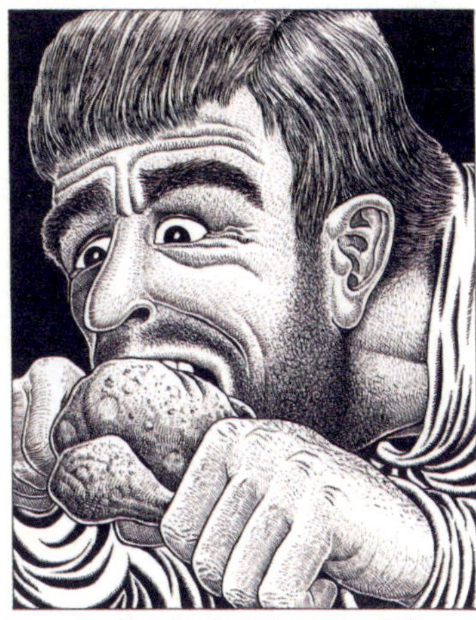

Many of the Israelites wolfed down the roasted meat as though they were starving!

Compare this 1961 drawing of an Israelite scarfing quail with our *10 a.m. Lunch Eater* of 1968. The Bible drawing is clearly the template for the lunch eater, seen here in its published version. With *Class Beauty* as its B-side, it was issued by Topps Chewing Gum as one of their Batty Book Covers, protective sleeves for notebooks, price five cents, bubble gum included. I remember using similar ones at PS 87, remember the waxy slickness of the coated paper and the origami fingers I needed to fold a tight fit.

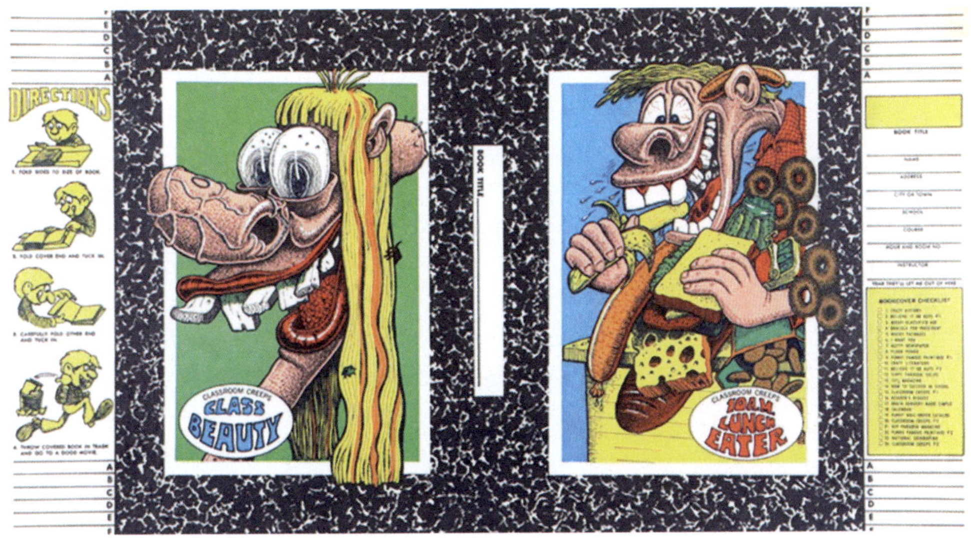

Now we can align the two sides of Wolverton. We see the profane side working for Topps, the spiritual side working for the Church of God. Both drawings are lessons in transgression, in sin. For the child reading *The Bible Story*, the lesson is: Obey the Lord or be buried in the Graves of Greediness. For the kid wrapping his schoolbook the lesson is: Be normal, be pretty, fit in—or you'll end up like this. For both: Curb your appetites or be destroyed.

The core teaching of the Church of God was the Second Coming, the End of Days. It was coming very soon, specifically in 1975. It would bring worldwide destruction in the form of floods, race war, nuclear holocaust, epidemics, mutations. World War II had been God's rehearsal. Only Church of God true believers would survive, as on a second Noah's ark. Here is what one member of the church said after she escaped the cult: "We were taught that after most of the world had been slaughtered, a great resurrection would take place—the dead would rise, including humans from ages past. The faithful members of our special religion would be rewarded with leadership positions. Those resurrected mortals that agreed with the teachings would be granted eternal life; the others would be thrown into a lake of fire."

The church taught that the Second Coming would bring racial purity. Take, for example, the lead article in the April 1957 issue of *The Plain Truth*, "The Race Question." It was written by Herman L. Hoeh, executive editor, Armstrong's right-hand man at the magazine. It begins by referring to the biblical Noah story: "The question arises: *why* were the different racial characteristics present in Noah's family? Doesn't this imply that there must have been racial intermarriage before the flood? *Indeed it does mean that there was RACIAL INTERMARRAIGE before the Flood!* That is exactly what brought the flood upon the world!" The article goes on: "Jesus Christ is coming to ABOLISH RACIAL DISCRIMINATION AND VIOLENCE. Jesus Christ is going to bring peace between the races. He is

—The Matson Photo Service, Los Angeles
Here is one of the most hideous and degenerate types of "facial beauty" imaginable. This is a native woman of Dar-es-Salam in Tanganyika. Notice the patterned face with permanent scars and the extended upper lip.

not going to do it by integration and intermarriage, but by segregation." The article features this illustration/caption.

Basil Wolverton said that his Bible and his End of Days drawings were the work for which he wanted to be remembered. But Wolverton's Church of God pictures are not the pictures for which he is remembered. They are moralistic, dogmatic, teacherly; they elicit the discomfort of the boring lecture; when we look at them, we feel fear and disgust, but no sympathy. Wolverton is remembered for *Lena the Hyena,* for *The Beautiful Girl of the Month,* for *Class Beauty* and *10 a.m. Lunch Eater.* Those works ring true. They continue to offer liberation to artists and adolescents young and old.

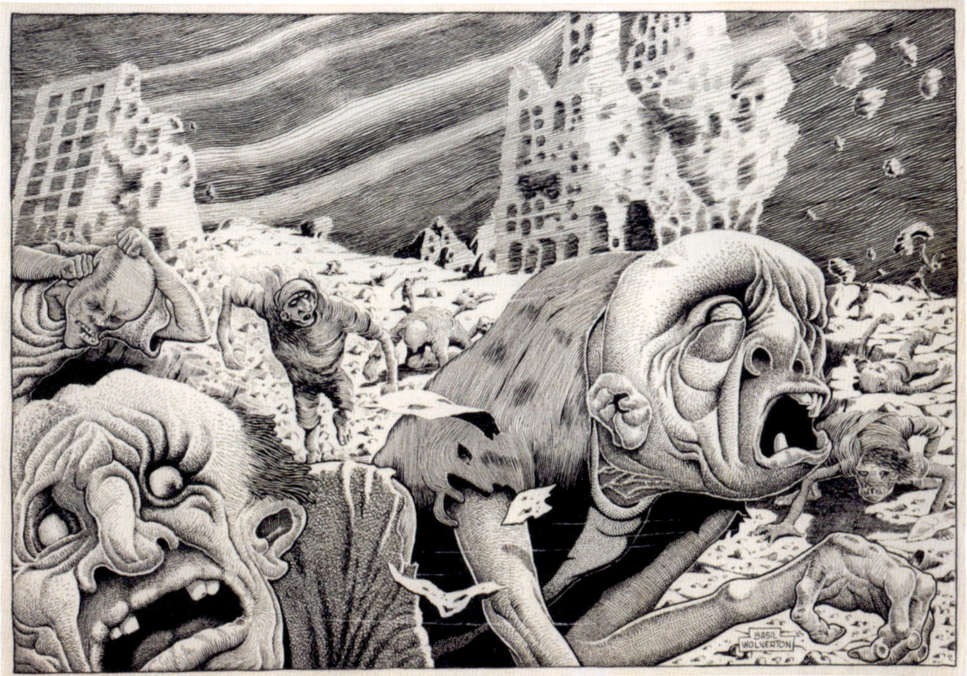

Take a look at these fucked-up-head drawings Wolverton made in the 1970s. Like no one before him, Wolverton performed grisly experiments on that thing we use to sense and think. He took the human head, mashed, sawed, knotted, inflated, exploded, strangled, stretched it, then reassembled it with the cool restraint and immaculate good taste of our Creator, the Creator of such beauty-contest winners as the vampire bat, the cockroach, the lobster.

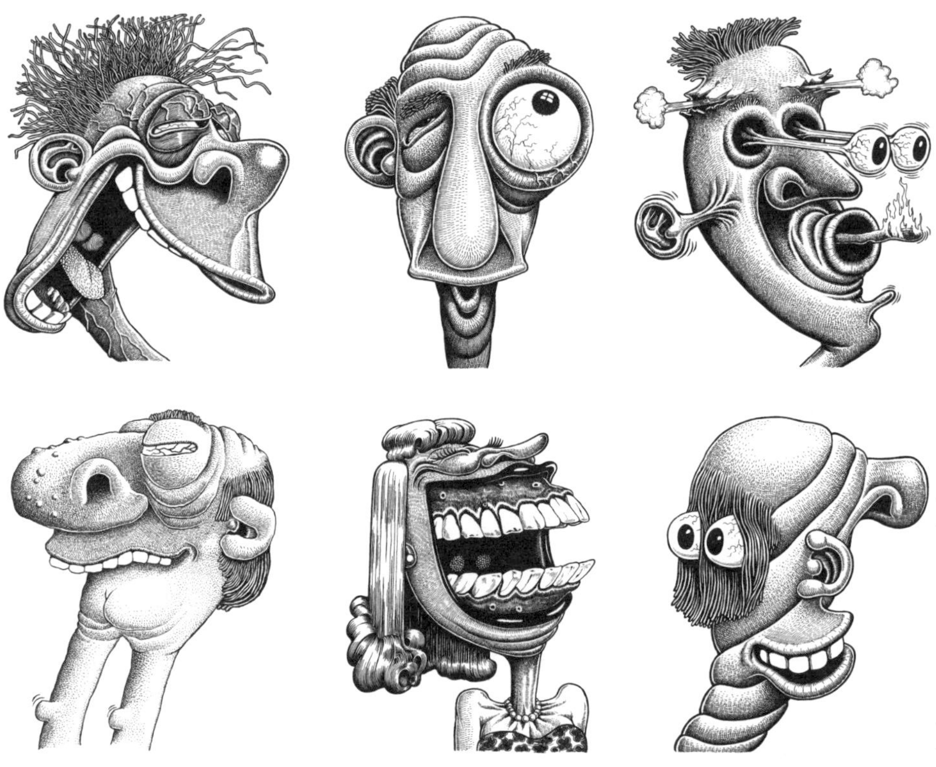

Wolverton's butchered heads are disgusting. They are nauseating. They are abysmal. They are born from the fecund cruel mind of a minister of a cruel and corrupt Aryan doomsday cult. They have captions like: "I'm all twisted up in my head" and "Who turned out the lights?" and "Who stole my Martini?" They represent what Buddhists call the three poisons: craving, ignorance, and hatred.

And these characters are funny. They are hilarious. They are cheerful. They affirm life. I cherish them.

And they are pathetic. They pull on our compassion, our kindness, our love. We recognize and embrace them, these distorted tortured sinners in the Church of God, these hungry greedy unfillable sinners. Waiting for the next apocalypse, worse than the last one. They are us. They are all of us.

There is a Wolverton who says: Pass the banana, please, pass the quail and the fat German sausage. It's 10 a.m. somewhere! Let's kick back and watch the wrestling. Of the Bad and the Badder, of the Ugly and the Uglier, of the Hungry and the Hungrier, of the Chosen People and the Even Choicer People. Let's chill and laugh our blasted heads off. It's almost 1975! It's almost over!

There is yet another Wolverton, the one who drew the pictures below, a catalog of the kosher and unclean animals listed in *Leviticus* and in Armstrong's laws of health. Pig, bear, shellfish are dirty. Cow, moose, pheasant are kosher, clean. These may be Wolverton's loveliest drawings, his most delicate, his kindest. Both the kosher and the unclean are treated tenderly. These Wolverton animals have a quality his humans don't have. They are not greedy, not deluded, not hating. The lamb lies down with the lobster. They are not under the pressure of God's laws. They are at peace.

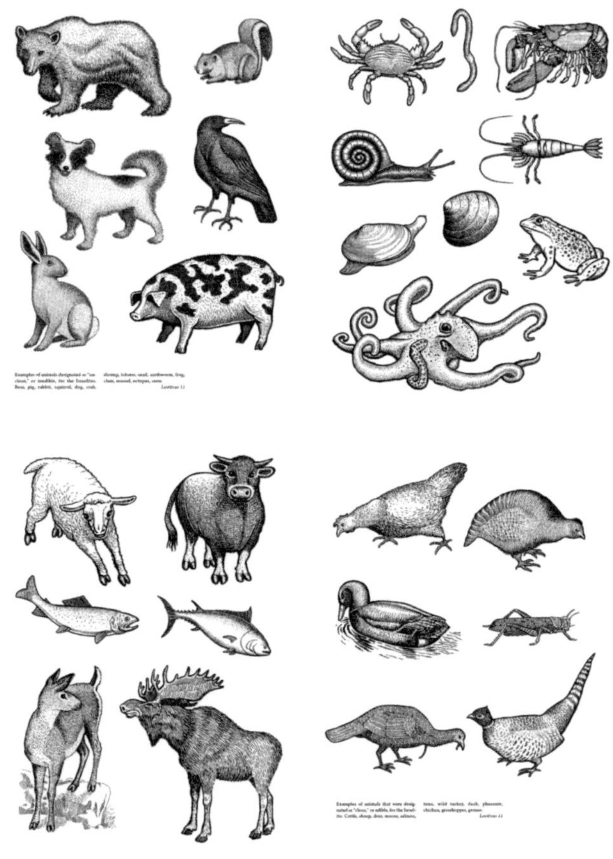

Warhol's Photograph of President Kennedy's Portrait

This is an apparently simple picture. It's an 8 × 10 inch black-and-white photograph of a painting. The painted image is of a man standing with crossed arms and bowed head. Moving out from the painted man, we see a gilt picture frame with a metal label. The framed painting is not straight in the photograph; a larger framing of uneven curved lines cuts off the picture frame at one corner. The painting—or is it the photograph?—looks faded, washed out.

We may recognize the painted man as President Kennedy. We may wonder who painted the painting, when was it painted, why. We may wonder where and when and why Andy Warhol saw the painting and decided to photograph it, along with thirty-five other things on a roll of film. He had his assistant Christopher Makos develop the film, snip the roll of negatives into strips, print a contact sheet. After Warhol studied that grid of thirty-six thumbnail photographs, why did he pick out this image to enlarge? Why create this skewed hallway—portal inside portal inside portal—leading to a pale image of a dead President? Why all the bother?

Some years ago I bought this stark photograph from the Andy Warhol Foundation on a whim, on a vague affinity. I'm interested in Andy Warhol, in President Kennedy, in painting, in photography, in framing, in death. I'm interested in how these things interact. I'm interested in untangling my threads of connection to this photograph, interested in weaving those threads into an understanding of all that I see and can see here.

American presidents were important to my Grandma Rose and Grandpa Justin. They were the paramount symbol of the rule of law in the country that gave them asylum. In 1938, after five years living under terror, they escaped Nazi Germany with nothing but their two young daughters, Margarete and Ursula, my future aunt and mother. My grandparents didn't talk about their

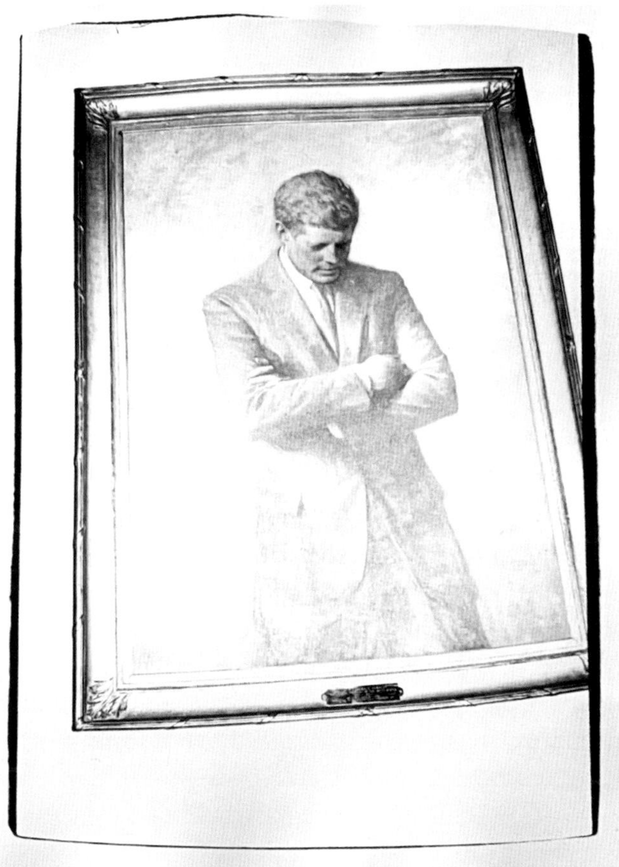

five years under the Nazis. They talked a lot about their devotion to the safety and freedom they found in the United States.

At home on the Upper West Side, summering in the Catskills—wherever she was, Grandma Rose bristled at any infraction of rule or law. She would raise her voice, berate the offender. She fired off letters to whatever official she felt held sway, from her Broadway grocer to the President of the United States. She taught us grandkids that no public good we enjoyed was a given; each required vigilance and protection.

Grandpa Justin—when we were kids, already divorced from Rose—would drive in twice a year from Jackson Heights to visit us on Central Park West. First thing, he would perch me on his woolen knee and test me. He had me list the Presidents of the United States in reverse order. The list grew longer

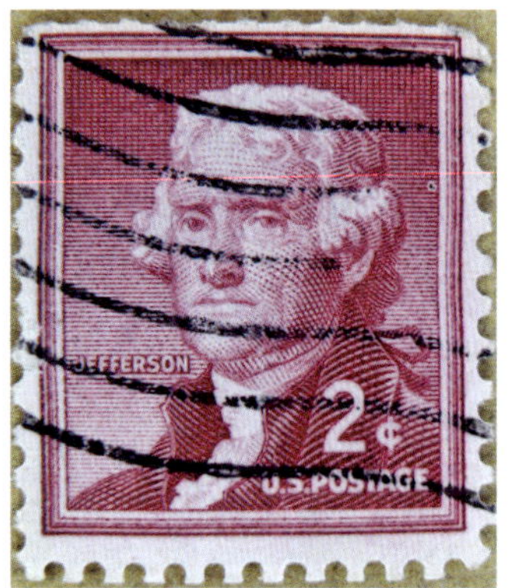

as I memorized more of the staccato syllables: Eisenhower, Truman, Roosevelt, Wilson . . . When I was around six, Grandpa Justin gifted me a small album for collecting postage stamps. He had filled the first page with heads of US presidents, penny stamps, each a single color, muddled green, chafed pink, tarnished yellow. My life as a collector of images began with those monochrome framed presidents.

Presidents were important to my father, too. His parents too had escaped to the US, fleeing the Russian pogroms. He too always feared the nipping of fascist teeth. I got a whiff of this as we watched the Nixon-Kennedy TV debate of 1960. Nixon was a primary supporter of Senator Joseph McCarthy. Dad was close to Madeline and Jack Gilford, a writer and actor who had been called to testify before McCarthy's House Un-American Activities Committee for their alleged Communist sympathies. They refused. They were put on the Hollywood blacklist; they couldn't find real work for years. Nixon continued to play the Communist-conspiracy card as he ran for President and went on TV to debate. But Kennedy was not much better, my dad said. John F. Kennedy had been the sole Democratic senator who did not vote to censure and thus depose Senator McCarthy. My Dad was skeptical of both Nixon and Kennedy.

Kennedy beat Nixon on TV, and became the first president on my list, but he was not special to me. John Glenn was. I thrilled at Glenn's launch into space— the first man to escape Earth! I compiled a three-ring binder of page after page crowded with clippings—my second image collection. There were maps of Earth and space, schematics of the trajectories, photographs of Glenn in his astronaut suit, in his capsule, the rocket, the launch, the orbit, the splashdown, the rescue at sea. It was never a given that Glenn would return alive. Glenn was a hero with whom a kid could identify.

I was in the library at PS 87 on a Friday afternoon when the loudspeaker announced that President Kennedy had been shot dead. I spent that weekend with Aunt Margie and Uncle Julie and my cousins in their Jackson Heights apartment. Sitting on the green carpet in the sun-drenched living room, we watched the continuous live television broadcast. Suddenly, the prisoner held as Kennedy's assassin was shot. My heart leaped up my throat.

The TV replayed the shooting again and again. Fear gave way to fascination. The shooting of Oswald brought home the terrible murder of the president, made him real to me. He was no longer just a name on a list, a head on TV, a stamp.

Andy Warhol reacted to the assassination by collecting press clippings of Jacqueline Kennedy in mourning. He transferred those images onto silkscreens and printed them again and again, mostly black paint on blue ground, titling them *Jackie*. They are as abstract as they are realist, as cold as they are hot, as shut down as they are emotional. They distill a murder, a family tragedy, a national crisis, an era.

It fell to Jacqueline Kennedy to commission the official presidential portrait of her late husband, and her own official first lady portrait too. She waited five years. In 1968 she hired Aaron Shikler. Why Shikler? Shikler's obituary says that she hired him after seeing portraits he made for her sister-in-law. That explanation leaves out what in Shikler attracted her. It was the year she married Aristotle Onassis, the year Nixon became President, the year her brother-in-law Robert Kennedy was assassinated, the year Martin Luther King was murdered, the year Andy Warhol was shot. Perhaps she was looking for safety. As Shikler's dealer said, "He does not seek out the avant-garde, and he is not a guest at SoHo painters' parties. But he will do 90 percent of the important portraits to be done in America."

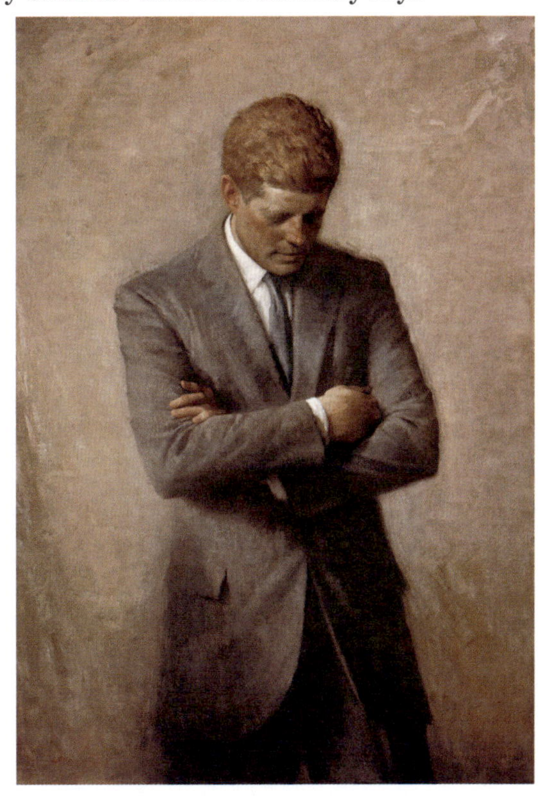

Shikler's painting of President Kennedy is unusual among official presidential portraits. It is the only one that obscures the eyes. It is the only one with bowed head. It is the only one with arms crossed over the body, as if protecting a wound. It is unique also in the looseness of the brushstrokes and in its nondescript space. It was the first not painted from life; it was painted from photographs. It is the most mournful of presidential portraits. It memorializes not only a national life but a national death.

Details about Shikler's two official portraits can be found on the very active website of the White House Historical Association—which was founded by Mrs. Kennedy Onassis. Shikler painted her from life in her Fifth Avenue apartment. He painted JFK in his 77th Street studio from five photographs provided by his widow.

When the portraits were finished, in 1971, Mrs. Kennedy Onassis and her two children, Caroline and John Jr., visited the White House for their initial hanging. It was Jackie's first (and only) return to her former home. The family admired the two portraits and agreed they had been beautifully hung, in the Green Room and in the Ground Floor Corridor respectively. The guests were served an intimate dinner, just them and the Nixons at table. The families of the archrivals ate richly; the first course was timbale of seafood américaine.

Aaron Shikler began his official portraits when I was starting high school; they were hung in the White House as I graduated. During those years I marched against the war in Vietnam, I admired the Black Panthers, I became a macrobiotic. My mother decorated our apartment with Andy Warhol silkscreens, including of Jackie. I hated that art. I thought Western painting had lost its spiritual compass after the Renaissance. Warhol's work was particularly galling. It felt heartless and commercial, it affronted my values. Its irony and pathos were lost on me.

My mother knew Aaron Shikler. I went to the same school as his kids. We could see his studio from our terrace if we looked south across the roof of the Museum of Natural History. My mother didn't like his painting, thought it old-fashioned. Though she dismissed his art, she admired his success. She was introduced to Shikler by Marian Goodman, whose son Michael was my kindergarten best friend. Marian and my mom became friends and business partners. They founded the avant-garde art gallery Multiples (which evolved into the iconic Marian Goodman Gallery). Marian and Aaron were close friends over many decades. They shared a once-a-week movie date until Aaron died in 2015. The friendship between the retardataire painter and the doyenne of the avant-garde is unexpected. Shikler painted like the nineteenth-century masters Degas, Sargent, Boldini. But he had studied at the avant-garde Hans Hofmann school and never lost interest in contemporary art.

Much information and insight about Warhol and the Kennedys was given to me by Bob Colacello. Bob was Andy's right-hand man in the 1980s. Andy liked having Bob around. He was editor of Andy's magazine *Interview*. He was also a photographer for the magazine; I represented his photographs in my gallery. He was a confidante to Warhol's rich and famous patrons. His 1990 memoir *Holy Terror: Andy Warhol Close Up* is terrific. Bob is a stellar raconteur. His stories have an arc like a whiplash with a snap at the end. He sets a golden icon on a pedestal, then topples it; it still glistens, but it's down to earth. Bob told me that Andy was not interested in JFK. Bob found this disinterest curious, since Warhol was very interested in the sex lives of A-listers and Kennedy was notorious for his sex life, especially with Marilyn Monroe, a central star in Andy's firmament. Andy was more interested in Nixon, Bob said, because Nixon, like Warhol, taped everything.

Warhol's interest in Nixon and disinterest in JFK can be seen in his art. In 1968 Warhol made of Nixon one of the funniest satirical portraits ever. He blew up Tricky Dick's head thrice life-size, then colored it turquoise and bile green against a Tropicana orange background. Beneath he scrawled two words: Vote McGovern. The portfolio of slapdash small silkscreens Warhol made about the JFK assassination are among his weakest works, inconsequential.

Warhol was always very interested in Jackie. His *Jackie* paintings are part of his trilogy of female icons: Jackie, Marilyn, and Liz. His paintings of these three muses are among the most important, most celebrated (and certainly the most expensive) portraits of our time. In these works Warhol found a way for art to readdress glamour, fame, death, and shared national mourning.

Warhol spent time with Jackie on several occasions, sometimes with Colacello in attendance. One day in 1974, as Bob recounts it, Andy and Bob picked up Jackie and her sister Lee Radziwill on Fifth Avenue across the street from the Metropolitan Museum of Art, where Jackie had an apartment on the fifteenth floor. A favorite driver of Andy's, Bobby Dalessandro, whose brother Joe was the star of several Warhol movies, drove them to an event in his beat-up station wagon. The Bouvier sisters got in the back with Andy, while Bob and Bobby sat up front. Bob told me he was amazed by what he heard. Jackie, in her breathy Marilyn Monroe whisper , the whisper she shared with her late husband's most notorious lover, asked Warhol to tell her, of all things, about Liz Taylor, whom Warhol had just visited in Rome. Bob was witnessing the exact moment when Warhol was in confluence with all three of his female icons. The stars were aligned.

In 1968, Valerie Solanas shot Warhol in the stomach and almost killed him. After recovering—which he never fully did—he became preoccupied with the rich and famous. He spent most of his waking hours courting them, cajoling them to get their portraits painted by him. His nightly socializing at Studio 54 or wherever was largely about chasing those commissions. In 1969 he co-founded *Interview*; as publisher and interviewer, he accessed more celebrity clients. His assistants, from Colacello on down, were hounded to bring in paying sitters; they were paid a percentage of each sale. Through the 1970s and into the 80s, Warhol produced with his staff of ten as many as fifty portraits per year. These portraits became the lifeblood of his studio output and the main stream of his income. Can we doubt Warhol would have loved the two commissions Jackie gave to Shikler? It must have vexed him that she paid someone else to paint her official portrait. Not to mention the official presidential portrait —painted from photographs! His thing! He would have risen above any disinterest in JFK.

Photography always played a key role in Warhol's work. Most of his major paintings were made from available press photos that he silkscreened onto canvas and overlaid with painted colors. Warhol first took his own photos to make his commissioned portraits. He bought his first camera, a Polaroid Big Shot, a clumsy tool designed to take close-up headshots. While Warhol was producing these prepaid celebrity portraits, critical reception of his painting hit bottom. Meanwhile, his interest in photography expanded. In 1976 Andy and Bob bought together their first 35 mm camera: the tiny, sexy, just-released Minox 35EL. "It looks like a James Bond camera," Andy said. Warhol's first shot, Bob's too, was of the remnants of a room-service lunch in a German hotel. A day or two later, in Naples, they both shot views of the famous bay. Warhol became excited. "We should do a photography book together, Bob.

We've got to take photographs of wherever we go from now on. It's work now, Bob."

From then on, Warhol photographed obsessively every day until his death. According to Bob, Andy shot at least one roll of film a day, and each week he picked around fifty images to be printed 8 × 10 inch. That would tally to over 25,000 prints. (In fact, there are over 22,000 prints in the Warhol photography archive at Stanford University, and hundreds or thousands have been sold.) Warhol's daily snapshot production accompanied his diary production. Every morning he dictated an entry to assistant Pat Hackett. In a third parallel production, Warhol made his Time Capsules. He filled 610 cardboard moving boxes, approximately one per week, with select mementos from his daily life. He kept a box at the foot of his desk and tossed in magazines, notes, postcards he had received, toys, business cards, invitations—whatever from the week's ephemera he chose to preserve. When he filled a box, it was taped up, dated, and stored away. His snapshots, tape recordings and Time Capsules made up a trinity of project to preserve his life beyond death. It was as if he were stocking his own burial chamber. He foresaw a posthumous opening of King Andy's Tomb.

Three years after he picked up his Minox, Warhol published his first photography book, *Exposures*. It reproduces over two hundred photographs and has text by Warhol and Colacello. (Some pictures credited to Warhol were actually shot by Bob.) Pictured are celebrities at festivities. The effect is rollicking, voyeuristic, gluttonous, like a fanatic let loose at the Oscars, dazed at his good luck, overindulging. But Warhol is also the North Star celebrity, the magnetic center of all the goings-on. We envy Andy his fun. We pity his compulsiveness; "It's work now, Bob."

Six years after *Exposures*, Warhol published his second photography book, *America*. He included his photo of the Kennedy painting. I had thought it was shot the evening of President Carter's inauguration, January 20, 1977. In fact, Warhol shot it on June 14 of that year, during an event at the White House celebrating artists who had supported Carter's election. Had he attended the inauguration, would Andy have noticed the Kennedy painting during the star-studded dance party that night? He did notice it on the quieter June afternoon. A news photograph shows Warhol and President Carter flanking a large

Warhol drawing of Carter. The theme of the day was presidential portraits, another reason Warhol would have noticed the Kennedy portrait. And so it became part of *America*.

"Andy always wanted to make abstract art that wasn't abstract," Bob says. For his art, Warhol took images we recognize, iconic images, what might be called clichés, and applied three operations: recontextualization, rescaling, and repetition. He moved a Campbell's Soup can from the grocery store to the art world, blew up its size, and serialized it. He did the same with news photos of Jackie. These operations moved iconic images from the realistic to the abstract, but not so far that we can't move them back. They oscillate.

After the publication of *America* and its less than sparkly book tour, Warhol began applying these operations to images that were not particularly iconic: his own snapshots. He made multiple enlargements of the same image and stitched them together with a sewing machine, four or more identical prints in a grid. He was treating his snapshots the way he treated iconic images in his paintings. The icon he was retooling this time was not "Campbell's Soup" or "Jackie" but "Photography." The sewn photographs were Warhol's first exhibited art photographs and made up his last exhibition, at Robert Miller Gallery, which closed less than a month before he unexpectedly died.

Warhol's photograph of Shikler's painting of JFK uses different means to render the image abstract, to pull it away from realism, to put itself in quotes. Warhol frames the framed painting on the diagonal—imagine a straight-on shot; it would just document the painting. Warhol bleaches the image—imagine it richly toned; it would not be so abstracted. It is a photograph of a generic portrait painting. It is a stark commentary by a new medium on an obsolete one. The photograph is an image of "Portrait Painting" abstracted.

But Warhol photographed not just any portrait painting. He photographed a painting of the shot Kennedy that the shot Warhol never painted. He printed a ghostly photograph of an unpainted Warhol portrait of a dead President. We see a photographed painting of a ghost photographed by a haunted painter who wanted to live forever, live forever as famous as any president. This plain photograph—fully abstract and fully realist, redolent with many meanings—is a surrogate self-portrait, a memento mori, and a tombstone.

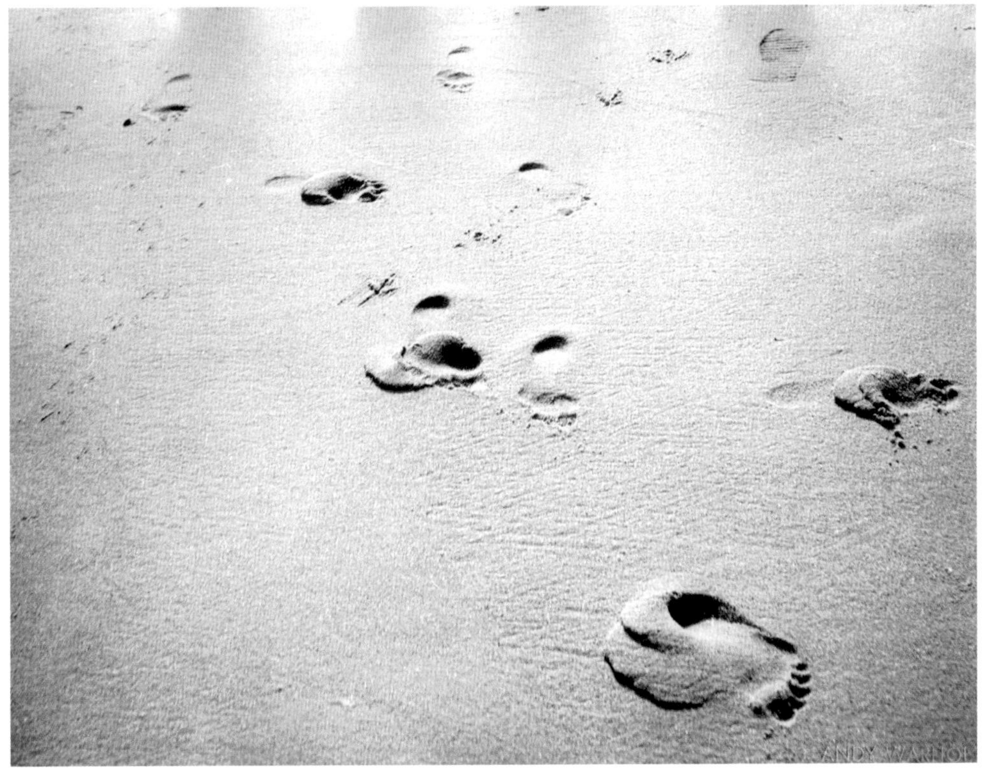

The other Warhol photograph that I have hanging at home was shot on the beach at Montauk, one town down from where I live. Warhol owned a summer home there on a bluff above the ocean beach. The picture shows us an unbordered expanse of sand. In the sand are footprints of a heavier barefoot person, a lighter barefoot person and a person in shoes. Their tracks are crossed by the footprints of a couple of seagulls. The sand is subtly crosshatched by the wind, wind that will surely wipe out these animal traces if the surf doesn't get to them first. The ocean waves implicit are mimicked by the waviness of the photograph's borderless paper.

Andy Warhol made very few works that can be called landscapes. There are some sunset paintings; they are "Sunset" paintings, paintings of the cliché. In the early 1980s he photographed and printed quite a few beach scenes: dunes, bluffs, surf, rocks, sand. He made them on visits to Cape Cod, to Deauville, to Fire Island, but most were shot near his Montauk home. On the contact sheets, next to every beachscape image, are pictures of the man who accompanied Warhol to those beaches: Jon Gould. Gould swims, walks, sunbaths, exercises, cavorts—occasionally nude, most often in a Speedo. Warhol met Gould in 1981. He immediately declared his love for Gould to his diary, "love" in quotes. The couple spent several years together. The relationship ended in 1985, after Gould was diagnosed with AIDS. In 1986 Gould died.

This picture, a borderless "bleed" print, is a study for an unexecuted sewn photo work of the type Warhol exhibited shortly after Gould's death. This has been confirmed by Christopher Makos, who made those prints and curated the show. Most of the sewn photos did not portray celebrities, but things more everyday: street scenes, still lifes, skulls, skeletons, cadavers, a blind man, trash cans. In these last works Warhol was again contemplating time and mortality, a contemplation he had begun with his earliest paintings. This photograph of sand and the Kennedy photograph are delicate adjuncts to that meditation.

Sand Dunes

This painting of sandpipers has been with me my entire life. I asked my mother to pass it down to me, and recently I passed it on to my grandson Jonah. It is a Fire Island beach scene painted on a driftwood plank found on that beach. The artist, Lester Garber, specialized in sandpipers painted on local driftwood. At the annual Ocean Beach Community Art Fair—pictures hung on wire fences, sculptures made of shells and beach stones—my mom picked this one out.

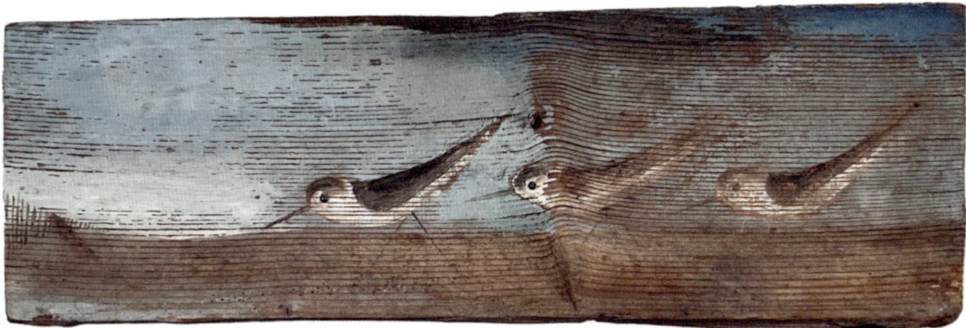

The picture has degraded. The birds' legs are now only slightly apparent or wholly erased. But we can still make out a rhythm, an attempt to convey their speedy patter: run and peck, to the surf and back, fly off in a flock: their special hilarity. If you look carefully at the knot on the left, you will see upright lines fading toward the horizon. This is the dune fencing that is the very emblem of Fire Island, the fencing that holds the dunes together, the dunes that protect the island from the surf. Fire Island is a sandbar, a barrier island always shifting, under threat of erasure. The Secatogues once inhabited the island. They called it "Sictem Hackey," Land of the Secatogues. A forgotten nation.

My mother hung the sandpiper picture in the sunny living room of our home perched on a Fire Island dune. The house was purchased when she married

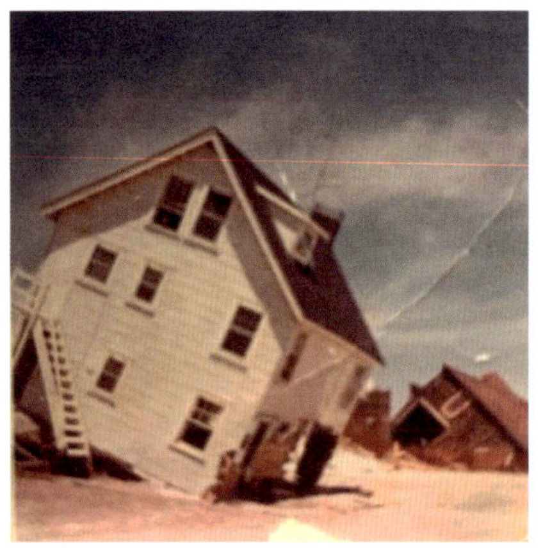

my stepfather. Here is the house after a hurricane. We were able to resuscitate it. Some years later, another hurricane washed it away, along with the dune and the other houses on it. Luckily, they had sold the house by then. So the sandpiper picture was saved.

You see the dune fencing again—and the also-emblematic dune grass, and the Town of Ocean Beach ocean—in this portrait of my mother and me. It was made by Dana Wallace Jr., "The Fire Island Photographer." I am one-and-a-half years old, with bright blond hair and a string monokini. My mom, Ursula, twenty-five years old, sports a stylish coif and wine-red lipstick. The scene is the dune by Wallace's house, his favorite location for a shoot. I remember him, perhaps apocryphally, in khaki shorts and a white-cotton collared shirt, Rolleiflex in hand, teasing us into position.

I have another picture from the same photo shoot. The flamingo would have been sun-washed pink, the citrus at my crotch bright orange. Again, the improbably platinum hair of a putto or child-Nazi. That globous belly is still with me; the columnar legs are now more twiggy, creaky.

In these pictures I am broadly happy. My mother's smile, if one looks with knowing eyes, is tinged with sadness, her sadness she always tried to hide.

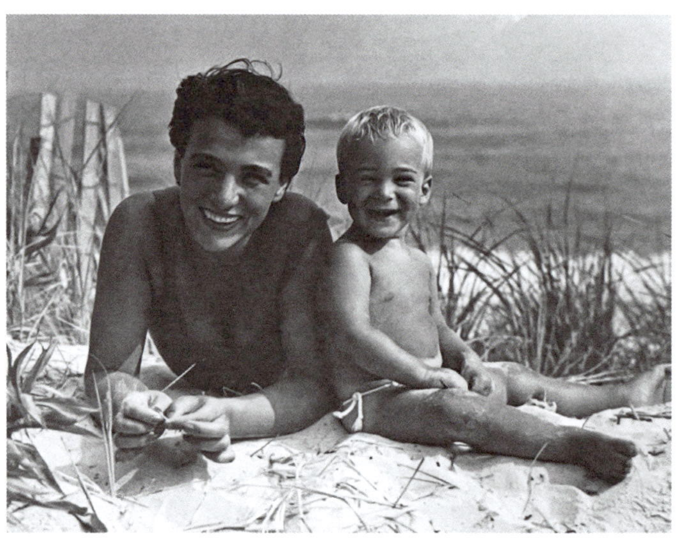

The vantage point of all these pictures is sand level. That's where we spent our summers. We lived in sand: sand in our toes, sand on our eyelids, itchy sand in our waistbands and our sheets at night, sand in our sandwiches. We'd be down in the sand digging up skittery sand crabs, collecting them in buckets, dropping them onto sandcastles, watching them bore back down into sand. The best sandcastles were made by my Uncle Del, the artist, my raffish hero. He was renowned on that beach for the precision and originality of his work. He built them sharp-walled, modernist, more Barragán than Balmoral. Washed away by dawn, they are unforgettable to me.

I own another painting of Fire Island, this one inherited from my father. The painting is by Victor Joseph Gatto, a Greenwich Village artist I write about elsewhere in this book. It hangs in my Amagansett home—on land of the Montaukett nation. This painting has its charms, but I don't fully embrace it. The figures are disproportionate to the beach and to each other. The dunes are too mountainous, too bushy, inaccurately missing the houses. There is a racial

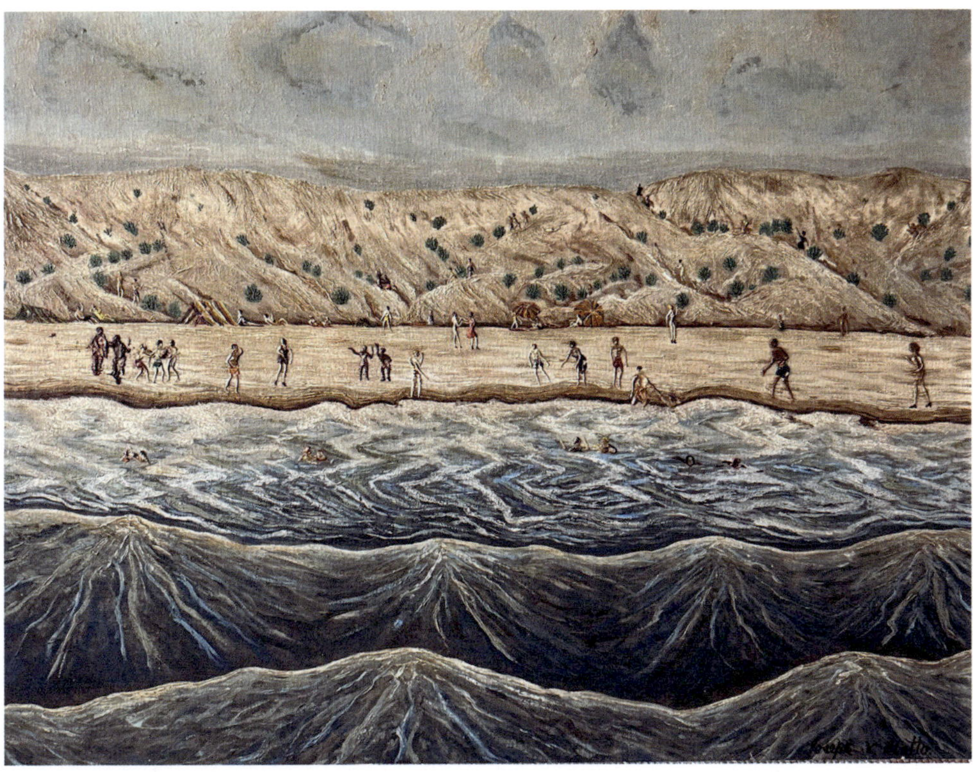

integration here that has not existed on Fire Island then or now—though I like that Gallo imagined it.

Still, this painting gives me back the waves of childhood summers. Days floating with friends buoyed up on crest after crest, riding the waves back to shore again and again. If we caught a wave wrong, we were churned under: jammed limbs, scraped backs, choking, panic. Finally, the miracle resurfacing. We called that "getting creamed," as in whipped by Neptune's whisk. We accepted that painful whipping as the price waves charge for giving us weightless joy.

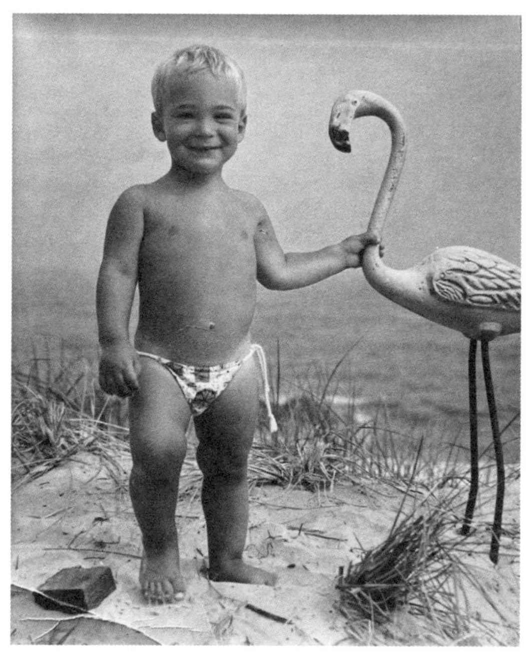

The Two of Us

In the summer of 2007 I introduced my mother to Günter Grass. At the opening of an exhibition of his graphics in my gallery, Mr. Grass stepped up on a wooden bench to toast the attending guests. When he stepped down I pulled my mother over to him. She smiled at him flirtatiously, tickled to be chatting with the famous author. She spoke to him in her childish German, a German that had not ripened since her flight from Germany seventy years prior. The great man smiled broadly, enjoying her. For my mother and Grass, the meeting was pleasant. For me it was an epiphany layered with ironies.

My mother, born Ursel Held, lived her first eight years in Frankfurt am Main. She remembered nothing from those years. She didn't remember grade school, nor being thrown out of school for being Jewish. She didn't remember being forbidden by German law to own a pet or a piano, to name just two of countless indignities. She didn't remember how, with her mother, father, and younger sister, she escaped in 1938 to London.

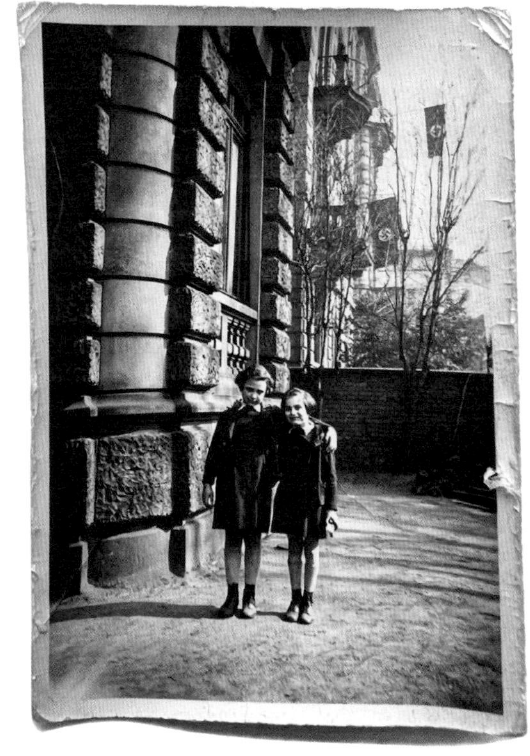

Here are the sisters on the eve of their departure. In matching outfits they pose in an embrace. The streets of their hometown are aflutter with the new German flag, the flag that two years prior had been decreed the sole German national flag. The flag was designed by Hitler himself. Red ground, white circle, black swastika. Hitler said that to see the flag is to see "in the swastika the mission of the struggle for the victory of

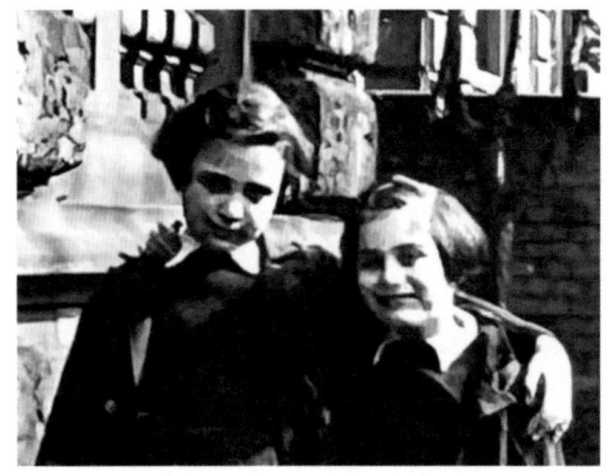

the Aryan man, and, by the same token, the victory of the idea of creative work, which as such always has been and always will be anti-Semitic." To Jews this flag said that the German state and all who subscribed to it wanted them gone. In the snapshot, we can see that Ursel is awkward, uncomfortable in her body, sad.

My mother did remember that she and her sister were sent away from London to escape the Nazi bombs, sent to live on a farm in the English countryside. She considered that banishment, being ripped from parents, as the greatest trauma. She spoke no English and the farmers spoke no German. She remembered their names, the Palathorpes. She remembered being put in charge of a dog named Jock, calling after the dog—*Jock! Jock! Komm her, Jock!*—terrified the dog would run away from her, terrified she would be blamed.

A well-off relative was persuaded to sponsor the family's emigration to New York. Max Stern had founded the successful pet company Hartz Mountain by sailing to America in 1926 with five thousand caged canaries. By 1934, head-quartered at Astor Place, he was the largest livestock importer in America. My mother remembered her terrifying stormy ocean passage to New York as one more trauma.

In New York the small family roomed in an apartment on 99th Street and West End Avenue. Ursula's foremost memory from those rooms was being caught stealing a chicken leg, her crime given away by the bone not well enough hidden. It is a story she liked to tell, with more pride than shame: she was hungry and bold. Even in her nineties she remained a great gnawer of bones. At family dinners she would lay claim to the chicken or turkey carcass, bag it for later devouring.

With time, the family could afford to move out of the boarding rooms into an ample apartment in the same building. Ursula's mother, Rosel (in America, Rose) worked as a saleslady at Fifth Avenue fancy-goods emporia such as Mark Cross and Bendel's. Grandma Rose was formidable behind those counters, armored in grey woolen suits she knitted herself. Her customers succumbed to the snobby authority of her English with its Old World accent. She climbed her way up, eventually heading the antiques department at Macy's. By the time I was born, Grandma Rose lived alone in that big West End Avenue apartment, where she loved to host her grandkids for sleepovers.

Grandpa Justin lived in Jackson Heights with his second wife. In Frankfurt he had been a traveling salesman of supplies to the surrounding farmers. He secured his first New York job at Independent Cordage Company, a wholesale distributor warehoused in what later became Tribeca. After the war, Justin opened his own business, a storefront at Canal Street and Broadway for buying and selling odd lots of zippers. His "wholesale only" store was still there when I lived in Tribeca as a young artist. It was catty-corner to the art supplier Pearl Paint; I would stop in to say hello, marveling at the zippers of all colors peeking out of dingy boxes shelved twelve feet high. I wanted to work some into collages, but never got up the nerve to ask. Grandpa Justin was miserly. When he died, his freezer held a frozen turkey stuffed with cash worth half a million dollars. In my dreams, Grandpa Justin appeared as an iron box surmounted by an iron imperial eagle.

Justin and Rose kept their congested German accents. But Ursula left Julia Richman High School wielding a shrewd Manhattan English, no whiff of the foreign. She found work as a dental assistant. She shared an apartment with her best friend, Faith Dane, an actress. Dane would become famous for her role in the Broadway and film versions of *Gypsy*, playing the hip-thrusting, bugle-blowing stripper Mazeppa. Her famous line: "You gotta have a gimmick if you want a check." Raising money for a play she was producing, Dane was introduced to Charles Kasher, a potential investor. Charlie and Faith's roommate took a shine to each other. I was conceived under the grand piano in pianist Leonid Hambro's apartment. Six months after that harmonious union, Ursula and Charlie married. Three years after that, living now in Great Neck as a suburban matron, pregnant now with my sister, learning that Charlie had been unfaithful to her yet again—with Faith Dane!—my mom divorced him. She married Sam Kalish, who, like her, had two young kids. The six of us moved into a big apartment on Central Park West.

It was in that apartment that my mother read Günter Grass's *The Tin Drum*, in 1961, when it came out in English. The way my mother spoke of *The Tin Drum* made me understand that a book could change a life. It has been called "the defining novel of the twentieth century" (by Darragh McManus) and "the greatest novel of the twentieth century" (by Eileen Battersby, 2015).

Its story takes place during the rise, dominion, and fall of Nazi Germany. The protagonist, Oskar, consents to exit his mother's womb—consents to enter the bloody twentieth century—only after he hears, from within the womb, his mother promise him a tin drum. Oskar comes to love the drum at the moment of his birth, because at that moment he hears a moth drumming its wings against a light bulb, a light bulb that kills it. Though Oscar agrees to be born, he doesn't agree to grow fully into adulthood. In this story of a German child never growing up, Ursula recognized something of herself. The book helped her touch, just barely, her unremembered childhood, gave her a glimpse of feelings she had shut away, of the trauma that had shut her feelings down.

The Tin Drum remains in print in over forty languages; it is assigned reading in schools all over the world. Grass gifted the royalties from the worldwide sales of *The Tin Drum* to his friend Gerhard Steidl. Steidl's art book business has been supported in large part by *The Tin Drum*, which therefore underwrote the eight books I made with Steidl. Gerhard told me this one day in Göttingen—a town many call "Steidlville"—after he stripped off his mad-scientist white lab coat for our walk past the Günter Grass Archiv-Haus on our way to eat a Wiener schnitzel lunch at Hotel Gebhards. He told me that he had published several volumes on Grass's visual art. He invited me to mount a Grass exhibition in my gallery, a show to coincide with the American publication of Grass's memoir, *Peeling the Onion*.

I was stunned. I considered the invitation a great honor. The author of *The Tin Drum*, the leading German left-wing public intellectual, the Nobel Prize Laureate! To be trusted with this task by his close associate, trusted with promoting the visual art of such an important figure! On the other hand, at just that moment critics were mauling Grass. In his memoir he had confessed that as a teenager he had served in the murderous Waffen-SS. He was accused of being complicit in war crimes, accused of hiding his past, papering it over with a righteous leftist persona. He was criticized for minimizing his guilt even while confessing, for not peeling back the onion to the core. Calls went up for his cancellation.

I wished Grass had owned up to more. But I didn't subscribe to cancellation. I believed his art and his public life should be reevaluated in light of his concealments and of his late revelations, but should remain precious. I signed on to mounting a show. I proposed an exhibition of his etchings and

woodcuts. The next step would be to meet
Mr. Grass at his home in Behlendorf, near
Hamburg.

But before we get to Behlendorf, let's
take a short detour. On one of my trips to
Steidlville, I stopped off in Frankfurt. I
had discovered the address of my mother's childhood home, Sternstrasse 25, on
the back flap of this envelope dug up from
Grandma Rose's photo box, which she had
bequeathed to me. With red crayon my
mother had written the address alongside

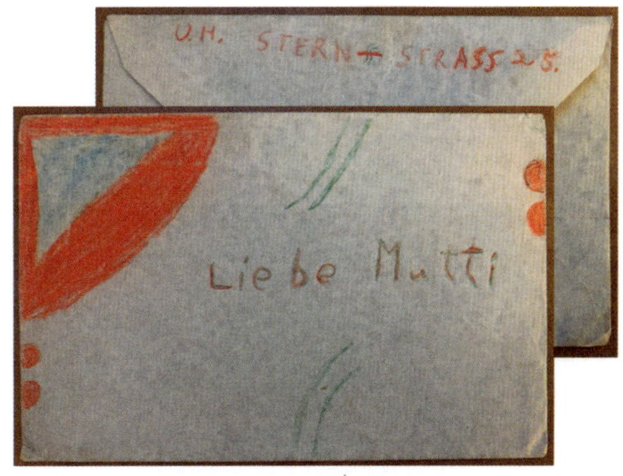

her initials, U.H. On the front she addressed the letter to Dear Mother. With
map in hand and a jumble of emotions in my chest, I found the street, just
north of the medieval city walls. Old arching trees, elegant small homes, flow-
ered yards. Not a sound. I lingered in front, feeling self-conscious and under
suspicion. In fact, a woman emerged from the house in question, or a neigh-
boring one, I'm not sure which—I was in a state—and gave me the eye. I held
back, my heart pounding, but what I wanted to do was shout at her, shout at the
whole twee neighborhood: "You fucking Nazi thieves! That's my house!"

I fantasized a twisted revenge. I would generously donate my anti-fascist
installation *The Art of Hitler*, the installation that begins with the photograph
of my mother, aunt, and flags, to the modern art museum in Frankfurt—on
condition they exhibit it periodically. In one blow, I would return my family,
symbolically, to my ancestral city, I would demonstrate forgiveness, I would
throw mud in German faces.

Back to 2007. I stopped off first in Lübeck at Günter Grass Haus, a museum
dedicated to the man and his work, then drove on to Behlendorf, to Grass's
rural home. Mr. Grass emerged from his studio and invited me in. He gestured
to the multiple worktables crudely built from wooden boards. They were designed for standing work; there was not a chair in the studio. Several tables held
old Olivetti typewriters, long obsolete but still Grass's chosen writing tool. He
asked me to keep a lookout for the vintage ink ribbons he needed; maybe I'd
find some stashed in some old desk drawer or at a flea market. He said he could

keep writing only so long as friends around the world found ribbons for him. A couple of worktables held drawing tablets, a couple held etching plates. One supported a lithographic stone. Grass had trained as a visual artist, had taken up writing later. Each day at his various workstands Grass alternated between images and texts.

We left the studio and retired to a stone patio amid fruit trees. Tea was served. I was greeted by Mrs. Grass, who was, I believe, the model for the woman in the etching seen below. Mr. Grass and I talked about his upcoming visit to New York and the exhibition we were planning. The opening would be followed by a dinner party. He talked about friends and relatives who lived in New York. I told him my mother was a fan.

The big Grass event in New York was at the Public Library. Several hundred people showed up for an evening titled "The Twentieth Century on Trial," a conversation between Grass and Norman Mailer. Mailer had just published what was to be his last book, *The Castle in the Forest*, a novel that traces Hitler's ancestry and youth. Onstage, the two writers were like old lions, still regal, still prowling their domains. In addition to the library conversation, Grass submitted to interviews, public appearances, book signings. He told me they were wearying.

At our gallery opening, Grass was in high spirits. He made a speech. He was sweet to my mother. We adjourned to the celebratory dinner, held in a friend's wine store on South Street, the rooms where Susan and I had hosted the rehearsal dinner for our wedding, its patio lit by lanterns. The guests were friends and relatives of Grass. The mood was warm and tranquil. Grass told me the party was his loveliest moment in New York.

I purchased this etching from our exhibition. It is titled *Wir zwei* (The Two of Us), 1979. It hangs prominently now in my living room. Though the woman's lineaments little resemble my mother's, this image is her truest portrait, the one that best explains her to me.

The eyes are permanently sad, speaking of some unhealing wound. They stare relentlessly, amazed that it still comes down to this. There is a fierceness in the visage, as if defenses must always be up. Her lips are sealed. Her arms are drawn in, constricting the breasts: more defensiveness. The hair is out of control.

The lobster: it is on her, it is before her, it threatens her. It is at her breast, at her neck, at her lips, at her eye. One disproportionate claw caresses her cheek,

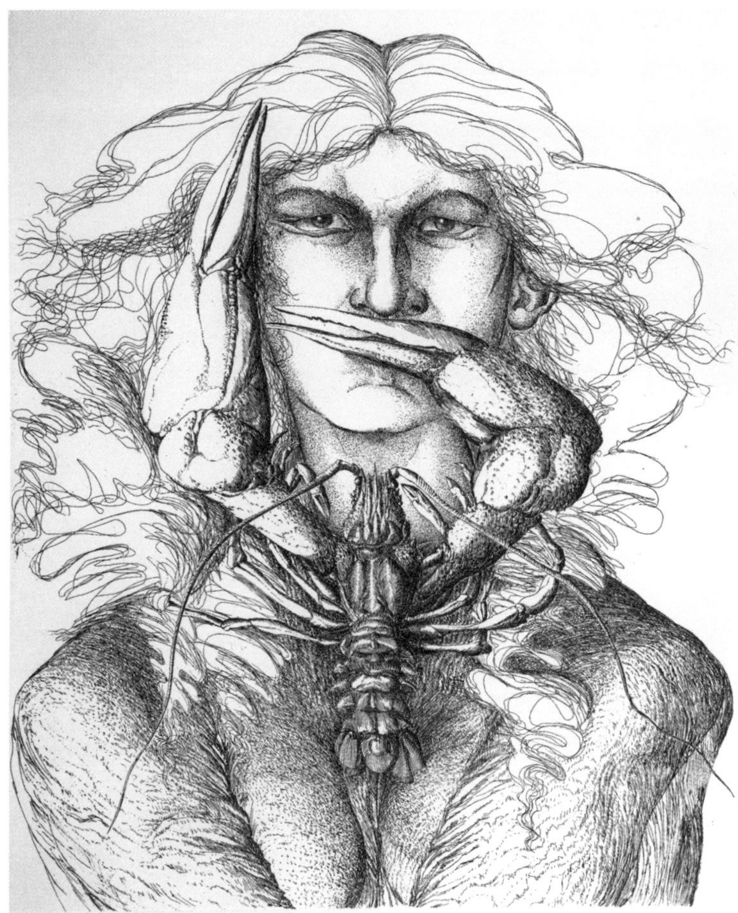

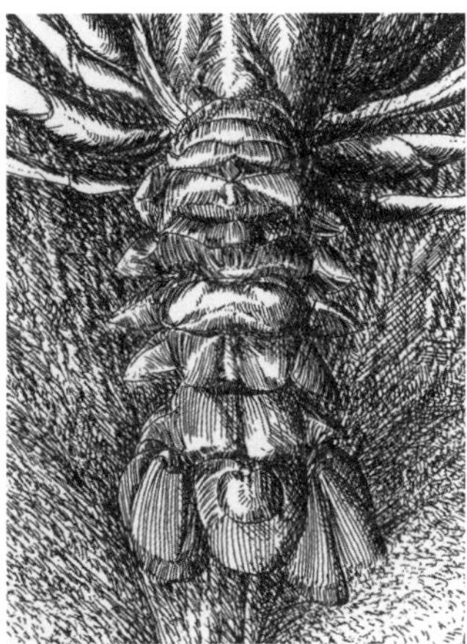

as smarmy as the villain in a 1940s film noir. The other claw both seals her lips and speaks sharply for her. The lobster is how she presents.

In the lobster's carapace one can make out a smaller face: a scowling Hogarthian hag. Once seen, this nasty face cannot be unseen. The small face and the bigger one are in dialogue.

Let me propose a little game; please play along. To what image can you trust your heart, knowing that it will not challenge or hurt you? Maybe blue sky, a fragrant flower, a pet, a child? What image can you conjure to console you? Pick something you love. Hold that image in mind. Take a deep breath—in, out. Take another slow breath—in, out. Feel your body soften, your heart release.

But what if there is a lobster guarding your heart, a clawing monster who will let nothing in? What if your heart is clenched like a scowling visage, disgruntled, never satisfied? What if you have crossed oceans and this lobster has never left your side, this menacing, frightening, piercing lobster? Then your heart is hard, life is harsh, joy is elsewhere.

When such a lobster attaches to your heart, you lock away your feelings. You turn the lobster toward the world. You present shell, armor, sharp parries, snaps, scratches. You enjoy your power to hurt. What your claw can't grab, you dismiss, deny it even exists. You never hug a dear thing to you, for fear you will cut it. You remember faintly that somewhere deep inside love exists. Tenderness, sweetness—they are there inside. You do not let them show. They are enshelled. You cannot break your shell. No child even can enter. You may feel it, but you will never say, "I love you."

My time with my mother was an endless duel. Me banging on her shell, begging her to come out, come out without armor. She, afraid to soften, flailing away at me armored and clawed. Then I would enshell and enclaw myself. And so the lobster fight went on. Apart, we had ways to signal our love. Back together, we clawed and scratched again. And so on.

And so that story might have ended. But then my mother took ill, took to dying. Along with my sister, I took up taking care of her. I would visit her daily, sit with her, do little chores like filling her pill boxes. I brought her little treats—cookies, cakes. It was difficult for me. She was nasty to her caregivers; she was sure they were stealing from her. She was angry and mean to me, sure I was taking the caregivers' side, sure I didn't really want to be there. Her lobster claws were snapping hard.

Over the sickly months, gaps opened up in the tension. I found it easier to breeze over whatever she said. Surprisingly, I could hold her transparent hand with tenderness. It became possible to tell her "I love you" with an unclenched heart. Once or twice she even said "I love you" back.

Those long-sought words sounded automatic, distracted, and had mild impact. What touched me was when she said, "Thank you, you are being a good son." Her son, her only son, had shown up, cared, loved. She said it calmly. Feeling her appreciation, I felt release.

I was with her at her deathbed. She was breathing hard, gasping, tossing. She seemed to be swimming against waves. I said to her, "Mom, you can relax now.

You can stop struggling. You can rest." I believe she heard me. Her breathing slowed. Her claw ungripped. As she released her last breath she seemed calm. She sank.

In life Mom wasn't much of a dancer. I never saw her do the twist or disco or anything like that. A couple of times on vacation in the Caribbean, she and Sam would take to the dance floor for some 1940s-style hand-on-waist moves. They looked romantic, but not too enthused, and would return to our table after a number or two.

Some weeks after my mom died I started dancing with her. One of my 5Rhythms teachers, Peter or Ariel or Kate, had once suggested dancing with ancestors. Thus prompted, I took my mom out on the floor. I invited her out gently. My impulse was to get her moving, loosen her up a bit, get her to smile. This worked quite well. We were connecting. I was showing her a good time. And I was showing myself that I wanted to show her a good time.

I danced with her like that for many months. I was kind to her and she responded. Then something else happened. I realized how cruel I had been to her. I felt the pain I had made her feel, that terrible pain I would feel if I were treated so by my daughter. I had so needed her to know how unhappy I was. But now my grievances were burned out, just ash. I no longer needed to hurt her. Remorse came, and I wept. I asked my mother to forgive me. She did, because she loved me.

Reaching for the Red Star Sky

My first girlfriend, Lisa Kraus, became a member of the Trisha Brown Dance Company. This is Nathaniel Tileston's plainly beautiful photograph of Brown's *Spanish Dance*. Five dancers in worn cotton shuffle small steps to Bob Dylan's cover of Gordon Lightfoot's "Early Morning Rain." At the end of the dance they pile up and reach for the sky. That's Brown in the middle, preceded by Wendy Perron. Lisa is in front. Lisa danced like a stranded angel.

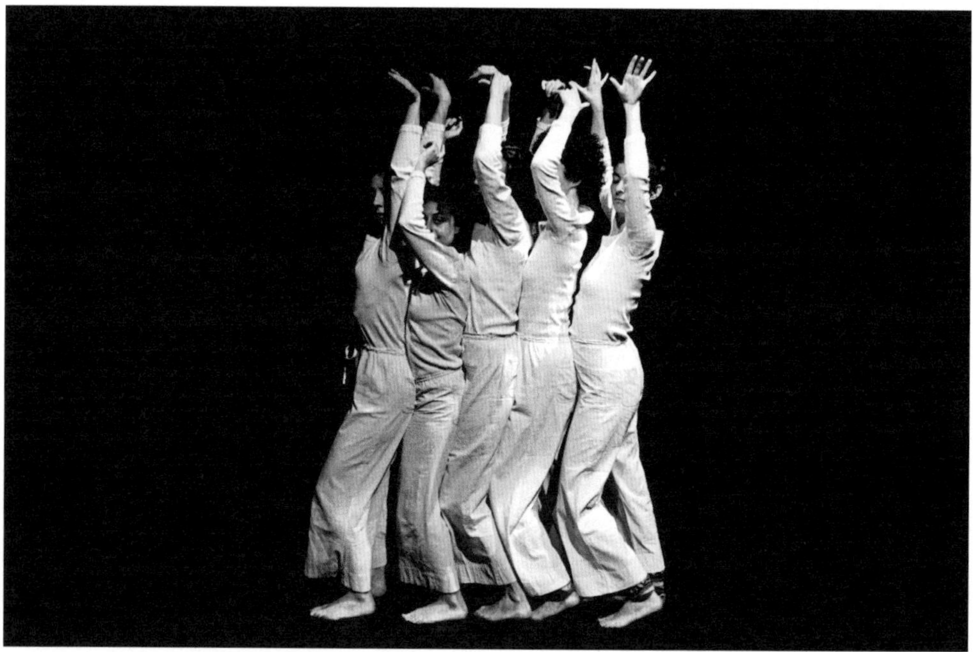

Lisa introduced me to modern dance and to Zen Buddhism. Lisa had studied with Merce Cunningham. Cunningham's partner, John Cage, had studied Zen with D. T. Suzuki, the man who brought Zen from Japan to America. Cage brought Zen to the Western avant-garde. Lisa gave me Cage's book *Silence*. She spoke of it in tones both reverent and nonchalant, spoke of it as an established classic—*Hamlet, Das Kapital*, the Torah. Cage called his performances Concerts or Lectures or Evenings. They call for a certain mode of attention. The spaces between sounds, words—the silences—come to the forefront of attention. We attend to the music of the sounds and silences. We learn from Cage to hear music everywhere, in ordinary rooms, on the street, consonant, dissonant, a symphony always there.

Cage applied Zen to his cooking and eating too. He was a Zen macrobiotic. Macrobiotics is a Zen-inspired diet based on the harmonizing of opposing forces, yin and yang. Macrobiotics proposes brown rice as the fulcrum staple food on which to balance the yin and yang elements of food and cooking. You can still find Cage's versions of thirty essential macrobiotic recipes at john-cage.org. As a teenager and in my early twenties, I was a macrobiotic. My bible was *Zen Macrobiotic Cooking* by Michel Abehsera. "You learn to yearn for an apple with a worm in it—the natural trademark of fruit free of chemicals and insecticides—so you will learn to spring to attention and direct all your impulse shopping to the tired, forlorn, limp vegetables on the way to the refuse bin." That lesson in the value of the pre-capitalist, the refused—that's still how I look at vegetables, and it's a big part of how I collect pictures.

Here's the first photograph I collected, dating back to my macrobiotic days. I was living in a loft between Avenues C and D, making paintings by day, working as a bartender by night. One evening on my way to work, I retrieved this photograph from the sidewalk. It is a battered and stained 8 × 10 inch print discarded from someone's darkroom. A thin man performing for the camera, framed by a ghostly tree. A leaping nerd, a nerd in flight, outstretched fingers fore and aft signifying something. This found picture reached out to me. Created who knows why, rejected for whatever reason, it could be given a second life. John Cage's friend Marcel Duchamp was on my mind. Duchamp was huge in the art world then for inventing the readymade, his

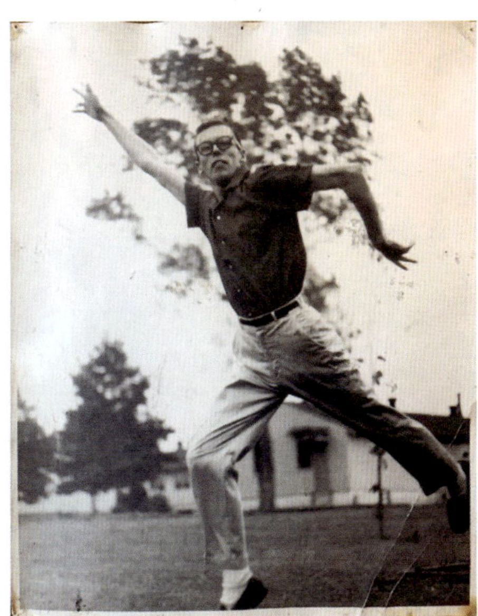

alchemy of turning not-art into art. By cherishing this picture, by picking it up and calling it art, I was creating a readymade. I was leaping into a dimension where noticing and making were one.

Here is a third image about dancing, leaping, ascending. This self-portrait is by Wendy Ewald and Denise Dixon, a collaborative art team of mentor and young photographer. Dixon set up the scene and asked a friend to snap the picture. Dixon put herself in motion, a windmill of limbs, an ecstatic gesture. She is echoed by the dizzy vectors of the cinder-block wall, the canted horizon lines, the crisscross hills. An unwanted plank points toward her feet. The smudge of her smile flies skyward. She is rooted and floating, grounded and groundless. A pose, a dance, worship? This image joins a chain linking back to prehistoric cave paintings, to Dionysiac dancers on Greek amphorae, to Titian's *Bacchus and Ariadne*, to Matisse's *Jazz*. Images of ecstatic dance, of private and communal trance.

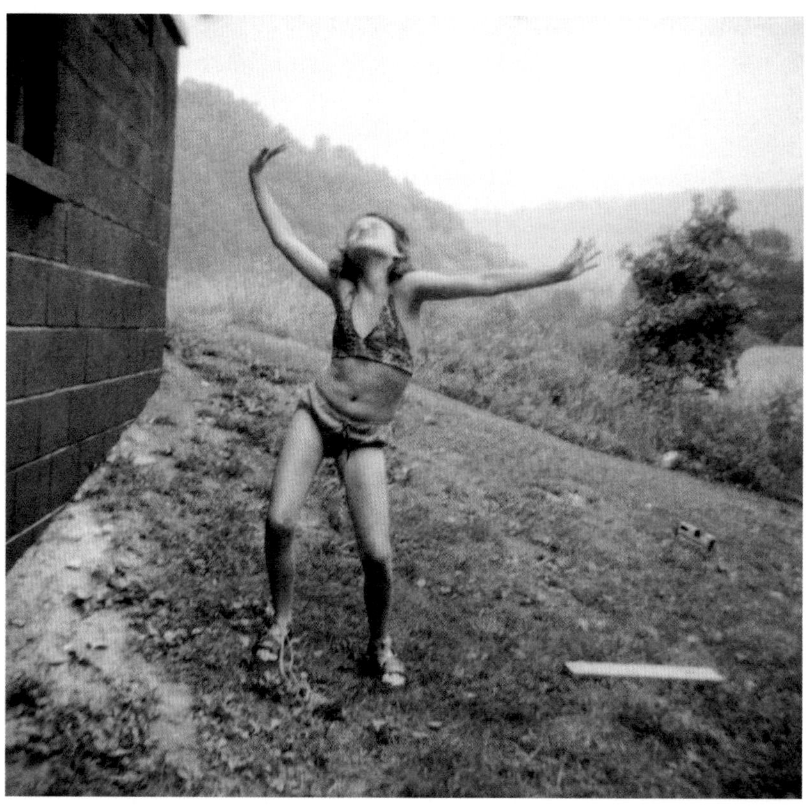

Dixon titled her work *Self Portrait Reaching for the Red Star Sky*. In an interview—she was twelve years old—Dixon described it:

I always think about what I'm going to do before I take the picture. . . . For some reason I was dancing in my bathing suit while the music was playing in the basement. I told my girlfriend, Michelle, how far away to stand and to take the pictures when I said. I like people in action, and I always look for a certain time to take a picture.

Snapped at the exact moment, with its unheard music and its calm ecstasy, *Self Portrait Reaching for the Red Star Sky* makes me think of Zen master Thich Nhat Hanh's "A Poem for Inviting the Bell":

> With body, speech, and mind in perfect oneness,
> I send my heart out with the sound of this bell.
> May the hearers awaken from forgetfulness,
> and transcend the path of anxiety and sorrow.

Twice a week I dance with friends and strangers in a tradition called 5Rhythms. It is a self-exploratory, communal, enraptured dance that comes out of Esalen, the spiritual education center that brought together Eastern philosophies and Gestalt psychology at Big Sur in the 1960s. We dance the five rhythms from flow through staccato, through chaos and lyrical to stillness. We let the music tighten us and release us, lift us up and put us down. We send ourselves out to the music with body, expression, and mind in perfect oneness. We dance upon and above the dust and gravel and cinder blocks and random planks of our daily ground.

Road Pictures

A-CHAN—Ayumi Furuta—and I met at the Steidl publishing house in Germany. We were both making books there. Ayumi lived in New York; she worked as a printer and assistant for Robert Frank on Bleecker Street. In the spring of 2013, I mounted two exhibitions of A-CHAN's photographs in my gallery. In *Vibrant Home* she showed color images she had shot in her native Japan, in *Off Beat* black and white images from her adopted city, New York. For the press release, I interviewed A-CHAN. "What is photography for you?" "For me it is more like things in a refrigerator next to scallion. But also a key to accept myself or to be a better person or something like that."

I bought this picture from Ayumi. I saw a hot, still day, reeds, a narrow road. I saw it as a cleansed vision, as in the Zen precept about enlightenment: "I see

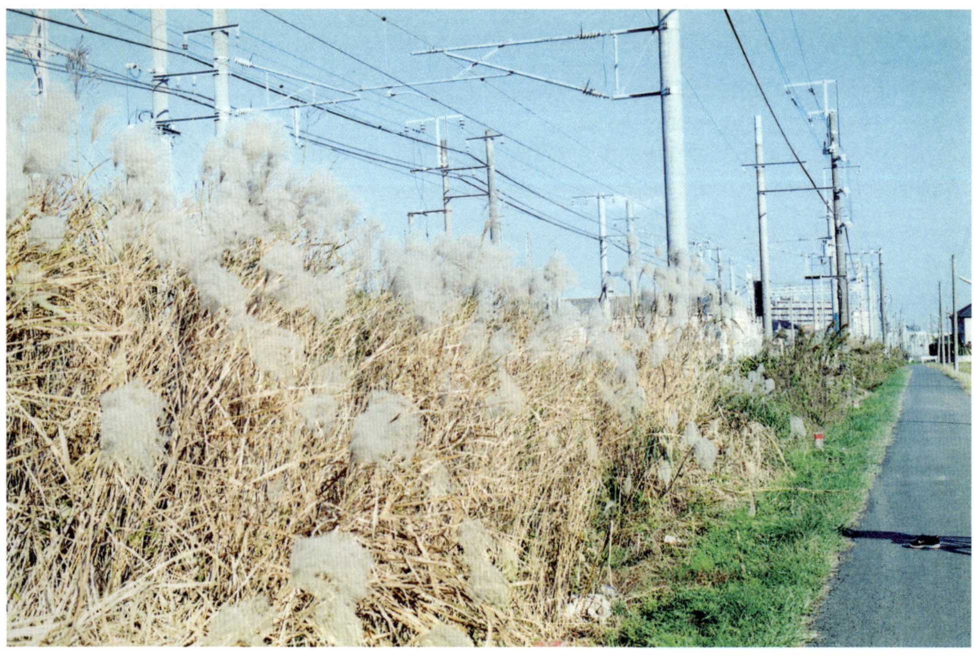

mountains once again as mountains, and rivers once again as rivers." I would pass the picture hanging on my wall and wonder why I liked it so much. Eventually I looked more carefully and saw more.

The reeds are familiar, and the narrow road, and the telephone poles. They remind me of Fire Island, where I spent my summers as a kid. It's a long, thin barrier island near New York City; no cars, no streets, just narrow walkways and sand. When the school year ended, we headed for the ferry. On board, we took our shoes off for the summer. For three months we would romp barefoot. Our only footwear was thickening callouses. Once a week, for tennis, we tied on canvas Keds. Accustomed to their freedom, our feet rebelled.

The stillness of A-CHAN's picture flutters when we notice the blurring of the reed tufts. The windblown reeds become ghosts of themselves. They remind me of classical Asian paintings of flying-dragon clouds, ghostly representations of nature's disruptive powers. I was struck by those when I stumbled upon them in a children's book.

It took years for me to notice the abandoned sneaker. It's off at the bottom right, hidden in a dark rupture in all that brightness, hidden in an island of shadow. Now the tranquil picture is disquieted, disturbed by a mystery. What casts that shadow? Can we make out the shadow of a bicycle? Whose bicycle? From whose foot has the shoe fallen? What calamity or crime is afoot? It's a Nike sneaker with its swoosh logo. Is this little Nike off at the edge actually the central point of the whole picture, the axis around which our readings should revolve? Does it matter here that Nike was goddess of Victory, the swoosh an abstraction of her transcendent wings? Or are the shoe and swoosh just scallion, just spicy garnishes to the main dish of this picture? Maybe the lost shoe and victorious swoosh are keys to help us accept ourselves, to be better people, or something like that.

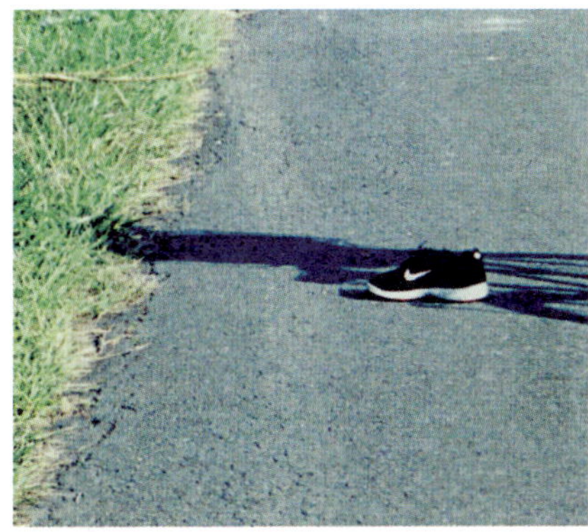

A-CHAN portrays a road that flows up from the base of her picture, from the bottom edge, the edge nearest to our perspective. She does this in a tradition of road photographs that includes two iconic ones by her mentor, Robert Frank: *US 285, New Mexico, 1956* and *Street Line/New York, 1951*, two empty roads leading to nowhere and everywhere. Another famous example is Roger Fen-

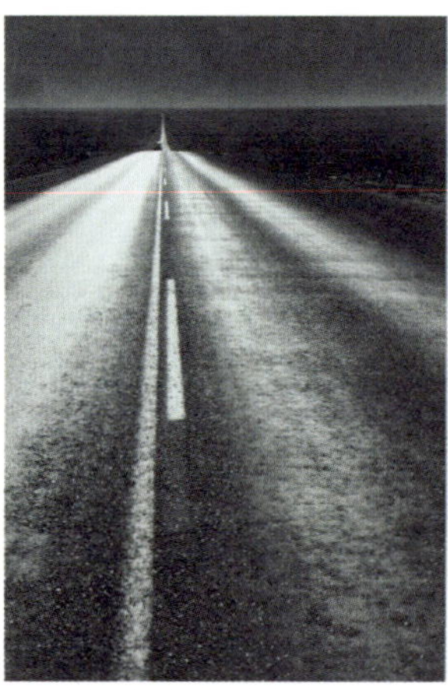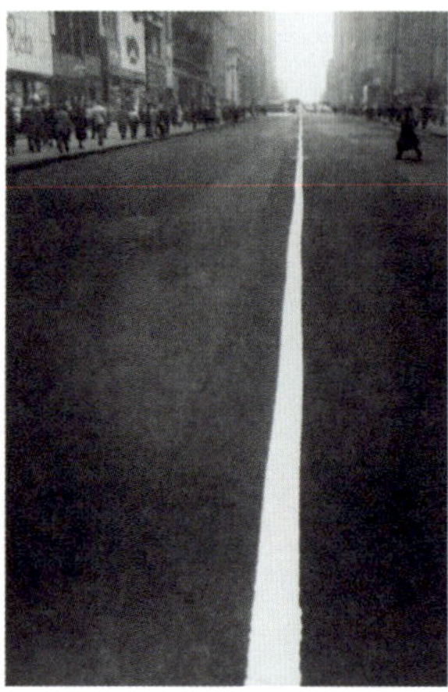

ton's *Valley of the Shadow of Death, 1855*, a stark depiction of an earthen road littered with cannonballs, each bearing a message of death. In road pictures like these, the path ends where the picture ends—at the horizon, at the edge beyond which we cannot see. Road pictures are shadowed by the end of the road, by the end of vision, by a vision of death.

In road pictures such as these, the photographer invites us to start at the bottom and travel a road; she offers us a journey. Using light and shadow, she reveals the textures of the road underfoot, invites us to feel the road, feel it as if walking it with shoes off. She invites us to give full attention to what we feel, what we feel before we are cut off. She reminds us of the Buddha's deathbed words: "Things fall apart. Be careful on the path."

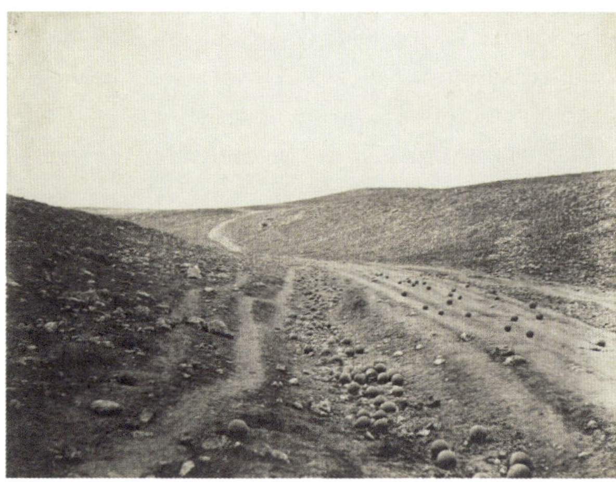

Accabonac Harbor

As things fell apart under threat of a deadly pandemic, my wife and I left New York City on March 13, 2020. I thought I'd return after a couple of weeks, then drive up to the Insight Meditation Society Retreat Center for a long-awaited ten days of silence. Susan was less optimistic about the return to normal. We have been living ever since in our home in Springs.

Most days I walk the same three-mile loop around Louse Point and back. Harbor Hill Lane, Winding Way, Old Stone Highway are edged with evergreens and scrub oaks. Small houses, some wizened, some renovation-fresh, sit behind privet or holly hedges. On Louse Point Road, I see to my right a grove of reeds much like in A-CHAN's picture from the previous essay. To my left I look through a stand of bamboo for the first glints of Accabonac Harbor. I pass an osprey nest on its pole and a copse of dead oak trunks draped in poison ivy. As the road butts against Gardiner's Bay, it narrows. Sand-blown now, it curves along between the choppier waters of the bay and the smoother waters of the harbor. To my right are squat junipers on dry dunes—what I call the Barren Heath. To my left are harbor dunes quilled with seagrass.

In 1963 Willem de Kooning relocated from New York City to Springs. De Kooning loved Louse Point. It is said he rode his bike there almost every day. A great 1963 painting, a pivotal painting, the first de Kooning acquired by any European museum (the Stedelijk), he titled *Rosy-Fingered Dawn at Louse Point*. His 1963 *Clam Diggers*, two voluptuous girls, pink and golden dissolving, is an evocation of Louse Point. His first large-scale sculpture, *Clamdigger*, a monumental bronze seemingly made of estuarine mud, is a tribute to the black mud shores of Louse Point.

Paddling west from Louse Point we will coast into Accabonac Creek. Living on the creek, Jackson Pollock and Lee Krasner made many of their greatest paintings. They first visited the neighborhood in August 1945, as the war was ending, invited out by Reuben and Barbara Kadish. Jackson and Reuben had been art school friends in LA (along with Philip Guston). The two couples shared an unplumbed, unelectrified rented shack on Louse Point; they spent an idyllic summer riding bikes, lazing in the sand, clamming. As summer ended, Pollock and Krasner thought about skipping out on New York and finding a winter rental in Springs. Hearing that their friends Harold Rosenberg and May Tabak had just bought a house there on Neck Path, they decided to buy too. They paid the $2,000 down payment with money advanced by Peggy Guggenheim. In 1950, Pollock told an interviewer from the *New Yorker* that when he moved to Springs, "Somebody bought one of my pictures. We lived a year on that picture and a few clams I dug out of the bay with my toes."

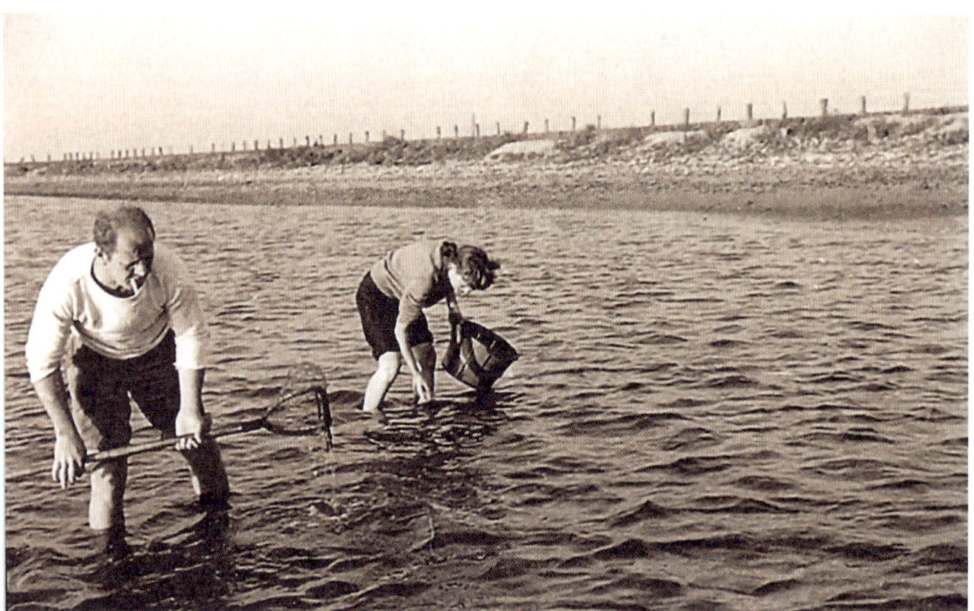

At Louse Point where de Kooning would have set down his bike is a grassy islet that is submerged at high tide. During the pandemic, my grandson Jonah and I dubbed it Squooshy Island. At low tide we would kayak out to it and step onto the black mud at its center. On Squooshy Lagoon we stomped around until the mud sucked us up—to my knees, to Jonah's groin. We washed off in the waters of the Accabonac and waded to a tinier islet the size of a big Jackson Pollock drip painting, what we called Taco Island. It was named for Jonah's younger brother, Milo, who was called Taco by all, though originally by Jonah, when he was still wrapped in my daughter's womb.

One must dig deep in the historical records to remember that Squooshy Island was once called Plato's Island. It is named so on one old map. Another document refers to "Isaac Plato—black of East Hampton—born free—is a free man." John Lyon Gardiner's *Account Book of Colours or Mulattos, 1799–1801* and his *Account Book No. 2, 1801–1806* (in the East Hampton Library's Long Island Collection) records the purchase by Plato of some of the Gardiners land in 1802 and 1803. These were "the earliest instances of documented land purchases by free people of color in the town of East Hampton," according to anthropologist Allison McGovern (dissertation, CUNY, 2015). McGovern also records: "Early on, the homes of Isaac Plato and Martin Plato were also located in Accobonack/Springs." And, "It looks like the early purchases by people of color in Accobonack are very close to Freetown and may in fact be the same place." Like Plato's Island, Freetown has disappeared from current maps, along with our memory of its free Black inhabitants.

Gardiner's Island, on the other hand, is on every map. The island is one of the largest privately owned islands in the US, and one of the country's most valuable properties. It was purchased from the Montaukets in 1639 by Lion Gardiner, the first English landowner in New York, for "a large black dog, some powder and shot, and a few Dutch blankets" and has remained in the Gardiner family ever since. A recently deceased owner, Robert David Lion Gardiner, said: "We have always married into wealth. We've covered all our bets. We were on both sides of the Revolution, and both sides of the Civil War. The Gardiner family always came out on top." Gardiner's Island was a plantation of enslaved and free people of color exporting cotton, lumber, and other products across Gardiner's Bay to the peninsula of Springs.

Before the white settlers arrived, Springs, with Accabonac Harbor at its heart, was home to a Native American nation. It is said "Accabonac" derives from the word for edible tubers in their Algonquian language. It is said that their land was a paradise of fine spring waters; of abundant deer, duck, and geese to hunt; of clams and fish from the waterways; of corn, squash, and beans to grow; wild grape, wild potato, cranberry, and beach plum to gather. It is said that this nation was overpowered by the Montauketts, their lands annexed, some two hundred years before the Montauketts were destroyed by the whites.

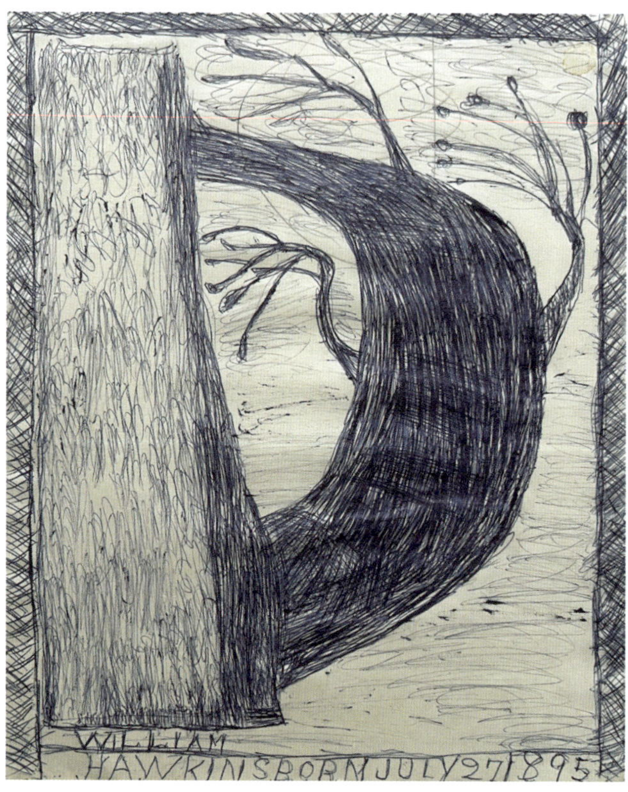

I take the same walk almost every day. It is never dull. This enchanted drawing by William Hawkins, *Trees and Road,* hangs in my studio. It evokes the ever-changing magic of my walk, the inseparability of road and trees. Have a good look at it. Hawkins, the Kentucky Insider artist, was a seer of estrangement and interbeing.

When I walk along the bay beach with Susan, I join her collecting sea glass. We walk alongside the white and green-blue Botticelli curls of the bay-beach wavelets. We scan the stone and shell rubble of the beach for sea glass. She is a master glasser, uncanny eyes; I'm semi-blind and oblivious. On a lucky day we find four or five rubbed glass shards between us. We collect sea glass because it is translucent and rare, because it is a compound of culture and nature, like us.

Different each day are the high tide and low, the shells and seaweeds they deposit, the deer and dog and human prints in the sand, all soon erased. I attend to the micro-changes of outer weather and inner. One moment the sky is a child's-eye blue, another a wolf gray. I might dwell on an agonizing dilemma—the pain of my dying mother, the debility of democracy. I might feel joy in a sly breeze, a smiling slant of light. I might look beneath the surface of a tree, beneath the thin veneer that reflects light back to the catchment of my eyes, unseeing with my mind's eye that luminous surface, seeing where light and eyesight don't reach, seeing the blackness that is everywhere underneath. I might compose a not-very-good poem, record it on my Notes app, a haiku all Japanese and Zen with crows, bare trees, and micro-seasons. Once I wrote a poem called "Paradise" about how lousy is Paradise, a shambles of suffering, a suffering that heals, a place continuously unforming and forming peace.

I walk through Springs, around Accabonac Harbor, past Plato's Island, along Gardiner's Bay. I walk these sands of enslavers and freed men, of abundance and suffering. I walk haunted by the lived, the living, and the yet unborn. I attend carefully to my path. At each step, I see what I see and don't see, I hear what I hear and don't hear, I feel what I feel and don't feel. I walk in the haunted paradise of the now.

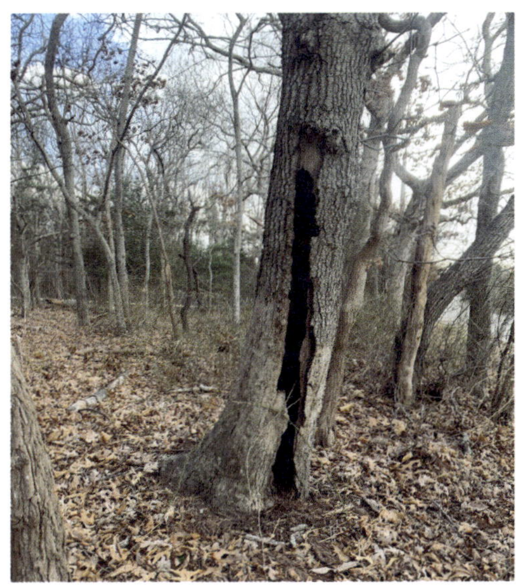

Acknowledgments

I bow to the artists whose images you see here, who inspired these words.

I thank you friends and colleagues who read drafts of these writings, took small bites or large. You read with kindness, offering me much-needed encouragement and correction. I could not have continued without you: Kay Larson, Teju Cole, Rachel Rickert, Vince Aletti, Laurie Anderson, Jim Cass, Ayumi Furuta, Jonathan Becker, Bob Colacello, Julian Cox, Chris DiMeglio, Andy Miller, Josh Sapan, Camille Kamoura, Eric Himmel, Nancy Rawlinson, Marvin Heiferman, Shira Spector, Monte Wolverton, Daile Kaplan, Deborah Bell, Geoffrey Dorfman, Emil Ferris, Gabrielle Bell, Lauren Weinstein, Aura Rosenberg, Brian Wallis, Alla Kovgan, Debi Cornwall, Daniel Lerner, Paul Barman, Accra Shepp, Adam Simon, Leo Rubinfien, Madison Smartt Bell, Stephen Fife, Gary Schneider, Andrew Mer, Chris George, Christopher Bonanos, Ella Spungen, Aliana Spungen, David Dechman, Scott Eder, Barret Oliver, Donald Newman, Ira Richer, Jenny Moore, Meryl Meisler, Rachel Liebling, Stephen Gill, Richard Pearlman, Christopher Makos, Brigitte Kenna, Andrew Pollock, Tara Booth, Leela Corman, Robert Reiner, Tahneer Oksman, Faith Cox, Eileen Boxer, Christopher Sweet, Michael Black, Andrew Friedman, Sarah Meister, Wade Hampton, Caveh Zahedi, Drew Sawyer, Jeff Rosenheim, Una Morera, Thea Giovanni, Walter Thomas, Dan Simon, Don Carleton, and any other dear friends who may have slipped my mind.

I'd like to salute the writers most on my mind while I was at work: George Saunders, Teju Cole, W. G. Sebald, Stephen Batchelor, Thich Nhat Hanh, James Baldwin, Fyodor Dostoevsky. And the *New York Times*; if the Buddha were around today, and he spoke English, and he only had time for one journal, he would read the *Times*.

To the teachers I sat or danced with, for waking me up: Arthur Byk, Chris Di-Meglio, Kamala Masters, Stephen Armstrong, Mark Nunberg, Akincano, Yuka Nakamura, Meredith Monk, Peter Fodera, Ariel Karass, Kate Sheela, Charlotte Preston, Tuere Sala, Greg Scharf, Brian Lesage, Jaya Rudgard, Andrea

Fella, Marjolein Janssen, Stephen and Martine Batchelor, Joseph Goldstein.

To my fellow practitioners, my sangha mates at St. Mark's Community of Mindfulness, at Morning Meditation, at the Insight Meditation Society, at Friday Morning Waves, at Tuesday Evening Group. I thank you for sharing your aspiration, your ardency, your vulnerability, your goodness.

To Sophie Crumb, for the perfect cover.

Thank you, copyright holders, for graciously allowing your images to appear in print here.

To all at Abbeville Press. Especially David Fabricant, master of many trades. And Nadine Winns, such a support.

To my darling Susan Spungen, who is my all and all.

Captions

Dedication

p. 4
Emil Ferris
Jonah and the Dragon, 2022
Ink on paper, 14 × 11 inches
Courtesy the artist

Big Cats, Under-Cats

p. 13
Victor Joseph Gatto
Jungle Scene, c. 1950
Oil on board, 20 × 24 inches

p. 14
W. Eugene Smith
Gatto with Lion Painting, 1948
Photograph
© 1948, 2025 The Heirs of W. Eugene Smith

p. 14
Henri Rousseau
The Sleeping Gypsy, 1897
Oil on canvas, 51 × 79 inches
Museum of Modern Art, New York

p. 15
Henri Rousseau
The Dream, 1910
Oil on canvas, 80 × 117 inches
Museum of Modern Art, New York

p. 16
W. Eugene Smith
Gatto at Dinner, 1948
Photograph
© 1948, 2025 The Heirs of W. Eugene Smith

p. 17
Anonymous
Al Pacino, Patsy Eboli, Al Lettieri, 1971
Photograph
Courtesy Giovannina Bellino

Genius

p. 19
Anonymous
Robert Berman, 1970
Offset lithograph from *The Mannikin,*
3 × 2 inches

p. 20
Anonymous
Robert Cullen, 1970
Offset lithograph from *The Mannikin,*
3 × 3 inches

p. 23
Robert Frank
Hollywood, California (Premiere in Hollywood), 1955
Gelatin silver print, 20 × 24 inches
© June Leaf and Robert Frank Foundation

p. 25
June Leaf
Centaur Drawing, 2013
Acrylic on canvas, 36 × 50 inches
© June Leaf and Robert Frank Foundation

The Artist, Then and Now

p. 27
Matthias Grünewald
The Crucifixion (detail of the Isenheim
Altarpiece), 1516
Oil on panel, full panel height 105⅝ inches
Musée Unterlinden, Colmar, France

p. 27
Matthias Grünewald
The Resurrection (detail of the Isenheim
Altarpiece), 1516
Oil on panel, full panel height 105⅝ inches
Musée Unterlinden, Colmar, France

p. 29
Lauren Weinstein
The Artist Then and Now, 2017
Ink on paper, 13½ × 13¾ inches
Courtesy the artist

p. 31
Lauren Weinstein
Preferences, 2017
Ink on paper, 13½ × 13¾ inches
Courtesy the artist

Lady Day

p. 33
Jerry Stoll
*Billie Holiday, Monterey Jazz Festival, Club
Nite, Back Stage*, 1959
Gelatin silver print, 14 × 11 inches
Courtesy Casey Stoll

p. 35
Jerry Stoll
*Billie Holiday and Pepi, Monterey Jazz
Festival, Club Nite, Back Stage*, 1959
Gelatin silver print, 14 × 11 inches
Courtesy Casey Stoll

Guston Unobstructed

p. 37
Philip Guston
White Painting I, 1951
Oil on canvas, 57⅞ × 61⅞ inches
San Francisco Museum of Modern Art
Artwork © The Estate of Philip Guston,
photo courtesy San Francisco Museum of
Modern Art

p. 39
Philip Guston
Painting, Smoking, Eating, 1973
Oil on canvas, 77½ × 103½ inches
Stedelijk Museum, Amsterdam
Artwork © The Estate of Philip Guston,
photo courtesy Stedelijk Museum,
Amsterdam

p. 40
Flyer for poster for 1974 Philip Guston
exhibition at the David McKee Gallery, with
Guston's *Smoking I*, 1973
Artwork © The Estate of Philip Guston

p. 42
Philip Guston
Untitled, 1980
Acrylic and ink on illustration board,
20 × 30 inches
Metropolitan Museum of Art, New York;
promised gift of Musa Guston Mayer
Artwork © The Estate of Philip Guston,
digital image © The Guston Foundation

p. 43
Sengai
Tiger and Cat, c. 1835
Ink on paper

John Chamberlain and Max's

p. 45
Anton Perich
John Chamberlain and Andrew Wylie at Max's, 1971
Gelatin silver print, 10 × 13 inches
Courtesy Anton Perich

p. 49
Takayuki Ogawa
John Chamberlain and Ultra Violet at MoMA, 1967
Gelatin silver print, 10 × 13 inches
Courtesy Akio Nagasawa Gallery, Tokyo

p. 50
Still from *Aguirre, the Wrath of God*, 1972, directed by Werner Herzog

p. 52
John Chamberlain
Bushland-Marsh, 1972–73
Painted and chromium-plated steel,
68½ × 90 × 83½ inches
Chinati Foundation, Marfa, TX
Photo: Alex Marks, courtesy The Chinati Foundation. © Fairweather & Fairweather LTD / Artist Rights Society (ARS), New York

Lou's The Past

p. 55
Lou Reed
The Past, 2005
Archival pigment print, 20 × 30 inches
Courtesy Laurie Anderson

Janis

p. 57
Robert Crumb
Cover of Big Brother and the Holding Company's *Cheap Thrills* (detail), 1968
Offset lithograph, 12⅜ × 12⅜ inches
Courtesy Robert Crumb

p. 58
Jim Marshall
Janis Joplin, Backstage at the Winterland, San Francisco, 1968
Gelatin silver print, 14 × 11 inches
© Jim Marshall Photography LLC

p. 61
Francesco Scavullo
Janis Joplin, 1969
Gelatin silver print, 20 × 16 inches

My Friend Ernest

p. 69
Anonymous
Ernest Withers and Talia Kasher, Steven Kasher Gallery, New York, 1997
C-print, 5 × 7 inches

The Fire That Won't Go Out

p. 72
Spread from "They Fight a Fire That Won't Go Out," *Life*, May 17, 1963, with a photograph by Charles Moore
Offset lithograph, 14 × 21 inches
Courtesy The Charles Moore Estate

p. 73
Charles Moore
Martin Luther King Jr. Arrested,
Montgomery, Alabama, 1958
Photograph, 11 × 14 inches
Courtesy The Charles Moore Estate

p. 74
Charles Moore
Firefighters Aiming High-Pressure Water
Hoses at Civil Rights Demonstrators,
Birmingham, Alabama, 1963
Photograph, 11 × 14 inches
Courtesy The Charles Moore Estate

Death War Protest Love

p. 75
Anonymous
Hunger Marchers Invade Ohio Capital,
May 15, 1935
Gelatin silver print, 8 × 10 inches

p. 76
Caption to *Hunger Marchers Invade Ohio*
Capital
Mimeograph, 2 × 6 inches

p. 77
Augustus Washington
John Brown, 1846–47
Daguerreotype, 7¾ x 4⅜ inches
National Portrait Gallery, Washington, DC

p. 78
Southworth and Hawes
The Branded Hand of Captain Jonathan
Walker, 1845
Daguerreotype, 2½ × 2 inches
Massachusetts Historical Society, Boston

p. 79
James Karales
Selma to Montgomery March, 1965
Gelatin silver print, 16 × 20 inches
© Estate of James Karales, Courtesy of
Howard Greenberg Gallery, New York

p. 80
Julio Cortez
Black Lives Matter Protester with US Flag,
Minneapolis, May 28, 2020
Digital photograph
Courtesy Associated Press

A Clayoquot Woman

p. 81
"War Bonnet Storage Case"
Spread from W. Ben Hunt, *The Golden Book*
of Indian Crafts and Lore (New York: Golden
Press, 1954)
Offset lithograph, 11 × 16 inches

p. 82
Edward S. Curtis
A Clayoquot Woman, 1915
Photogravure, 7 × 5¼ inches

p. 83
Saloon Scene at the Karl May Museum, near
Dresden, Germany, 1933–45
Uncredited photograph from John Toland,
Hitler: The Pictorial Documentary of His Life
(New York: Ballantine, 1976)

Tintypes and Disfarmers

p. 87
Anonymous
Two Men, c. 1875
Tintype, 4 × 2½ inches

p. 112
Leela Corman
Life Is an Ambush (detail of page 1 of 2), 2016
Graphite, ink, gouache, watercolor, and
acrylic on vellum Bristol, 18¾ × 11¾ inches
Courtesy the artist

p. 112
Leela Corman
Life Is an Ambush (detail of page 2 of 2), 2016
Graphite, ink, gouache, watercolor, and
acrylic on vellum Bristol, 18¾ × 11¾ inches
Courtesy the artist

p. 113
Leela Corman
It Only Masquerades as Entertainment
(detail of page 3 of 4), 2017
Graphite, ink, gouache, watercolor, and
acrylic on vellum Bristol, 14 × 11 inches
Courtesy the artist

p. 114
Leela Corman
You Are Not a Guest (page 2 of 7), 2021
Graphite, ink, gouache, watercolor, and
acrylic on vellum Bristol, 14 × 11 inches
Courtesy the artist

p. 115
Leela Corman
Ruthless Ruby (detail of a page from *Victory
Parade*), 2018–21
Graphite, ink, gouache, watercolor, and
acrylic on vellum Bristol, 14 × 11 inches
Courtesy the artist

p. 116
Leela Corman
Faces of Ruby/Ruth/Rivke (details from
Victory Parade), 2018–21
Graphite, ink, gouache, watercolor, and
acrylic on vellum Bristol, each page
14 × 11 inches
Courtesy the artist

p. 117
Leela Corman
Hands (details from *Victory Parade*), 2018–21
Graphite, ink, gouache, watercolor, and
acrylic on vellum Bristol, each page
14 × 11 inches
Courtesy the artist

p. 118
Leela Corman
"You Checked This Room Yet?" (detail of a
page from *Victory Parade*), 2018–21
Graphite, ink, gouache, watercolor, and
acrylic on vellum Bristol, 14 × 11 inches
Courtesy the artist

Preposterous Pictures of Peculiar People

p. 120
Basil Wolverton
The 10 a.m. Lunch Eater, 1968
Pen on paper, 8½ × 8½ inches
Courtesy Monte Wolverton

p. 120
Philip Guston
Untitled, 1980
Acrylic and ink on illustration board,
20 × 30 inches
Metropolitan Museum of Art, New York;
promised gift of Musa Guston Mayer
Artwork © The Estate of Philip Guston,
digital image © The Guston Foundation

p. 121
Anonymous
Four women eating bananas, c. 1880
Tintype, 2$\frac{1}{2}$ × 3$\frac{1}{2}$ inches

p. 122
Anonymous (Acme School of Drawing)
Become a Cartoonist, 1908
Offset lithograph in *Popular Mechanics*,
2 × 3 inches

p. 123
Basil Wolverton
Powerhouse Pepper in "Eatin' for Beatin'"
(page 2 of 8), 1968
Pen on paper, 14$\frac{1}{4}$ × 10$\frac{3}{4}$ inches
Courtesy Monte Wolverton

p. 124
Basil Wolverton and Al Capp
Li'l Abner, October 21, 1946
Offset lithograph, 3 × 6 inches
Courtesy Monte Wolverton

p. 125
Basil Wolverton
Cover of *MAD* magazine, May 1954
Offset lithograph, 10 × 7 inches
Courtesy Monte Wolverton

p. 127
Basil Wolverton
*Many of the Israelites Wolfed Down the
Roasted Meat as If They Were Starving!*, 1961
Offset lithograph, from *The Bible Story* in *The
Plain Truth*, November 1961, 7 × 5$\frac{1}{2}$ inches
Courtesy Grace Communion International

p. 127
Basil Wolverton
Batty Book Cover, 1968
Offset lithograph, 10 × 18 inches

p. 128
Anonymous (Matson Photo Service)
Woman of Dar-es-Salam, 1936,
from *The Plain Truth*, April 1957
Offset lithograph, 4 × 3 inches

p. 129
Basil Wolverton
Mutants, c. 1954
Pen on paper, 14$\frac{1}{2}$ × 20$\frac{1}{2}$ inches
Courtesy Monte Wolverton

p. 130
Basil Wolverton
6 pages from *Common Types of Barflyze*, 1974
Offset lithographs, 7$\frac{1}{4}$ × 5$\frac{1}{2}$ inches
Courtesy Monte Wolverton

p. 131
Basil Wolverton
Unclean and Clean Animals, c. 1960,
from *The Bible Story*
Courtesy Grace Communion International

Warhol's Photograph of President Kennedy's Portrait

p. 133
Andy Warhol
Portrait of President Kennedy, 1977
Gelatin silver print, 10 × 8 inches
© 2025 The Andy Warhol Foundation for the
Visual Arts, Inc. / Licensed by Artists Rights
Society (ARS), New York

p. 134
US Postal Service
Liberty Series stamp of President Thomas
Jefferson (after portrait by Gilbert Stuart),
1954
Offset lithograph, canceled in ink,
1$\frac{1}{2}$ × 1 inches

p. 135
Aaron Shikler
John F. Kennedy (official White House
portrait), 1970
Oil on canvas, 50 × 33 inches
Courtesy The White House

p. 141
Andy Warhol
Footsteps on Beach, Montauk, 1977
Gelatin silver print, 10 × 8 inches
© 2025 The Andy Warhol Foundation for the
Visual Arts, Inc. / Licensed by Artists Rights
Society (ARS), New York

Sand Dunes

p. 143
Lester Garber
Sandpipers, c. 1960
Tempera on wood, 7½ × 20½ inches

p. 144
Anonymous
*Kasher/Kalish Home after the Hurricane,
Ocean Beach*, 1962
C-Print, 3½ × 3½ inches

p. 144
Dana Wallace Jr.
Ursula and Stevie Kasher, 1955
Gelatin silver print, 8 × 10 inches

p. 145
Victor Joseph Gatto
Fire Island, c. 1950
Oil on board, 20 × 24 inches

p. 146
Dana Wallace Jr.
Stevie Kasher, 1955
Gelatin silver print, 14 × 11 inches

The Two of Us

p. 147
Anonymous
Ursel and Margarete Held, Frankfurt, 1938
Gelatin silver print, 3½ × 2½ inches

p. 148
Ursel Held
Envelope addressed to her mother, 1938
Crayon on paper, 4½ × 6½ inches

p. 151
Günter Grass
Wir zwei (The Two of Us), 1979
Etching, 25½ × 19¾ inches
© 2025 Artists Rights Society (ARS),
New York / VG Bild-Kunst, Bonn

p. 153
Günter Grass
Wir zwei (The Two of Us) (detail)
© 2025 Artists Rights Society (ARS),
New York / VG Bild-Kunst, Bonn

Reaching for the Red Star Sky

p. 156
Nathaniel Tileston
Trisha Brown's Spanish Dance, c. 1980
Gelatin silver print, 8 × 10 inches
© The Estate of Nathaniel Tileston

p. 157
Anonymous
Leaping Man, c. 1975
Gelatin silver print, 10 × 8 inches

p. 158
Denise Dixon / Wendy Ewald
Reaching for the Red Star Sky, 1979
Gelatin silver print, 10 × 8 inches
Courtesy Wendy Ewald

Road Pictures

p. 160
A-CHAN
Untitled, Fujishiro, 2004–6
C-print, 8 × 10 inches
Courtesy the artist

p. 161
A-CHAN
Untitled, Fujishiro (detail)
Courtesy the artist

p. 162
Robert Frank
34th Street, New York City, c. 1948
Gelatin silver print, 14 × 11 inches
© June Leaf and Robert Frank Foundation

p. 162
Robert Frank
U.S. 285, New Mexico, 1956
Gelatin silver print, 14 × 11 inches
© June Leaf and Robert Frank Foundation,
from *The Americans*

p. 162
Roger Fenton
Valley of the Shadow of Death, 1855
Salted paper print, 8 × 10 inches

Accabonac Harbor

p. 164
Herbert Matter
*Jackson Pollock and Lee Krasner Clamming,
Accabonac Harbor*, 1947
Gelatin silver print, 8 × 10 inches
Courtesy Pollock-Krasner House and Study
Center, East Hampton, NY

p. 166
William Hawkins
Trees and Road, c. 1980
Ink on paper, 12 × 9 inches
Copyright 2026 Ricco/Maresca Gallery

p. 167
Steven Kasher
Tree, Louse Point Road, 2020
Digital photograph

Index

Design: Steven Kasher and Misha Beletsky
Layout: Julia Sedykh and David Fabricant
Production editor: Kayla Hassett
Prepress: Ada Rodriguez
Production manager: Louise Kurtz

First edition
10 9 8 7 6 5 4 3 2 1

ISBN 978-0-7892-1530-7

Library of Congress Cataloging-in-Publication Data available upon request

For bulk and premium sales and for text adoption procedures, write to Customer Service Manager, Abbeville Press, 655 Third Avenue, New York, NY 10017, or call 1-800-ARTBOOK.

Visit Abbeville Press online at www.abbeville.com.